Equally Yoked

EQUALLY YOKED

*A Premarital Counseling Primer
for Multiethnic Christian Couples*

MATTHEW R. AKERS

WIPF & STOCK · Eugene, Oregon

EQUALLY YOKED
A Premarital Counseling Primer for Multiethnic Christian Couples

Copyright © 2016 Matthew R. Akers. All rights reserved. Except for brief quotations in critical publications or reviews, no part of this book may be reproduced in any manner without prior written permission from the publisher. Write: Permissions, Wipf and Stock Publishers, 199 W. 8th Ave., Suite 3, Eugene, OR 97401.

Wipf & Stock
An Imprint of Wipf and Stock Publishers
199 W. 8th Ave., Suite 3
Eugene, OR 97401

www.wipfandstock.com

PAPERBACK ISBN 13: 978-1-4982-2949-4
HARDCOVER ISBN 13: 978-1-4982-2951-7

Manufactured in the U.S.A.   02/29/2016

To Glenda

The embodiment of Proverbs 31.
Our multiethnic journey is one of the greatest joys of my life.

Contents

1 Introduction | 1

2 Multiethnic Marriage in the Old Testament | 7

3 Multiethnic Marriage in the New Testament | 43

4 A Historical Survey of Attitudes Toward Multiethnic Relationships in North America | 73

5 Challenges of Multiethnic Couples | 104

6 Premarital Counseling Propositions for Multiethnic Couples | 122

7 Conclusion | 136

Bibliography | 139
Author Index | 159
Subject Index | 161
Scripture Index | 167

1

Introduction

DURING THE PAST FIFTY years, Western culture has experienced a significant shift in its overall stance regarding multiethnic marriage. As late as 1966, seventeen of the fifty states still enforced laws that prohibited certain types of racial intermixing within the bonds of matrimony.[1] The following year, however, the Supreme Court rendered such statutes unconstitutional after hearing the groundbreaking case *Loving v. Virginia*.[2]

The Commonwealth of Virginia was one of the states that did not permit couples from dissimilar ethnic backgrounds to wed. In 1958 Richard Loving (a Caucasian) and Mildred Jeter (an African American with Rappahannock heritage) held their wedding ceremony in Washington, DC, because the district had no such restrictions.[3] Their attempt to curtail their state's law, however, met with resistance when they returned to their Virginia residence.

Law enforcement agents in the small town of Central Point raided their home in the middle of the night. The sheriff arrested them and ordered that they serve a jail sentence of one year for their disregard of Virginia law. The judge offered to suspend the punishment if the Lovings would agree to

---

1. For helpful figures that list the states that forbade multiethnic marriage between 1866 and 1966, see the photographs that appear between pages 146 and 147 in the following work: Wallenstein, *Tell the Court I Love My Wife*. For an informative analysis of the historical factors that led to a gradual dismantling of the objections regarding multiethnic marriage in the United States, see Romano, *Race Mixing*, 12–43.

2. "U.S. Supreme Court: Loving v. Virginia, 388 U.S. 1 (1967)."

3. Sollors, *Interracialism*, 28.

leave the state for twenty-five years, but instead they decided to appeal the original ruling.[4]

Nine years later, their case appeared before the Supreme Court, and, after a unanimous decision in favor of the Lovings, Chief Justice Warren opined:

> Marriage is one of the "basic civil rights of man," fundamental to our very existence and survival . . . To deny this fundamental freedom on so unsupportable a basis as the racial classifications embodied in these statues, classifications so directly subversive of the principle of equality at the heart of the Fourteenth Amendment, is surely to deprive all the State's citizens of liberty without due process of law. The Fourteenth Amendment requires that the freedom of choice to marry not be restricted by invidious racial discriminations. Under our Constitution, the freedom to marry, or not to marry, a person of another race resides with the individual, and cannot be infringed by the State.[5]

As a result of this decision, multiethnic marriages became legal in all fifty states. The percentage of such unions continues to rise.[6]

THE MOTIVATION FOR THE STUDY

The primary motivation for this study is the sheer number of multiethnic unions presently occurring in the early twenty-first century. According to a 2010 study conducted by the Social and Demographic Trends division of Pew Research, "14.6 percent of all new marriages in the United States in 2008 were between spouses of a different race or ethnicity from one another."[7] A measurable rise of multiethnic marriages in Canada,[8] as well as the fact that nearly two-thirds of Mexicans are mestizos,[9] indicates that the blending of peoples is a significant North American trend.

4. Spickard, *Mixed Blood*, 280.

5. "U.S. Supreme Court: Loving v. Virginia, 388 U.S. 1 (1967)." The court heard the case on April 10, 1967, and issued a decision on June 12, 1967.

6. Wang, "The Rise of Intermarriage."

7. Passel et al, "Marrying Out."

8. Proudfoot, "Number of Mixed-Race Couples." Statistics show 5.1 percent of marriages in Canada's urban centers are multiethnic, as compared to only 1.4 percent in rural areas.

9. "North America: Mexico." The word *mestizo* refers to people of Spanish and Native American descent. For a discussion of their origin, see Cope, *The Limits of Racial*

Introduction

Research indicates multiethnic unions are becoming more common in the North American branch of Christendom. Joshua Tom and Brandon Martinez, researchers at Baylor University, analyzed the data from 12,000 marriages and made two interesting observations regarding wedding trends. First, they concluded evangelical and mainline Protestants are as likely as their non-religious counterparts to marry someone of another ethnicity. Second, they noted almost twice as many Catholics versus other demographic blocs chose to wed a person of a different ethnicity.[10]

A secondary motivation for the study is the author's own marriage. This writer is a Caucasian male whose family has resided in the same rural region of the Midwest for over two centuries.[11] His wife, on the other hand, is of Salvadoran extraction. She is a descendent of Native American, African, and European ancestors[12] who converged in Central America as a direct result of what many historians refer to as the Homogenocene Era.[13] Accordingly, the author is part of the growing North American tendency to marry across ethnic lines. Not surprisingly, the writer's interest in the subject of multiethnic unions—particularly within Christian circles—is a significant impetus for this work.

THE RELEVANCE OF THE STUDY

A work that focuses on multiethnic marriage is necessary for at least three reasons. First, as the previous section of this study reveals, significantly more North American Christians have elected to choose spouses from different ethnicities or cultures in the twenty-first century. Thus, this study provides a timely addition to the field of biblical counseling.

Domination, 14–15.

10. Briggs, "The Ties that May Not Bind."

11. Carter, *The Territory of Louisiana-Missouri*, 360. The author's ancestor, James Britton Sr., appears in a petition that residents of the Louisiana Territory delivered to the Federal Government in 1810.

12. This statement finds confirmation by means of her family's oral history and DNA testing.

13. *Homogenocene* refers to the interaction and blending of diverse peoples from distant regions that occurred as a result of Columbus's fateful voyages to the Americas. Soon after the initial meeting of New World and Old World civilizations in 1492, representatives from each culture cohabitated and produced offspring. For a discussion of the consequences of this intermingling, see Mann, *1493*, 17–19, 24–26.

Second, multiethnic couples must prepare for the challenges and permanency of matrimony. Scripture depicts marriage as an institution that should endure as long as both partners remain alive. Jesus, for example, permitted divorce only in the case of immorality (Matt 19:3–9).[14] Paul explained a Christian partner no longer is bound to an unbelieving spouse who abandons the marriage covenant (1 Cor 7:15).[15] These cases are exceptions to the rule, however, because believers must "let no one separate that which God has joined together" (Matt 19:6b).[16]

Every marriage encounters trials, but multiethnic partners experience stressors that are unique to their situation. While some pressures are external in nature (e.g., potential familial or societal rejection), others originate from a failure to consider cultural differences (e.g., worldview, gender roles, communication). This study is relevant because its objective is to make multiethnic couples proactively aware of the issues their marriages could encounter. Such knowledge is key to responding to the complications in a manner consistent with scriptural principles.

Third, because few works address multiethnic marriage from a Christian perspective, the topic is important. The writer's preliminary research demonstrated that relatively few published volumes concentrate on the needs of ethnically diverse husbands and wives.[17] Furthermore, the author failed to locate a premarital counseling resource that examines multiethnic pairings from a scriptural perspective.[18] Consequently, the current offering makes a unique contribution to the field of counseling.

---

14. One should note that Jesus never commanded a spouse to divorce an immoral partner. Rather, He noted that the Torah permitted such an action when the guilty party refused to repent and remained in sin. For a helpful discussion of Jesus' teachings regarding divorce, see Molldrem, "A Hermeneutic of Pastoral Care," 46.

15. Thiselton, *The First Epistle to the Corinthians*, 530.

16. Each biblical quotation in this study is the author's translation of the text.

17. See Alupoaicei, *Your Intercultural Marriage*; Breger and Hill, *Cross-Cultural Marriage*; Bystydzienski, *Intercultural Couples*; Grearson, *Swaying*; Crohn, *Mixed Matches*; Littlejohn and Karazin, *Swirling*; Leslie, *How to Survive an International Marriage*; Romano, *Intercultural Marriage*; Shelling, *In Love But Worlds Apart*. Two details are worth nothing about this list: 1) The earliest contributions appeared in print less than twenty years ago, indicating that the field of multiethnic marriage research is relatively new; 2) The only resource in this footnote that is exclusively Christian in its orientation is Alupoaicei's volume, *Your Intercultural Marriage*.

18. Although Alupoaicei devoted a thirteen-page chapter to the subject of multiethnic marriage from a Christian perspective, the section examines the topic in an anecdotal fashion rather than systematically. Additionally, she included only three brief Bible references without offering an exegesis of the texts.

Introduction

THE PURPOSE OF THE STUDY

The purpose of this study is to offset the deficit of volumes by producing a work that emphasizes premarital preparation for multiethnic Christian couples. As Charles Wood said, such proactive counseling is "an effective and lasting resource [for] couples who are getting married."[19] This project seeks to help counselees to build healthy and lasting marriages that weather the potentially destructive effects of cultural collision. In short, the study prepares multiethnic partners for the struggles they will experience, and provides them with tools to respond to these difficulties.

Additionally, this document endeavors to equip North American biblical counselors to assist the rising number of multiethnic couples they will encounter. In order to offer effective premarital guidance, counselors must understand the key issues and communicate them to counselees in a comprehensible, systematic fashion. Thankfully, the Bible is not silent on the matter of multiethnic marriage. The Word of God addresses the theme with clarity, attesting once more that "all Scripture is inspired and is useful for instruction, for reproof, for correction, for instruction in righteousness" (2 Tim 3:16; cf. 2 Pet 1:19–21).

THE ORGANIZATION OF THE STUDY

Chapter 2 of the study considers Old Testament teachings regarding multiethnic marriages. After examining pertinent Toranic texts (e.g., Deut 7:1–6; 21:10–14), the author investigates marriages that occurred between Israelites and Gentiles in the Old Testament era. This section categorizes the pairings according to ambiguous examples, negative examples, and positive examples before considering the implications of the research's findings.

Chapter 3 concentrates on New Testament teachings concerning multiethnic relationships. The chief objective of this unit is to review New Testament principles regarding ethnicity, as well as to examine the kinship that exists between Jews and Gentiles who follow Jesus Christ. This inspection considers the implications of the teachings.

Chapter 4 contains a historical survey of attitudes toward multiethnic relationships in North America. The author divides the investigation into four categories: 1) the colonial era (1492–1775); 2) The late eighteenth and nineteenth centuries (1776–1900); 3) The twentieth century prior to *Loving*

---

19. Wood Jr., "Premarital Counseling," 44.

v. Virginia (1901–1966); and 4) North American attitudes after *Loving v. Virginia* (1967–present). Finally, the assessment summarizes prominent North American stances toward multiethnic marriage.

Chapter 5 outlines the challenges multiethnic couples encounter. In addition to familial and societal acceptance, this portion of the study also focuses on worldview differences such as identity, values, conceptions of time, and male and female roles. Furthermore, the section reflects on potential difficulties such as communication and day-to-day tasks.

Chapter 6 synthesizes the findings of the aforementioned portions of the study in order to offer premarital counseling propositions for multiethnic couples. This division of the treatise examines principles and paradigms of multiethnic marriage as well as appropriate applications of the biblical material to the subject of culturally dissimilar couples. Finally, chapter 7 serves as the study's conclusion.

2

Multiethnic Marriage in the Old Testament

INTRODUCTION

ON JANUARY 6, 1959, trial judge Leon Maurice Bazile charged Richard and Mildred Loving with willfully disregarding the laws of the Commonwealth of Virginia by marrying across racial lines. He cited supposed Christian teachings as the reason why the statute existed: "Almighty God created the races white, black, yellow, malay and red, and he placed them on separate continents. And but for the interference with his arrangement there would be no cause for such marriages. The fact that he separated the races shows that he did not intend for the races to mix."[1] Bazile's interpretation of Scripture was not unique; numerous American Christians agree with his assessment.

For example, from the 1950s to March 2000, Bob Jones University, a non-denominational fundamentalist school in Greenville, South Carolina that boasts an enrollment of 3,000,[2] banned its students from dating across ethnic lines.[3] In 2011, the Pew Research Center for the People and the Press asked participants whether or not interracial marriage was good for

---

1. Brazile, "Indictment for Felony."
2. "Fast Facts."
3. "Bob Jones University Drops Interracial Dating Ban."

society. While 16 percent of Anglo evangelicals responded negatively to the question, only 9 percent of Americans in other brackets agreed with this statement. Mainline Anglo Protestants and Anglo Catholics disapproved of intermarriage at a rate of 13 percent and 9 percent respectively.[4] A percentage of Anglo evangelicals who disapprove of multiethnic marriages likely hold this view because they believe the Bible embraces this position.

Prolific author and avowed atheist Richard Dawkins cited this supposed doctrine as one of the principal reasons why he rejected Christianity:

> The God of the Old Testament is arguably the most unpleasant character in all fiction: jealous and proud of it; a petty, unjust, unforgiving control-freak; a vindictive, bloodthirsty ethnic cleanser; a misogynistic, homophobic, racist, infanticidal, genocidal, filicidal, pestilential, megalomaniacal, sadomasochistic, capriciously malevolent bully. Those of us schooled from infancy in his ways can become desensitized to their horror.[5]

Dawkins's acerbic paragraph is his subjective opinion rather than a research-driven analysis of the biblical material, but his estimation reflects that of numerous critics. Although each issue he addressed requires a thorough, informed response,[6] the narrow confines of this study permits only an exploration of his claim that Scripture promotes a racist outlook. Accordingly, this chapter will explore Toranic teachings regarding multiethnic marriage and analyze Old Testament examples of the practice.

TORANIC TEACHINGS REGARDING MULTIETHNIC MARRIAGES

Deuteronomy 7:1–6

In the book of Deuteronomy, Moses prepared the sons of Israel to enter the land of Canaan after they had wandered in the desert for forty years due to their disobedience. God prepared them for their next stage of existence by providing a historical review of his interactions with them and their

---

4. Grant, "Opposition to Interracial Marriage." Interestingly, unaffiliated Protestants and African American Protestants both scored at about 3 percent each, significantly below the national average.

5. Dawkins, *The God Delusion*, 51.

6. For an excellent rebuttal to *The God Delusion*, see McGrath and McGrath, *The Dawkins Delusion*, 1–118.

Multiethnic Marriage in the Old Testament

ancestors (Deut 1:1—4:49). Chapters 5–11 contain a treatise that reiterates the laws God gave Israel in the book of Exodus. Within this context appears Deut 7:1–6, a section that prohibits intermarriage between Israelites and the residents of Canaan.

In addition to charging the sons of Israel to dispossess the seven nations of Canaan (Deut 7:1), God warned his people not to intermingle with them politically or personally: "And the LORD your God will put them before your face, and you will smite them to the point of extermination. You shall make no covenant with them or show them mercy, and you shall not intermarry with them. You shall not give your daughter to his [a Canaanite's] son and you shall not take his daughter for your son" (Deut 7:2–3). In the ancient Near East, families typically arranged marriages for their children.[7] God warned parents, therefore, that he did not permit such unions between his covenant people and the inhabitants of Canaan.

The remainder of the pericope specifies why God found this type of intermarriage particularly abhorrent: "For they will cause your son to turn aside from Me and serve others gods, and the anger of the LORD will kindle against you and He will hasten to destroy you" (Deut 7:4). Accordingly, God directed his people to make a preemptive strike against the Canaanites' negative religious influences by destroying their sacred objects (Deut 7:5). Because the Lord had chosen Israel as his unique possession, the people were to remain separate[8] from other nations by devoting themselves to him.

While some commentators accuse the Torah of expressing ethnocentric viewpoints because of passages like Deut 7:1–6,[9] this concern is not the intention of the text at hand. Rather than citing the Canaanites' dissimilar ethnicity as the impetus for rejecting them as spouses, verse 4 cites their aberrant worship practices as the reason why God directed the Israelites to reject them. Under Moses' leadership, the Israelites already had succumbed

---

7. Bratcher and Hatton, *A Handbook on Deuteronomy*, 152. Any attempt to secure a spouse without the cooperation of one's parents was a breach of social etiquette.

8. The word the author translated as *separate* is *qādôsh*. Although the term often carries the idea of holiness, its base meaning is *separate* or *set apart*. This usage fits the present context because the pericope emphasizes the importance of the sons of Israel remaining distinct from the pagan inhabitants of Canaan. For a helpful listing of the various usages of *qādôsh* in the Old Testament, see Brown et al, *Enhanced Brown–Driver–Briggs Hebrew and English Lexicon*, 872.

9. E.g., Glick and Pi-Sunyer, "Acculturation," 138–41; Haddad, "The Biblical Basis," 97–113; Netanyahu, "Américo Castro," 398–404; Stulman, "Encroachment in Deuteronomy," 613–32; Boyarin and Boyarin, "Diaspora," 709–13.

to both Egyptian and Moabite idolatrous practices (cf. Exod 32:1–6; Num 25:1–3). They were susceptible to Canaanite religion as well. God refused to share his glory, so "competing allegiances [were] to be vigorously avoided."[10]

Deuteronomy 21:10–14

Deut 19:1–22:8 contains a sequence of civil laws that was to govern Israel after the nation inhabited Canaan.[11] In the middle of the unit is a section that regulated the treatment of female war captives by Israelite soldiers. Deut 21:10–14 permitted these warriors to marry women of other ethnicities under certain circumstances.

Gerhard von Rad held that the passage contradicted the interethnic marriage restrictions of Deut 7:1–6,[12] but a careful reading of the entire book demonstrates otherwise. While the Israelites were to exterminate every resident of Canaan (Deut 20:16–18), God allowed them to relate differently to the inhabitants of distant regions that belonged to non-Canaanites (Deut 20:10–15). Only if a city refused the covenant nation's terms of peace by declaring war must Israelite soldiers kill all males while taking the women, children, animals, and spoil for themselves (Deut 20:13–14).

If a warrior found among the captives a beautiful woman that he desired, he must respond appropriately rather than taking advantage of her vulnerable status by sexually mistreating her.[13] The enamored man must: 1) take her as his wife rather than regard her as a sexual slave; 2) bring her to his home; 3) shave her head; 4) trim her nails; and 5) allow her to mourn her parents for an entire month (Deut 21:11b–13). Only after observing this rigid formula could the soldier consummate the marriage with his foreign bride. This procedure served the dual purpose of "cutting off all ties to the [woman's] former life,"[14] including any idolatrous religious associations, as well as allowing the foreign woman time to acclimate to her new cultural context.

---

10. Earl, "The Christian Significance," 49. Earl noted that the proper reaction to God's love was "responsiveness . . . in terms of allegiances (and holiness)."

11. Merrill, *Deuteronomy*, 19.

12. Rad, *Deuteronomy*, 137; cf. Kaminsky, "Did Election Imply," 414.

13. Diamond, "The Deuteronomic," 62–63. The writer disagrees with many of the article's conclusions, but Diamond was correct to note that Deut 21:10–14 protected non-Israelite women from sexual mistreatment.

14. Merrill, *Deuteronomy*, 291.

If, for whatever reason, the husband was displeased with his new wife and sought a divorce,[15] he could not sell her or treat her badly. Rather, he had no choice but to set her free (Deut 21:14). In essence, the foreign wife's status as the bride of an Israelite man afforded her a measure of legal protection as well as personal dignity.[16] In this sense, her value was identical to the wife who was a descendant of Abraham, and by extension a beneficiary of Yahweh's covenant with the patriarch (cf. Deut 24:1–4).

Implications

Several observations are worth noting. First, Deut 21:10–14 clarifies the marital restrictions of Deut 7:1–6. Because Israelite soldiers could marry the non-Israelite women who lived in distant cities, the Torah did not forbid all multiethnic marriages. In other words, the prohibition against marrying Canaanite women was not racial in nature.[17]

Second, the problem with Canaanite women, as outlined in Deut 7:4, was that they would entice the Israelites to forsake the true Lord by venerating false gods. The concern of the Torah, then, was not the ethnic disparity of Israelites and Canaanites, but their religious differences. As covenant people, the nation of Israel could have no other gods or worship carved images (Deut 6:7–8) because the Lord was a jealous God who refused to share his glory.[18]

Third, the foreign brides of Israelite men enjoyed the same marital status as native Israelite wives. Rather than possessing the status of slaves or concubines, they received the same treatment as Israelite women.[19] For all intents and purposes, the Torah depicted multiethnic spouses as equally yoked, provided that neither one of the partners worshiped false gods.

---

15. Deut 21:14 does not advocate divorce, but rather contains an if/then clause that is one of the hallmarks of casuistic (case) law. Accordingly, the passage does not approve of the foreign wife's expulsion (or any other type of divorce for that matter), but provides a strict policy for the husband to follow if he stubbornly insists on taking this course of action. For a helpful discussion of the nature of casuistic law as it applies to Toranic teachings, see Guenther, "Interpreting the Silences," 42.

16. Phillips, *Deuteronomy*, 141; Thompson, *Deuteronomy*, 228.

17. Wright, *Deuteronomy*, 238.

18. Cf. Deut 4:24; 5:9; 6:15; 32:16, 21.

19. Goodnick, "She Shall Mourn," 200–201. Goodnick correctly recognized one of the pericope's chief aims: "The whole episode appears . . . to enhance the status of women, no matter what their original source or status."

EQUALLY YOKED

AMBIGUOUS EXAMPLES OF MULTIETHNIC MARRIAGE

The Old Testament catalogs more multiethnic marriages between Israelites and non-Israelites than one might expect. While most accounts portray any given pairing in either a negative or positive light, a few examples describe such unions ambiguously. These cases hail from the entire spectrum of Old Testament Israelite history.

Abraham and Keturah

After the death of his wife Sarah, Abraham took a concubine[20] named Keturah (Gen 25:1–6). Although the book of Genesis does not contain an overt reference to her ethnic identity, of help is a genealogical section that traces her progeny through several generations (Gen 25:2–4). The fact that descendants such as Midian settled in Arabia, along with the discovery of a number of South Arabian inscriptions that employ the same names that appear in Keturah's lineage,[21] points to this territory as her likely place of origin.

The brief unit that details Abraham and Keturah's relationship offers no narratory judgment regarding their decision to marry. Rather, the paragraph, along with the subsequent family histories of Ishmael and Isaac (Gen 25:12–18; 19–34) alludes to God's promise that Abraham would be the progenitor of innumerable descendants (Gen 22:17). Scripture reveals Jacob's children were the exclusive recipients of the Abrahamic covenant, but the patriarch's offspring through Ishmael, Esau, and Keturah became mighty peoples as well (cf. Gen 25:1–6; 36:9–43).

Joseph and Asenath

Once Joseph gained Pharaoh's trust by predicting Egypt's upcoming famine and suggesting a course of action that would save the nation (Gen 41:14–44), the grateful ruler gave Joseph an Egyptian name (Zaphenath-paneah) as well as an Egyptian bride. Asenath was the daughter of Potiphera, the

---

20. While Gen 25:1 refers to Keturah as Abraham's wife (*'ishāh* also translated in other contexts *woman, female*), 1 Chron 1:32 calls her his concubine (*pilegesh*). The two statements are not contradictory because "a concubine was a true wife, though of secondary rank" (Harris et al, *Theological Wordbook*, 724).

21. Kidner, *Genesis*, 150.

priest of On, a city in which the gods of the midday sun and the evening sun (Re and Atum respectively)[22] received praise.[23] Egyptian scholars concur that *Asenath* means "belonging to Neith,"[24] a reference to the goddess of "watery preexistence."[25] This linguistic information indicates that both Potiphera and Asenath were staunch adherents to Egyptian religion rather than the God of Israel. The text of Genesis is silent, however, on whether or not Joseph's marriage to the pagan priest's daughter resulted in her conversion to monotheism.[26]

As in the case of Abraham and Keturah, the book of Genesis neither approves nor condemns this multiethnic union. Once more, the text merely reports the event occurred, noting the pairing resulted in the birth of Ephraim and Manasseh, two of the patriarchs of the twelve tribes of Israel. Of interest is Samuel Curtiss' remark: "There were dormant sympathies in the blood of Ephraim which [king] Jeroboam awoke, when he made Jehovah the object of worship in his kingdom under the form of a steer"[27] (cf. 1 Kgs 12:25–33). Nevertheless, a demonstrable link between the idolatry of Asenath and the aberrant worship practices of her offspring almost a millennium later is impossible to prove conclusively.

Huram-Abi's Parents

Second Chron 2:13–14 does not provide the names of Huram-Abi's parents. The passage does, however, identify his mother as an Israelite from the tribe of Dan.[28] His father was a Gentile who originated from Tyre, a costal

---

22. Assmann, "Re," 689–92. The last syllable of the word *Potiphera* is a theophoric element that marks him as a worshiper of Re.

23. Mathews, *Genesis*, 764.

24. Hamilton, *The Book of Genesis*, 508.

25. Assmann, "Neith," 616–18.

26. Although the pseudepigraphical work *Joseph and Aseneth* (ca. first cent. BC to AD second cent.) recounts that Joseph's wife ultimately rejected idolatry before he would allow consummation of the marriage to take place, this interpretation of the Genesis material appears to be a later rabbinical justification for the marriage. For an excellent translation and commentary that highlights rabbinical thought concerning Joseph's marriage, see Burchard, "Joseph and Aseneth," 177–247.

27. Curtiss, "Delitzsch on the Pentateuch," 2.

28. The parallel account in 1 Kgs 7:13–14 records that his mother was from the tribe of Naphtali rather than Dan. These two statements do not contradict each other. Rather, the difference more than likely is the result of one reference providing genealogical information, while the other notes residency. Similarly, Scripture describes the prophet

city that lay to the northwest of Israel. Hiram, the ruler of Tyre, loaned the master craftsman[29] Huram-Abi to King Solomon in order to assist in the construction of the Jerusalem Temple because of his considerable expertise in engraving, weaving luxurious textiles, and molding precious metals.

Richard James Coggins opined that the mention of Huram-Abi's maternal heritage "may be stressed so as to avoid the implication of a major role in the building of the temple being played by one of foreign descent."[30] Nonetheless, such an interpretation is unlikely when one recalls that 2 Chronicles makes no effort to suppress the Gentile side of his ancestry. While the author of 1–2 Chronicles clearly emphasizes the admiration Hiram and Solomon had for Huram-Abi's matchless craftsmanship, no evaluation of his parents' multiethnic marriage—either positive or negative—appears in the account. Of interest, though, is Solomon's indifference to the biracial status of the man who guided the construction of the most important building in Israelite history.

Ahasuerus and Esther

The book of Esther records how God used a Jewish woman to save the Israelite exiles during the Persian period of Old Testament history. When King Ahasueres held a contest to decide who would replace Vashti, his deposed queen, he chose Hadassah/Esther because he loved her more than all other candidates (Esth 2:17). Unknowingly, Ahasueres wedded across ethnic lines because he was unaware of Esther's Jewish heritage. Her cousin Mordecai had advised her to conceal her familial roots because of the discrimination Jews experienced in Persia (Esth 2:10).

Rabbinical commentators of a later era found Esther's marriage to a non-Jewish man unsettling:

> One of the most troublesome features of the Esther story is the very fact that a Jewish woman married a Gentile, even if he was a king. The idea of a Jewish woman letting herself be taken, apparently

---

Samuel's father as both an Ephraimite and a Levite (cf. 1 Sam 1:1; 1 Chron 6:33–38). See Selman, *2 Chronicles*, 302.

29. For a discussion of how *abi* may mean "master craftsman" in this context, see Thompson, *1–2 Chronicles*, 212.

30. Coggins, *The First and Second Books of the Chronicles*, 152.

without protest, into the harem of a Gentile king did not sit well with the sages or with many of our medieval exegetes.[31]

In order to justify Esther's supposed indifference to the situation, Jewish interpreters suggested a number of explanations for her behavior that range from the plausible to the bizarre.[32] As in previous cases, the text offers nothing more than a retelling of the incident.

While the Bible neither celebrates nor denounces Esther's marriage to Ahasueres, the event was pivotal in Jewish history. When it appeared the Jews' enemies had the advantage over their opponents and would exterminate the covenant people, Esther revealed her identity to her surprised husband and secured permission for the Jews to defend themselves against their oppressors (Esth 7:1–6; 8:9–14). Regardless of the morality of Esther's multiethnic marriage, God used the union to preserve the Jews during an age of extreme persecution.

Implications

In three of the above instances, the covenant marriage partner made a positive contribution to the well-being of Israel. Abraham was the father of the Israelites, while Joseph and Esther saved their kinsmen during times of great distress. In the fourth case, the son of a multiethnic couple guided the construction of Solomon's Temple. These examples indicate intermarriage did not necessarily alienate participants from their fellow Israelites. Scripture, however, depicts these marriages neither positively nor negatively.

NEGATIVE EXAMPLES OF MULTIETHNIC MARRIAGE

In addition to depicting various examples of multiethnic marriage in an ambiguous manner, the Old Testament also condemns a number of cross-cultural pairings. This list is comparable to the sampling of ambiguous matrimonial unions in that negative instances originate from the patriarchal period to the post-exilic period. In this section, the writer examines the reasons why Scripture denounces each particular marriage.

---

31. Walfish, *Esther in Medieval Garb*, 122.

32. Ibid., 122–24. Walfish provided a helpful survey of the explanations influential medieval rabbis offered for the apparent lack of objections on Esther's part.

EQUALLY YOKED

Abram and Hagar

After the Lord had sworn to give Abram descendants as plenteous as the stars, the elderly and childless man believed God, "and He accounted it to him as righteousness" (Gen 15:5–6). When the ensuing years brought no son, Abram's wife Sarai began to despair. In an attempt to bring the prophecy to completion through human means, Sarai gave her Egyptian maid Hagar to her husband in order to bear children vicariously (Gen 16:1–3). According to ancient–Near Eastern documents, this convention was commonplace when one's wife could bear no offspring.[33]

Even though Abram and Sarai acquiesced to a culturally acceptable practice in order to secure progeny, and an initial reading of Gen 16 may appear to present a straightforward narrative,[34] the tone of the account differs greatly from the one that relates Keturah's later betrothal to the patriarch (cf. Gen 25). Several textual clues indicate that God did not approve of Abram's marriage to Hagar.

First, Gen 15 recounts two momentous occasions: 1) the Lord's promise that Abram would father an heir; and 2) the ceremony in which God affirmed the Abrahamic covenant. The reference to Abram's impregnation of Hagar in the chapter after which these significant events occur is no coincidence. The juxtaposition of these incidents points to a lack of faith on the part of Abram and Sarai.[35]

Second, David Cotter noticed another striking difference between chapters 15 and 16, along with other portions of the book of Genesis:

> In the preceding chapter, God had been relatively talkative with Abram. In this chapter, God is silent, except for the extended dialogue with Hagar. When had God been silent before? When humanity acts . . . contrary to God's will, e.g., in Genesis 3, when the Man and the Woman transgressed God's command, and in Genesis 4, when Cain brought his brother into the field. In this way, our author sets a scene that renders what follows as both unnecessary and unwilled by God.[36]

---

33. Arnold, *Genesis*, 163.

34. Cotter, *Genesis*, 102.

35. Brueggemann, *Genesis*, 151. Polygamy also contradicted God's plan for marriage (cf. Matt 19:4–6).

36. Cotter, *Genesis*, 102–3.

Multiethnic Marriage in the Old Testament

To put it another way, the Lord's muteness regarding Abram's decision to concede to Sarai's demands implies he was displeased with the resultant marriage to Hagar.

Third, an intriguing relationship exists between Gen 3:17 and 16:2.[37] The connection between these two verses is more than superficial due to their comparable linguistic structure. Whereas in Gen 3:17 God censured Adam because he listened to the voice of Eve and ate the forbidden fruit (*shāmaʿĕtā lĕqôl ʾshĕkā*), Gen 16:2 recounts that Abram listened to the voice of his wife and took Hagar as his bride (*wayyishĕmaʿ ʾbĕrām lĕ sārāy*). This verse appears to echo the phraseology of 3:17 in order to paint Abram's decision to heed Sarai's counsel as sinful.

Fourth, the Lord's response to Abram (now Abraham) in Gen 17 clearly portrays his union with Hagar as erroneous: "And Abraham said to God, 'O that Ishmael might live before Your presence.' But God said, 'No. Rather, Sarah your wife will bear for you a son and you will call his name Isaac. And I will establish My covenant with him for an everlasting covenant for his offspring after him'" (Gen 17:18–19). The inference is that Sarai's strategy for circumventing her barrenness by providing her husband with an additional spouse was unacceptable. Accordingly, in Gal 4:21–31 Paul continues to develop this theme by drawing a clear distinction between the offspring of Hagar and Sarah.[38]

Undoubtedly then, Gen 16:1–3 depicts Abram's marriage to Hagar in a negative light, but not because of its multiethnic nature. While verses 1 and 3 note Hagar's Egyptian roots, these references are descriptive identifiers rather than pejorative in nature.[39] God's promise that her son Ishmael would be the ancestor of countless descendants (Gen 16:10), along with the Lord's acknowledgement of the affliction that Hagar had received at the hand of Sarai (Gen 16:11), indicates that she was the innocent party and that her ethnicity was not a cause for concern. Rather, God found fault with Abram and Sarai because they manipulated and abused her due to their faithlessness.[40]

---

37. Mathews, *Genesis*, 178.

38. In Gal 4, Hagar represents the concept of bondage, while Sarah embodies the idea of freedom.

39. One should note, for example, the manner in which Potiphar's wife used the term *Hebrew* to disparage Joseph's ethnicity when she accused him of rape (Gen 14:13). See Akers, "What's in a Name," 693.

40. Dozeman, "The Wilderness," 28–29.

EQUALLY YOKED

Esau and His Hittite Wives

When Jacob was ready to take a wife, his father Isaac commanded him not to consider Canaanite women as potential brides. Instead, he was to make the long voyage to his grandfather's ancestral homeland and choose one of his maternal uncle's daughters as a spouse. Before the young man began his life-altering journey, Isaac bestowed upon Jacob and his descendants the blessing of the Abrahamic inheritance of the land of Canaan (Gen 28:1–5).

After Esau heard the instructions his father gave his twin brother, he realized his two Hittite wives displeased Isaac. In an attempt to gratify his father, Esau sought to emulate the directive Isaac had given Jacob by marrying Mahalath, Ishmael's daughter. Because Ishmael was Isaac's half-brother, Esau reasoned that selecting a relative as a bride might soften Isaac's discontentment with him due to his two existing marriages (Gen 28:6–9; cf. 26:34).

Although some modern commentators sympathize with Esau's plight because they perceive him to be a pitiable outcast,[41] the juxtaposition of Jacob's attainment of an acceptable bride and Esau's failure to do so until he obtained a third wife demonstrates his culpability. The implication of Gen 28:1–9 is Canaanite women were not suitable helpmeets for the heirs of the Abrahamic covenant.

Walter Brueggemann observed that a number of Western Christians find this pericope troubling:

> This text will seem odd to tolerant "melting pot" America, which has worked hard to overcome destructive religious sectarianism and has learned to practice ecumenism and even "mixed marriage" with some degree of humaneness . . . But in principle, the text requires the faithful community to recognize that "Canaanite/Hittite" alternatives can be dangerous to the community. There are times when concrete steps of discipline must be taken for the purpose of identity and survival.[42]

Although Brueggemann wrote these words thirty-five years ago, he presciently described the misconceptions that modern readers sometimes have regarding Gen 28:6–9. Each of his points, therefore, requires a scripturally informed response.

---

41. E.g., Abraham, "Esau's Wives," 258; Cotter, *Genesis*, 206; Mathews, *Genesis*, 441.
42. Brueggemann, *Genesis*, 239.

Multiethnic Marriage in the Old Testament

First, North Americans who look to the passage as proof the Bible prohibits multiethnic marriage misunderstand the text's purpose. In reality, Esau's offense stemmed in part from his disregard for the ancient–Near Eastern practice of allowing parents to arrange one's marriage (cf. Gen 26:34–35).[43] More importantly, he had ignored God's promise to his grandfather Abraham that he would give the land of Canaan to the covenant people because of the inhabitants' iniquitous practices (Gen 15:12–16). In other words, the idolatry of the Canaanites was the primary reason why Esau's marriage to Hittite women was immoral.

Second, the charge that Jacob's family despised non-endogamous marriages[44] because it wished to ensure the tribe's survival ignores his lineage's history. For example, Abraham himself took as wives an Egyptian and an Arabian, and he was not the last of his line to wed women who were ethnically dissimilar. The difference in tenor between Abraham's marriage to Keturah (ambiguous) and his grandson Esau's marriage to the Hittite women (negative) shows that endogamy is not the concern of Gen 28:6–9.

Third, North Americans who suspect that the Esau narrative promotes sectarian ideology are correct. One of the key themes of the book of Genesis is the exclusivity of the worship of Yahweh according to his standards, so he strictly forbade idolatry and syncretism.[45] Esau breached this demand of complete commitment by betrothing himself to two women who did not worship Yahweh.

Shechem and Dinah

Genesis 34 is one of the most intriguing and troubling passages in the Torah. The chapter relates the double tragedy of Dinah's rape by prince Shechem and the subsequent massacre of the entire male population of his city.[46] When Dinah went out to visit the daughters of Canaan, Shechem forced her to lie with him before deciding he loved her. As a result of his

---

43. Prewitt, "Kinship Structures," 93.
44. E.g., Arnold, *Genesis*, 241; Feldman, "Josephus' Portrait of Jacob," 128.
45. Brueggemann, *Genesis*, 238.
46. Modern scholars debate whether one should interpret Shechem's sexual encounter with Dinah in Gen 34:2 as rape or as consensual. The language of the verse, however, is almost identical to that of 2 Sam 13:14, a text that recounts Amnon's violation of his half-sister Tamar. This linguistic parallelism indicates Shechem's actions were predatory and forced upon Dinah. For a summary of modern interpretations of Gen 34:2, see Barth, "The Dinah Affair," 36–37.

infatuation with Dinah, he convinced his father, Hamor, to negotiate a marriage contract with her father, Jacob (Gen 34:1–4).

When Dinah's family learned of her mistreatment, they were furious. The brothers insisted that every male resident of Shechem's city undergo the rite of circumcision before they would give their consent to the marriage proposal. Hamor and his son reasoned that such an alliance would enrich them because of Jacob's great wealth. They agreed to this condition and directed their followers to submit to the procedure (Gen 34:5–24). Rather than gaining riches, Dinah's brothers Simeon and Levi repaid Shechem's evil act by extracting Dinah from the prince's house and slaughtering the men of the city while they were too sore from their surgeries to defend themselves. Jacob rebuked his sons for their bloodthirsty act, but they indignantly justified their actions (Gen 34:25–31).[47]

Scholars debate whether or not Shechem officially had married Dinah by the time Simeon and Levi massacred the city's males.[48] Even if the actual ceremony had not taken place by this time, both families had agreed upon the necessary prerequisites for the union. This factor justifies the inclusion of Gen 34 in the list of case studies that examines the topic of multiethnic marriage in the Old Testament.

In addition to Dinah's appalling rape, the text condemns this marriage for other reasons as well. First, Shechem was a Hivite, one of the seven nations of Canaan God later would instruct the Israelites to drive out (Deut 7:1). As emphasized earlier in Gen 15:12–16, God described the Canaanites as iniquitous and idolatrous. Because they were devotees of false gods, they made unsuitable marriage partners.

Second, the mention of the Hivites' uncircumcised condition is significant (Gen 34:13–17). Decades earlier God had required Abram and his male descendants to undergo circumcision as a sign of his covenant with

---

47. Hamilton, *The Book of Genesis*, 353. Hamilton wrote that the Old Testament traces children through their mother's lineage a total of seven times, one of which occurs in Gen 34:1. He astutely observed that the purpose of identifying Dinah as the daughter of Leah in this verse was to remind the reader that she was the full sister of Simeon and Levi. This close kinship was the reason why Simeon and Levi took it upon themselves to avenge Dinah. Also worth noting is Jacob's strong disapproval of his sons' actions (cf. Gen 34:30; 49:5–7).

48. The question is whether Dinah's presence in Shechem's home (Gen 34:26) signifies their marriage already had occurred or whether Shechem's family had held her hostage after her rape in order to strengthen the possibility that Jacob would consent to the marriage. For helpful surveys of the possible interpretations of verse 26 see Cotter, *Genesis*, 253; Hamilton, *The Book of Genesis*, 359; Mathews, *Genesis*, 607.

them (Gen 17:1). The allusion to the Hivites' ignorance of this custom is an intentional reminder that they had no alliance with the God of Israel.[49]

Third, the marriage posed the risk of associating Jacob and his family with Canaanite paganism.[50] The pact with Shechem's kin would have provided the sons of Israel with a more permanent residential status in the land of Canaan (cf. Gen 34:21), but at the cost of ignoring God's covenantal promise to secure the territory on his terms (Gen 17:8). In essence, intermarriage with the Hivites would have signified a lack of faith, a breach of the Abrahamic covenant, and a disregard for the exclusive worship of Yahweh.[51] Accordingly, Gen 34 condemns Dinah's marriage to Shechem on religious—rather than ethnic—grounds.

David and Bathsheba

Second Samuel 11 introduces readers to Bathsheba and her husband Uriah. While Uriah is a Hebrew name, his description as a Hittite likely points to his family's country of origin.[52] His classification as one of David's mighty men (cf. 2 Sam 23:39) indicates assimilation was possible for non-Israelites during the United Monarchy period of Israel's history.

The etymology of the word *Bathsheba* is uncertain. While *bat* means *daughter*, the second component of the name (*sheba'*) possibly signifies *seven* or *oath*.[53] The word also might denote "a foreign god, which may indicate the family of Bathsheba was of non-Israelite origin."[54] First Chronicles 3:5 refers to Bathsheba as Bath-shua, which also was the name of Judah's Canaanite wife (1 Chron 2:3).[55] This point of linguistic contact may suggest a non-Israelite origin for Uriah's wife, but identifying one's ethnicity solely on the basis of his or her name is problematic.[56]

49. Earl, "Toward a Christian Hermeneutic," 41.
50. Arnold, *Genesis*, 294–95.
51. Pummer, "Genesis 34," 187.
52. Hertzberg, *1 and 2 Samuel*, 310.
53. Brown et al, *Hebrew and English Lexicon*, 124, 987–88.
54. Achtemeier, *Harper's Bible Dictionary*, 97.
55. Only two Old Testament passages refer to Bath-Shua the Canaanitess (Gen 38:2, 12; 1 Chron 2:3). Because the texts mention her only in passing, insufficient material exists to warrant an examination of her marriage to Judah within this chapter.
56. Even if Bathsheba was a native Israelite, she still qualifies for inclusion in this chapter because her first marriage was to a Hittite. From this perspective, her multiethnic marriage would fall under the category of ambiguity because Scripture never condemns

While Uriah fought a distant war for the crown of Israel, David remained at home because his military advisors were concerned his enemies might kill him in battle (2 Sam 21:17). One late afternoon from his high perch on the palace rooftop, the king happened to look down into the courtyards of the houses that surrounded his citadel and saw a woman bathing. Instead of looking away, lust for the woman grew in his heart. When David's inquiries revealed that Bathsheba was Uriah's wife, he ignored her marital status and committed adultery with her (2 Sam 11:1–4).

David's rash act led to Bathsheba's pregnancy. His frenzied attempt to conceal his wickedness ultimately led to Uriah's murder (2 Sam 11:5–25). In a move that made him appear to be a compassionate rescuer rather than the heartless executioner that he really was, the king married Bathsheba in order to conceal his wickedness. Ultimately David repented when the prophet Nathan exposed his sin (2 Sam 12:13; cf. Ps 51), but his transgression carried lifelong consequences.

Undoubtedly, Scripture denounces David's marriage to Bathsheba (cf. 2 Sam 12:9–10). The condemnation does not arise from the possible multiethnic aspect of their relationship, but rather from its adulterous beginning, as well as its murderous consequences. Accordingly, although Bathsheba became the mother of king Solomon and an ancestress of the Messiah, both the Old and New Testaments draw attention to David's illicit activities by reminding the reader that she originally had been the wife of Uriah the Hittite (2 Sam 12:15; Matt 1:6).

Solomon and His Foreign Wives

Scripture's portrayal of Solomon provides two insights regarding multiethnic marriage. First, if Bathsheba was of non-Israelite extraction, Solomon then would be the offspring of ethnically diverse parents. The ramification of this potential scenario is significant, for it would demonstrate that Israelites approved of multiethnic marriage under certain circumstances. On the other hand, an eventuality in which Bathsheba was an Israelite by birth still establishes that the widow of a foreigner could become the mother of a Davidic heir who sat on Israel's throne. This corollary implication of Solomon's reign provides helpful interpretational context for the primary Solomonic contribution to the topic of multiethnic marriage.

---

her relationship with Uriah.

Multiethnic Marriage in the Old Testament

Second, 1 Kgs 11:1–2a reveals that Solomon's polygamous conquests included more than Israelite women: "And Solomon the king loved many foreign women in addition to the daughter of Pharaoh: Moabite, Ammonite, Edomite, Sidonian, Hittite, from the nations that the LORD said to the sons of Israel, 'You shall not associate with them, nor they with you. They will turn your hearts after other gods.'" In spite of this prohibition, Solomon eventually accumulated seven hundred royal wives and three hundred concubines (1 Kgs 11:3).

Subject and rival nations alike evaluated ancient–Near Eastern kings in part by the size of their harems and the number of political alliances they negotiated.[57] Rulers paired these criteria together by offering their daughters to each other as tangible symbols of their peace treaties. Wayne Brindle argued Solomon's participation in these commonly practiced activities can only mean that he "wanted to be a king like all the other nations that he so admired. For this reason he amassed enormous wealth, a large number of wives, and built several fortress cities."[58]

Although society encouraged—and even expected—rulers to behave in this manner, God prohibited Israelite kings from obtaining multiple wives (Deut 17:17). Furthermore, he forbade all Israelites from intermarrying with the pagan nations that surrounded them (Deut 7:1–6). Consequently, Solomon willfully defied God's counsel, likely justifying his rebellion by convincing himself that his deeds strengthened his kingdom.[59] Instead, his disregard for God's admonition proved disastrous.

In his old age, Solomon's wives convinced him to worship their idols. In addition to venerating Ashtoreth, the goddess of the Sidonians, he honored Milcom, the god of the Ammonites. Near the Temple Mount, he built shrines for the Moabite deity Chemosh and the Ammonite deity Molech. These pagan sanctuaries had a damaging and lasting effect on Israel. They remained in operation until King Josiah destroyed them over three centuries later.[60]

Jerome Walsh vividly described the effect Solomon's polytheist undertakings had upon his relationship with God: "In verse 4 Solomon's heart 'was not true' to Yahweh. The Hebrew word for 'true' here is *šālē*, a pun on Solomon's name (*šĕlōmōh*). In turning away after other gods, Solomon

---

57. Olley, *The Message of Kings*, 115.
58. Brindle, "The Causes of the Division," 229.
59. Rice, *1 Kings*, 87.
60. Inrig, *1 and 2 Kings*, 81.

leaves behind not only the example of David but his own deepest identity as well."[61] This devastating breach resulted not only in the Lord dividing the kingdom in two as a sign of his judgment (1 Kgs 11:9–13), but also in a pervading spiritual darkness that led his people to commit the twin offenses of polytheism and syncretism. As God had prophesied, intermarriage with nonbelievers led to religious apostasy (Deut 7:4).

Like previously examined texts in this section, the focus of 1 Kgs 11:1–13 is not the wholesale condemnation of all non-Israelites or a polemic against multiethnic marriage. Rather, the common denominator of each of Solomon's foreign wives was that they worshiped idols instead of the God of Israel. Consequently, failure to recognize Yahweh as the only true Lord is the emphasis of this passage.

Ahab and Jezebel

Ahab, son of Omri, ruled the northern kingdom of Israel during the period of the Divided Monarchy, some six decades after Solomon's death.[62] His reign parallels that of David's son in that he made treaties with the nations that surrounded his realm. His most significant partnership was with Eth-baal, the king of the Tyre and Sidon, who gave his daughter Jezebel to Ahab as a wife (1 Kgs 16:29–33). This alliance proved disastrous for the spiritual well-being of the northern kingdom.

Eth-baal operated as a typical ancient–Near Eastern ruler in that he served as both the king and the high priest of his people.[63] He devoted himself to Baal Melqart, the city god of Tyre,[64] from which derives the *baal* component of his name. His daughter's devotion to his deity is obvious because *Jezebel* contains the same theophoric element present in Eth-baal's name.

History reveals that Ahab's reign "experienced unprecedented political stability, strength, and prosperity."[65] From God's standpoint, Ahab's kingship was a failure for two reasons. First, Ahab followed the wicked example of Jeroboam, the idolatrous founder of the northern kingdom

---

61. Walsh, *1 Kings*, 135.
62. Davis, "Ahab," 36–37.
63. Prentice, "Elijah and the Tyrian Alliance," 33.
64. Ribichini, "Melqart," 563–65.
65. Rice, *1 Kings*, 138. Rice noted that "1–2 Kings ignores these achievements, for according to his theological criteria, Ahab did 'evil in the sight of the LORD.'"

Multiethnic Marriage in the Old Testament

(1 Kgs 16:31). Second, Jezebel's pagan influence enticed Ahab to worship Baal, erect an altar to the deity in his capital city of Samaria, and construct Asherah poles that honored the goddess of fertility (1 Kgs 16:32). Ahab's paganistic tendencies provoked the Lord more than any of the Israelite kings who had reigned before him (1 Kgs 16:33).

While from a human standpoint Ahab's partnership with Eth-Baal appeared to strengthen the northern kingdom, in actuality his marriage to a pagan woman weakened the country. After Ahab's reign, the deity Israelites most often courted when they drifted from the God of Abraham was Baal.[66] Accordingly, the author of 1–2 Kings depicts Ahab's marriage to his Sidonian bride in such a way that it mirrors Solomon's marriage to countless foreign women half a century earlier.[67] Both kings' spouses drew their hearts away from God and ultimately damaged their nations' spiritual fortitude.

While verse 31 relays Jezebel's ethnic origins, this information serves an informational purpose rather than as a condemnation of her non-Israelite ancestry. Worth noting is that the Sidonians do not appear in the list of seven nations that the Lord prohibited his people from marrying. Nevertheless, Jezebel's polytheism disqualified her from espousing an Israelite. Consequently, Ahab's marriage was not abhorrent because of its multiethnic nature, but because it prompted the king to worship idols instead of the God of Abraham.

Jewish Men and Their Foreign Wives

Ezra 10:1–4 is one of the most controversial passages in the Old Testament. After Ezra led the second group of exiles back from Captivity (ca. 458 BC), he learned of a social problem that threatened Israel's existence and future as God's covenant people.[68] Many of the Jews had disobeyed God's admonition not to marry the inhabitants of the surrounding nations (cf. Deut 7:2–4). Rather than enforcing this command, Israel's priests and Levites had been foremost in practicing this forbidden mingling (Ezra 9:2).

The problem with the mixed marriages of Ezra's time was that a number of Jewish men had joined themselves to women who worshiped false gods and were spiritual adulterers (Ezra 9:1). Religious intermixing in

---

66. Walsh, *1 Kings*, 218.
67. Brueggemann, *1 and 2 Kings*, 202.
68. Brown, "The Problem of Mixed Marriages," 438.

EQUALLY YOKED

Israel's past had led to apostasy,[69] and would have the same effect again if left unchecked. In response to the dilemma, Ezra tore his garments, pulled some of the hair from his head and beard, and confessed the trespass to God (Ezra 9:3, 6–15). Coggins noted that Ezra's "prayer concludes with a direct appeal to God, and the use once again of the theme of a remnant."[70] The preservation of this vulnerable remnant would be the primary motivation for what Israel did next.

In an attempt to preserve the spiritual integrity of the covenant people "at any cost,"[71] Shecaniah the priest impelled the men to make a covenant with God to put away their foreign wives and children (Ezra 10:3). Chapter 10 lists Shecaniah's father Jehiel as one of the transgressors (10:26), which may indicate that he had divorced his Israelite wife so that he could marry a pagan woman.[72] After hearing Shecaniah's message, the offenders recognized their wrongdoing and divorced their idolatrous foreign wives.

Two observations are in order. First, one should note that each Jew must divorce his unbelieving wife "according to the Law" (Ezra 10:3). This reference to the Law (*tôrāh*) is an allusion to the injunction not to intermarry with other nations (Deut 7:3). The Jewish offenders were guilty of intentionally disregarding God's edict for selecting appropriate wives, so Ezra required them to separate from the pagan women according to the regulations of the Mosaic law.

Second, in no other biblical period does one find the explicit command to divorce a spouse. The reason for this unique circumstance was Israel's vulnerability in the early post-exilic era. During this stage of Israelite history the nation's population was dangerously low, hence the repeated usages of the term *remnant* in the book of Ezra.[73]

Given the extent of the list of offenders (cf. Ezra 10:18–44), cohabitation with unbelievers was perilous. After the Assyrian conquest of 722

---

69. Breneman, *Ezra*, 164. Cf. 1 Kgs 11:1–40.
70. Coggins, *The Books of Ezra and Nehemiah*, 59.
71. Kidner, *Ezra and Nehemiah*, 70.
72. Throntveit, *Ezra–Nehemiah*, 57. Another possible explanation is that Jehiel remained married to Shecaniah's mother while taking a second wife from the surrounding nations. Polygamy was a common practice before the Exile, and may have been a concern in the post-exilic era as well. In either case, Jehiel sinned against God's law because he had married a woman who worshiped false gods.
73. The word *remnant* appears four times in the immediate context of Ezra 10:1–4 (cf. Ezra 9:8, 13, 14, 15). Apart from Jer 44 (cf. vv. 7, 12, 14, 28), Ezra 9 contains the highest concentration of remnant language in the entire Old Testament.

BC, the residents of the northern kingdom intermarried with pagans and produced the syncretistic Samaritans. Thus, in the southern kingdom "the survival of the Jewish faith seemed at risk. Drastic measures were necessary to purify the community from a growing corruption."[74] In other words, desperate times required desperate measures because so many Jewish men had married women who worshiped false gods.

Implications

This systematic analysis of Old Testament passages that portray certain multiethnic marriages in a negative light reveals several things. First, in four of the seven cases (Esau, Dinah, Solomon, post-exilic Jewish men), the unions violated God's injunction against intermarrying with representatives of the seven nations of Canaan (Gen 15:12–16; Deut 7:1–6). Two of the instances (Esau, Dinah) allude to the spouses' non-covenantal standing before God, while the other two (Solomon, post-exilic Jewish men) explicitly highlight the religious apostasy that resulted from marrying people who worshiped false gods. Additionally, Scripture reveals that Dinah's brutal encounter with Shechem the Hivite was reprehensible because he raped her.

Second, although Jezebel did not originate from one of the seven Canaanite nations with which God forbade intermarriage, her commitment to Baal excluded her as an eligible marriage partner. Ahab's apathetic stance toward her religious beliefs initially led to his adoption of Baalism, and then to the northern kingdom's implementation of polytheism. The result was similar to Solomon's plight and that of the post-exilic Jewish men because the consequence of Ahab's marriage to Jezebel was religious apostasy.

Third, two of the cases (Abram and David) emphasize disobedience. In Abram's case, God had promised an heir, so his marriage to Hagar was unnecessary and indicated a lack of faith. Bathsheba already was the wife of another man, so David did not have a right to take her. Both Abram and David deliberately snubbed God's express will in order to pursue their selfish desires.

In summary, none of these examples have as their concern the complete prevention of the comingling of distinct people groups. Rather, the motivation in most of the above cases was Israel's religious purity. God required the absolute and unwavering devotion of his covenant people, so he refused to share his glory with any idol (Exod 20:4–5). The Lord also

---

74. Larson and Dahlen, *Ezra, Nehemiah*, 119.

expected his people to trust him and abide by his directives regarding morality (Exod 20:14; cf. Heb 11:6). To disobey his commands amounted to spiritual rebellion. In short, God required the Israelites to honor him in every aspect of their lives, including their selection of suitable marriage partners.

POSITIVE EXAMPLES OF MULTIETHNIC MARRIAGE

In addition to ambiguous and negative examples of multiethnic marriage, the Old Testament also contains numerous positive instances of the practice. This list is different than the sampling of ambiguous and negative matrimonial unions in that all cases originate from before the pre-monarchal period (prior to ca. 1050 BC) rather than within the entire scope of Israel's history. In this section, the writer will examine the reasons why Scripture approves of each particular marriage.

Moses and Zipporah

After Moses fled Egypt to escape his punishment for murdering an Egyptian taskmaster, he settled in the land of Midian (Exod 2:15). The biblical material, along with archaeological evidence, suggests that the Midianites dwelled in the southern part of the Transjordan as well as northwestern Arabia.[75] In this country, Moses adopted a pastoral lifestyle and married Zipporah, the daughter of Reuel, who was the priest of Midian (Exod 2:16–21).

The book of Genesis identifies the Midianites as descendants of Abraham's wives Hagar and Keturah (Gen 25:1–4; 37:28). Over half a millennium and untold generations separated them from the Israelite line of the family tree. In the intervening centuries, the different divisions of Abraham's progeny had developed into distinct people groups. The patriarch's faith appears to have had a lasting effect on at least a portion of his Midianite descendants, for Reuel believed in the God of Israel.[76] Because he was a follower of Yahweh, he was able to serve as a trusted spiritual advisor to his son-in-law when Moses led the sons of Israel during their time in the

---

75. *The NIV Archaeological Study Bible*, 88.

76. Meyers, *Exodus*, 45. "Friend of God," the meaning of his name, reveals much about Reuel's religious affiliation.

wilderness of Sinai (Exod 18:17–27).[77] Presumably, Zipporah was a believer as well. Scripture portrays her positively rather than as an idolater.

On the other hand, a number of Midianites worshiped false gods, at one point prompting the covenant people to bow to Baal of Peor at Shittim in Moab (Num 25:1–9). After sending a plague to punish the Israelites who had revered the idol, Yahweh directed his people to strike down the Midianites. The Lord ordered their destruction because they had enticed Israel to stray from worshiping him (Num 25:16–18).

This dual portrayal of the Midianites in the Torah prompted Adriane Leveen to ask an important question: "Taken together, the stories of Jethro and that of the [other] Midianites allow one to ask 'upon what basis is one sort of outsider to be tolerated and another to be banned?'"[78] The answer to this inquiry is straightforward and provides a clue as to why certain multiethnic marriages were acceptable in Old Testament times and others were not.

On the one hand, God set himself against the Midianites at Shittim not because they were foreigners, but because they venerated idols and taught the sons of Israel to do so as well. On the other hand, no such denunciation of Reuel or his family appears in Scripture because of their commitment to the God of Abraham. Although her relatives certainly were "marginal to Israelite society,"[79] Zipporah the Midianite was an appropriate marriage partner for Moses the Israelite because she recognized Yahweh was the only Lord.

One final detail worth noting is Moses' unique relationship with God. The book of Deuteronomy regards him as a great prophet like no other because he knew Yahweh "face to face" (Deut 34:10). Additionally, only he was privileged to receive a glimpse of God's glory because he had found favor in the Lord's sight (Exod 33:17–23). Moses was not a perfect man, however, because Scripture records his two great sins (Exod 2:11–12; Num 20:8–13). Absent from this list is his marriage to Zipporah. In other words, multiethnic marriage to a woman who was a fellow believer received no censure because God approved of the union.

---

77. Leveen, "Inside Out," 397.
78. Ibid.
79. McNutt, "The Kenites," 109.

EQUALLY YOKED

Shelomith's Son

Lev 24:10–16 introduces readers to a young man whose mother Shelomith was an Israelite of Danite extraction, while his father was an Egyptian. Considering the amount of time the sons of Israel resided in Egypt, one might expect they frequently intermarried with the native Egyptians, as well as with African and Asiatic slaves who derived from distinct ethnic populations.[80] The reference to the mixed multitude that exited Egypt alongside the Israelites during their exodus corroborates this proposal (Exod 12:38).[81]

During Israel's wanderings in the desert, Shelomith's son quarreled with a full-blooded Israelite. In his anger, the multiethnic young man blasphemed the name of Yahweh and cursed (Lev 24:10b–11). Because of his dual ancestry, the Israelites were unsure how to proceed and placed him into custody until the Lord revealed how they should respond to his breaking of the third commandment (cf. Lev 24:12; Exod 20:7).

Through Moses, God directed everyone who had heard the young man's curse to lay their hands upon his head in order to verify that the accusation was truthful. The witnesses confirmed the guilt of Shelomith's son, after which God provided the protocol for this and future cases that involved people of mixed heritage: "As the sojourner, so the native. Whenever he blasphemes the Name, he shall be put to death" (Lev 24:16b). In other words, one rule governed all people regardless of their heritage.

One may find it odd that the author categorizes the text in which Israel puts Shelomith's son to death as a positive example of multiethnic marriage, but justification exists for this decision. First, although Martin Noth wrote that the son "remains a foreigner, even if he has an Israelite mother,"[82] this interpretation of Lev 24:10–16 is incorrect. Verse 10 initially identifies Shelomith's son as having an Egyptian father, but thereafter, the text identifies him as the offspring of an Israelite woman numerous times (cf. Lev 24:10b, 11a, 11b). The pericope clearly demonstrates his association with Israel through his mother's side of the family. This relationship is one of the

---

80. Stuart, *Exodus*, 303–4.

81. Cole, *Exodus*, 113. Cole noted that the identity of the mixed multitude in Exod 20:7 "would either be the result of intermarriage, or else kindred Semitic groups who seized the opportunity to escape."

82. Noth, *Leviticus*, 179. Noth appears to have ignored cases such as Moses' biracial son Gershom and David, the descendant of Ruth the Moabitess.

Multiethnic Marriage in the Old Testament

reasons why Lev 24:11 provides detailed information regarding Shelomith's pedigree (i.e., "the daughter of Dibri, of the tribe of Dan").

Second, commentators who view Shelomith's son as "the product of an unlawful mixture"[83] or disparage him on the basis of his status as a "half-breed"[84] import into Lev 24 concepts that are not native to the chapter. The passage never condemns Shelomith's marriage or her son's multiethnic heritage; it only addresses the wicked action of blaspheming Yahweh's name. His dual ancestry serves only to explain why the Israelites had difficulty deciding how they should react to his flagrant sin.

Third, God's response to the young man's infraction signifies that his law is unchanging whether one is a full-blooded Israelite, half-Israelite, or non-Israelite (cf. Lev 24:16, 22). In other words, while some of the sons of Israel viewed the young man differently because of his mixed parentage, God did not. The same standard pertained to Shelomith's son as everyone else.[85] Accordingly, this example portrays the concept of multiethnic marriage in a positive light.

Moses and His Cushite Wife

Num 12:1–15 reveals that during the time of Israel's desert wanderings, Moses married a Cushite woman. Scholars often identify the region of Cush as modern-day Ethiopia, which signifies she was of African extraction.[86] The woman likely was part of the mixed multitude who escaped Egypt alongside the sons of Israel (Exod 12:38), and her non-Israelite background prompted Moses' siblings Miriam and Aaron to speak out against him (Num 12:1).[87]

When Miriam and Aaron jealously objected that the Lord had spoken through them as well, God ordered the three to gather before him in Israel's tent of meeting (Num 12:2, 4). He chastised Moses' siblings and declared that their brother had a special relationship with Him. Only he had beheld

---

83. Sherwood, *Leviticus*, 82.
84. Vroom, "Recasting Mišpāṭîm," 27.
85. Bellinger, *Leviticus, Numbers*, 146.
86. Ibid., 226.
87. The placement of Miriam's name before Aaron's in Num 12:1 implies she was the instigator of the criticism directed toward their brother Moses, and Aaron merely was following her lead. For this reason the Lord decided to punish only Miriam instead of Aaron.

"the form of Yahweh" (Num 12:8). As punishment for her presumptuous arrogance, God struck Miriam with leprosy so her skin became "as white as snow" (Num 12:10). Ultimately, Moses' pleadings to heal Miriam prompted God to heal her seven days later (Num 12:13–15).

An analysis of Num 12 divulges several pertinent facts. First, although some commentators understand Miriam's disdain of the Cushite woman as nothing more than an excuse for attacking Moses' authority,[88] Scripture does not validate this interpretation. Num 12:1 explains Miriam and Aaron questioned their brother's leadership "because (*'odôt*) of the Cushite woman." The Hebrew term *'odôt* denotes causality,[89] proving that Moses' marriage to the woman from Cush was the primary motivation for this particular confrontation.

Second, if his marriage to the Cushite woman had been a legitimate cause for concern, one would expect Num 12 to expose Moses' error. Instead, the Lord expressed his wholehearted approval of his servant while, at the same time, excoriating his siblings for daring to bring a false accusation against Israel's leader. In other words, Moses' multiethnic marriage was well within the bounds of what God considered acceptable behavior.

Third, the double reference to the woman's Cushite origins (Num 12:1) leads the reader to conclude that Miriam's problem with her was that she was not an Israelite by birth. In essence, her impetus for questioning Moses' authority stemmed from a racist denunciation of his wife.[90] The fact that God struck Miriam with a disease that made her skin as white as snow may be significant as well. Perhaps, as William H. Bellinger Jr. suggested, the whitish pallor of her diseased skin was an appropriate punishment for loathing an African woman whose hue was much darker than Miriam's.[91] This proposition may be difficult to prove objectively, but in any case Yahweh defended Moses' multiethnic marriage.

Salmon and Rahab

Joshua 2 relates that, during the period of the Conquest, Israel's spies received assistance from an unexpected source after they entered Jericho with the purpose of identifying its weaknesses. When the city's king became

---

88. Wenham, *Numbers*, 111.
89. Brown et al, *Hebrew and English Lexicon*, 15.
90. E.g., Sherwood, *Leviticus*, 155; Allen, *Numbers*, 798.
91. Bellinger, *Leviticus, Numbers*, 226.

Multiethnic Marriage in the Old Testament

suspicious of the mysterious visitors, Rahab, a harlot, hid them among the stalks of flax that were drying on her roof. She convinced the ruler's search party that the two spies already had escaped Jericho and were headed in the direction of the Jordan River (Josh 2:3–7).

Rahab's motivation for protecting the spies stemmed from the dual realization that Yahweh had given the land of Canaan to the Israelites, and he was God of both heaven and earth (Josh 2:9–11). This confession amounted to a rejection of her Canaanite idols and an unwavering commitment to the God of Israel.[92] The result of Rahab's courageous actions and her newfound faith was a treaty with the covenant people that saved her and her entire family from the Israelite extermination of Jericho's population (Josh 2:12–14, 17–20).

After their deliverance, Rahab and her relatives resided "outside the camp of Israel" for a time (Josh 6:23b), but assimilation into the covenant people soon occurred. Josh 6:25b records, "She dwells in the midst of Israel to this day because she hid the messengers whom Joshua sent to explore Jericho." Rahab also married an Israelite man named Salmon and became an ancestor of the Messiah.[93]

Some scholars take the reference in Josh 6:23b to mean that non-Israelites who became followers of Yahweh often remained marginalized, dwelling on the fringes of society as distinct ethnic populations.[94] However, the fact that Rahab lived "in the midst" of Israel (Josh 6:25) instead of remaining on the periphery appears to contradict this assertion. Richard Hess put it well when he explained how non-Israelites could unite with the covenant people:

> [Rahab] is not distinguished from, but is part of, Israel. She has ceased to be a Canaanite or non-Israelite and has now become an Israelite . . . The text stresses that Rahab rejected her past associations with the Canaanites and transferred her loyalty to Israel. By so doing, it demonstrates how Israel could receive others with kindness.[95]

---

92. Howard, "Rahab's Faith," 276. Howard rightly noted that the spies' treaty with Rahab was not sinful because she had rejected the religion of the Canaanites.

93. Although the Old Testament preserves Salmon's name in a genealogical record (cf. 1 Chron 2:11), only the New Testament identifies him as Rahab's husband (Matt 1:4).

94. E.g., Hawk, *Joshua*, 104; Woudstra, *The Book of Joshua*, 116; Kaminsky, "Did Election Imply," 413.

95. Hess, *Joshua*, 134.

Thus, Rahab's conversion from paganism to the worship of Yahweh wove her into the fabric of Israelite society.

While in a genetic sense Rahab remained a Gentile, Salmon was free to marry her because in a religious sense she was an Israelite. For this reason the book of Joshua does not condemn the spies' treaty with her as it does in the case of the nation's spurious associations with the pagan Gibeonites (cf. Josh 9:1–27).[96] The New Testament's favorable portrayal of Rahab (Heb 11:31; Jas 2:25) also serves to demonstrate that Scripture depicts her multi-ethnic marriage to an Israelite in a positive manner.

Caleb's Family

Because of his unwavering faith, Caleb is one of the most celebrated figures of the pre-Monarchic era of Israel's history. Of the dozen spies who originally scouted out the land of Canaan prior to the forty years of desert wandering, only he and Joshua reported to the people that they should have faith in God's promises and take the land (Num 14:6–9). When the conquest of Canaan finally occurred, he and his family occupied the hill country of Hebron south of Jerusalem and exterminated the giants who lived in the region (Josh 14:1–14; 15:13–19).

Interestingly, Caleb's identification as the son of Jephunneh the Kenizzite (Josh 14:6) appears to point to a non-Israelite heritage. Admittedly, family designations are not always an accurate gauge of one's cultural background because the nomenclature of diverse people groups' often overlap. The term *Kenizzite*, however, may be the gentilic form of *Kenaz*, a name that appears both in Edomite genealogical lists and centuries later in the branch of the Judahite tribe that sired Caleb (Gen 36:11; 1 Chron 4:13).[97]

Alternatively, Caleb's father may have pertained to the Kenizzites who resided in Canaan during Abram's lifetime (Gen 15:19).[98] A definitive answer as to which people group spawned Caleb's ancestors may not be

---

96. In reality, Rahab typifies the grafting of Gentile believers (represented as wild branches) into the olive tree that symbolizes Israel (cf. Rom 11:1–36). For a discussion of how early Christians such as Origen and Theodoret regarded Rahab as a prototype for Gentile believers of the New Testament era, see Auld, *Jesus Son of Nauē in Codex Vaticanus*, 139.

97. Gray, *Joshua*, 131.

98. Woudstra, *The Book of Joshua*, 227.

possible, but E. John Hamlin's detailed analysis of Caleb's family provides convincing evidence that his family was of foreign extraction rather than native Israelites: "In the group of peoples associated with Caleb, we find Korah (1 Chron 2:43), whose name is also borne by an Edomite chief (Gen 36:16), Rekem a Midianite (Num 3:18; Josh 13:21), and Shema a Kenite (1 Chron 2:55)."[99] Whether Caleb's bloodline was Edomite or Canaanite, his forefathers likely were members of the mixed multitude that departed Egypt with the sons of Israel (Exod 12:38).

Some critical scholars find it problematic that in different texts Scripture describes Caleb as both a Kenizzite and a Judahite,[100] but no contradiction exists. In much the same manner that a man from Nigeria who obtains United States citizenship can refer to himself simultaneously as a Nigerian and an American, Caleb's clan became so intertwined with the tribe of Judah that the appellations of Kenizzite and Judahite concurrently were accurate.[101] This close association ultimately led to intermarriage and complete assimilation, which explains why Caleb appears in Judah's genealogy (1 Chron 2:42).[102]

Caleb's heroic portrayal in the book of Joshua, along with the absorption of his family line into the tribe of Judah, reveals several insights about multiethnic marriage in the pre-Monarchic era. First, Israel welcomed foreigners who regarded Yahweh as the only true God. Such persons could obtain a position of honor within the covenant people, as evidenced by Caleb's representing the tribe of Judah as one of the original twelve spies who infiltrated the land of Canaan (Num 14:6–9).[103]

Second, Caleb's reception of territory in Hebron with the blessing of Joshua (Josh 14:13–14) confirms non-Israelite believers could integrate themselves fully into the nation of Israel instead of merely remaining on the fringes of society. His ownership of a tract of land that God had promised to the descendants of Abraham is substantial evidence he enjoyed the

---

99. Hamlin, *Joshua*, 122.

100. E.g., Dahlen, "The Savior and the Dog," 222.

101. Similarly, the book of Genesis depicts the men who enslaved Joseph as Ishmaelites and Midianites (Gen 37:28) because both descriptors were true.

102. Miller and Tucker, *The Book of Joshua*, 117.

103. One also should recall that Othniel, the first judge of Israel, was one of Caleb's blood relatives (cf. Josh 15:17; Judg 1:13; 3:9). Furthermore, Shamgar, Israel's third judge, possessed a non-Semitic name (perhaps Hittite or Hurrian) that also implies a foreign heritage (Judg 3:31).

same benefits as natural born citizens.[104] For all intents and purposes, Caleb became an Israelite because of his unwavering commitment to the God of Abraham.

Third, as Hamlin observed, "Caleb's special place in the Joshua story emphasizes the importance of the faithfulness to Yahweh . . . rather than blood relationship to Israel."[105] Accordingly, the intermarriage of Caleb's line into the tribe of Judah was acceptable because his family members were followers of God rather than idolaters. As in the case of Rahab, Caleb's account discloses that multiethnic marriage was acceptable for an Israelite when the partner worshiped Yahweh because God examined one's heart rather than one's outward appearance (1 Sam 16:17).

Samson and His Philistine Wife

Samson proved to be one of the most rebellious representatives of God in the book of Judges. Although the angel of the Lord had directed his parents that he must observe the Nazirite vow for the entirety of his life (Judg 13:3–5; cf. Num 6:1–21), he disregarded every aspect of the oath.[106] Additionally, the anarchic judge married a woman who was not an Israelite.

Judg 14:1 records that Samson became enamored with a Philistine woman who resided in Timnah, a village on the border of Danite territory. During this period of time, the Philistines were the predominant oppressors of Israel (cf. Judg 13:1; 14:4). Contrary to the ancient-Near Eastern tradition of fathers securing spouses for their offspring, Samson insisted his parents acquiesce to his demands for a mate (Judg 14:2).[107] When his father and mother protested that an Israelite wife would make a more appropriate bride than the daughter of an uncircumcised Philistine, Samson refused to listen. He maintained his choice for a spouse was "right in [his] eyes" (Judg 14:3b), a phrase that mirrors the people's practice of doing what was right in their own eyes during the era of the judges (cf. Judg 17:6; 21:25).[108]

---

104. Harris et al, *Joshua*, 86.

105. Hamlin, *Joshua*, 122.

106. Judg 14–16 emphasizes that Samson deliberately disregarded his Nazirite vow by: 1) consuming grape products at his wedding feast (Judg 14:10–11); 2) touching dead bodies (Judg 14:9; 15:15; 16:7); and 3) allowing Delilah to cut his hair (Judg 16:19).

107. Schneider, *Judges*, 205.

108. McCann, *Judges*, 101.

Samson's parents objected to the wedding because it conflicted with Mosaic legislation that prohibited associating with idolaters,[109] but "they did not know that it was from the LORD, for He sought an opportunity against the Philistines" (Judg 14:4a). In other words, their son's betrothal to the Timnite woman was part of God's divine plan to prompt his judge to attack the people of Philistia.[110] Soon Samson would strike by setting fire to the Philistines' crops after his father-in-law gave his wife to another man (Judg 15:1–5). In response to this act, the Philistines burned his ex-wife and her father, and Samson once more sought revenge against them (cf. Judg 15:6–8).

Shimon Bakon referred to Judg 14:1–4 as "a magnificent paradox [because] providence decrees for a certain purpose that Samson choose a Philistine wife, yet the fact that he follows his own inclination is considered a rebellion against God."[111] This explanation, however, is a misreading of the text. One must recall that a major theme of the book of Judges is God's control over Israel in spite of the nation's frequent rebellion against its sovereign Ruler. Samson's mutinous actions were no different.

In every instance in which his people rebelled against him, God sent foreign oppressors who ultimately achieved his purpose by prompting Israel to repent and return to their Ruler.[112] Similarly, the Lord used Samson's defiant, selfish actions to motivate him to become the judge the Lord had prophesied he would be (cf. Judg 13:5).[113] Consequently, Judg 14 contains no inconsistency, but underscores God's ability to accomplish his plans regardless of the circumstances, without sanctioning the events (cf. Gen 50:20; Rom 8:28).

Judges 14:4 makes two assertions. On the one hand, Samson's marriage to a Timnite woman was deplorable on a personal level because she

---

109. The region of Philistia was not one of the nations Yahweh explicitly prohibited in Deut 7:1–6, but the fact that its inhabitants served idols made Samson's choice of a Timnite bride unacceptable. For a helpful discussion of abhorrent practices that disqualified the Philistines as marriage partners for the Israelites, see Howard, "Philistines," 239–40, 248–49.

110. Luciani, "Samson," 324.

111. Bakon, "Samson," 36.

112. Virtually all Old Testament scholars recognize the cyclic nature of the book of Judges. The text explains that each occupation by a foreign enemy was a visible manifestation of Yahweh's response to Israel's rebellion. Oppression led to Israel's repentance, after which the Lord raised up military saviors to deliver His covenant nation from its persecutors. For a discussion of this motif see Klein, *The Triumph of Irony*, 34.

113. Block, *Judges, Ruth*, 426–27.

was not a follower of Yahweh. On the other hand, the result of Samson's union with a pagan non-Israelite was positive on a theological level because it provoked him to enact God's desire to deliver his people from the Philistines.

Boaz and Ruth

Perhaps the most familiar Old Testament case of multiethnic marriage is Ruth's betrothal to Boaz. Because of a severe drought in the land of Israel, an Israelite named Elimelech sojourned in the land of Moab with his wife Naomi and his two sons. While living there, Mahlon and Chilion married Moabite women who worshiped idols. When Naomi's husband and sons died within a short period of time, she decided to return to Israel, and her daughter-in-law Ruth expressed her interest in accompanying her (Ruth 1:1–14).

At first, Naomi urged her daughter-in-law to return to her Moabite family and seek another husband, but Ruth insisted that she was resolute in her decision: "For wherever you go, I will go. And in the place you abide, I will abide. Your people are my people, and your God is my God" (Ruth 1:16b). In essence, Ruth forsook her pagan religion in order to join herself to the people of Israel, subsequently embracing their God as hers.[114]

In Naomi's hometown of Bethlehem, Ruth labored in Boaz's field so she could provide for her mother-in-law (Ruth 2:1–2). Providentially, Boaz was one of two close kinsmen of Ruth's father-in-law Elimelech. When the other relative forfeited his legal right to redeem Elimelech's inheritance, Boaz accepted the obligation and married Ruth so he might produce an heir who would perpetuate a family line that otherwise would go extinct (Ruth 4:1–10; cf. Gen 38:8; Deut 25:5–6). Three generations later, this union led to the birth of King David (Ruth 4:18–22). The lineage's most important descendant was Jesus Christ, who was born a millennium later (cf. Matt 1:1–17).

Rabbinical commentators often found Boaz's marriage to Ruth to be an embarrassment because of the Toranic prohibition against permitting Moabites into Israel's assembly "even to the tenth generation" (Deut

---

114. Hubbard, *The Book of Ruth*, 117. Hubbard's claim that Ruth "renounced her ethnic . . . roots" is flawed because the book repeatedly calls her a Moabitess (Ruth 2:2, 21; 4:5, 10).

23:3–4),[115] and the fact that David, Israel's most celebrated king, was part Moabite because of his great-grandmother's ancestry.[116] Because of this perceived quandary, ancient Jewish scholars argued that either the Deuteronomic polemic against Moabites pertained only to males,[117] or the book of Ruth was "a silent protest against intermarriage."[118] However, both attempts to reconcile the book of Ruth to Deut 23:3–4 are incorrect.

First, the women of Bethlehem overwhelmingly supported Ruth's marriage to Boaz because they imparted on her the blessing of fruitfulness. Their mention of Rachel and Leah (Jacob's wives; cf. Ruth 4:11), together with Perez (the progenitor of the Judahite line; cf. Ruth 4:12), demonstrates that they had accepted Ruth as one of their own. Essentially, they had adopted her into the tribe of Judah. The author's inclusion of this account alongside David's genealogy (Ruth 4:18–22) indicates he shared the Bethlehemite women's approval of the marriage.[119]

Second, the injunction forbidding Moabites from entering the assembly of Yahweh in Deut 23:3–4 does not apply to Ruth. Because Boaz functioned as a kinsman redeemer, his son Obed counted as Elimelech's heir rather than as a Moabite. This arrangement circumvented Deut 23:3–4 and explains why his lineage (including David) legitimately could sit upon the throne of Israel although Moabite blood flowed through its veins.

Third, Ruth's rejection of Moab's national deities and her subsequent commitment to Yahweh made her a suitable bride for Boaz. Accordingly, Hamlin put it well when he wrote, "The book of Ruth is a bold challenge to readers in every age to open themselves to different evaluations of a foreign people usually considered as evil, even to the possibility that God could use a foreigner like Ruth in his plan for all nations!"[120] One must add to

---

115. The context of this prohibition was the Moabite attempt to snare Israel first by hiring Balaam the son of Beor to curse the people (Num 22:1—24:22) and then by successfully enticing them to become sexually involved with Moabite women and serve Baal (Num 25:1–16).

116. For a summary of rabbinic explanations regarding why Ruth's inclusion in the Davidic family line did not contradict Deut 23:3–4, see Magonet, "Rabbinic Readings of Ruth," 155.

117. Ibid.

118. Cundall and Morris, *Judges and Ruth*, 250.

119. No justification exists for the assertion that the book of Ruth depicts the titular character negatively. For an unconvincing attempt to paint Ruth as a seductress who manipulated Boaz, see Ostriker, "The Redeeming of Ruth," 217–19.

120. Hamlin, *Ruth*, 10.

Hamlin's perceptive observation that the Old Testament's unchangeable requirement for portraying a non-Israelite or a multiethnic marriage positively is the participants' belief that no God exists but Yahweh. Ruth fulfilled this prerequisite admirably.

Implications

This survey of Old Testament multiethnic weddings that receive a commendable evaluation helps to define the contours of what makes a marriage between people of two ethnicities acceptable. Except for the cases of Samson and his Philistine bride (which teaches that God can overrule a rebellious act to accomplish his purposes), and Shelomith's son (which specifies that the same standard applies to Israelites, half-Israelites, and non-Israelites), the other examples in this section express the same theme. Although Yahweh made a special covenant with Abraham and his descendants, people of foreign descent who forsook the gods of their nations in order to serve him could find acceptance in the Israelite community.

As God-fearers, these Gentiles participated in the religious life of Israel and enjoyed the blessings of the Abrahamic covenant. Furthermore, they could reside within Israel without any stigma attached to them (e.g., Rahab), become Israelites in every sense of the word (e.g., Ruth), possess territory in the Promised Land (e.g., Caleb), and become the spouse of one of the nation's most godly heroes (e.g., Zipporah). Moreover, Yahweh defended Moses' Cushite wife when Miriam despised her because of her foreign ethnicity. In summary, multiethnic marriages between Israelites and non-Israelites were just as valid as Israelite–Israelite unions under the proper circumstances.

IMPLICATIONS FOR PREMARITAL COUNSELING

The preceding investigation provides Christian counselors with a biblically centered means by which to evaluate the practice of multiethnic marriage. First, contrary to the opinions of some ancient, medieval, and modern commentators (such as Dawkins), the God of Israel did not express xenophobic tendencies in the Old Testament era. Undoubtedly, he warned the Israelites about associating with the people groups that surrounded them, but not because of their racial makeup.

Multiethnic Marriage in the Old Testament

Yahweh rejected certain ethnic groups because they worshiped false gods. He commanded his followers not to make treaties with these nations or intermarry with them. In instances in which Israelites ignored this decree, Scripture portrays the resulting multiethnic marriages negatively.

Second, foreigners who recognized the error of worshiping graven images could become followers of Yahweh. God welcomed these religious immigrants warmly and encouraged his people to do so as well. The prophet Isaiah recorded Yahweh's invitation for the Gentiles to acknowledge him as the only true God:

> And the sons of the foreigner who is joined to Yahweh, to serve Him and to love the name of Yahweh, to become His servants, all who keep from profaning the Sabbath and hold firmly to My covenant, even them will I cause to come to My holy mountain, and cause them to rejoice in My house of prayer. Their whole burnt offerings and their sacrifices will obtain favor on My altar, for My house will be called a house of prayer for all peoples. The utterance of the Lord GOD who gathers the outcasts of Israel: "Yet I will gather unto him those who are to be gathered to him." (Isa 56:6–8)

In other words, Yahweh desired people from all ethnic backgrounds to become God-fearers.

Scripture portrays marriages between Israelite and Gentile believers more positively than unions in which his covenant people took pagans as spouses. While God issued an unequivocal mandate to avoid interfaith unions, no such command existed for believers who derived from disparate ethnic backgrounds. The implication is that God was more concerned that spouses have a mutual commitment to him than a similar racial heritage.

These factors indicate biblical counselors must develop a balanced approach to the issue of multiethnic marriage. On the one hand, the Old Testament contains no universal condemnation of intermarriage. Counselors, therefore, should not decline to provide premarital counseling solely because the couple possesses distinctive ethnic or cultural characteristics.

On the other hand, counselors should not agree to every multiethnic couple's request to receive premarital instruction. The faith of people who seek marriage is a crucial factor in determining if their objective is biblically acceptable. Scripture prohibits the marriages of potential husbands and wives who do not share a mutual commitment to Christ. Consequently, biblical counselors must not endorse such unions by conducting counseling sessions or officiating at their wedding ceremonies.

Before counselors consent to offer premarital training, their task is to determine if both candidates are believers. Two topics to explore in this pre-counseling consultation are the couple's understanding of salvation and their testimonies of how they became Christians. Their present relationships with Christ also are important matters to consider (cf. Matt 7:21; 2 Cor 5:17).

Counselors need to listen carefully to these answers in order to determine whether participants understand the gospel correctly. Counselors also should be aware that people sometimes give the responses they think their interviewers would like to hear in order to secure their participation in the impending marriage ceremony. In cases in which reservations arise about one of the participants' relationships with Christ, evangelism—rather than pre-marital counseling—will become the counselor's goal.

In summary, multiethnic couples who exhibit an authentic Christian faith are suitable candidates for premarital counseling because their marriage is scripturally permissible. However, multiethnic couples who do not have the same relationship with Christ are incompatible marriage partners. Under these circumstances, biblical counselors should not provide pre-marital counseling.

3

Multiethnic Marriage in the New Testament

INTRODUCTION

SLAVERY WAS A FIERCELY debated subject during the era of the American Civil War (1861–65). Opponents of the institution vociferously denounced treating fellow humans as property. In response, supporters warned emancipation ultimately would lead to marriages between African Americans and Anglos,[1] an alarming thought to slaveholders. For this reason, pro-slavery Democrats attempted to malign Abolitionists in particular, and Republicans in general, by portraying both groups as proponents of intermarriage.

In 1864, David Goodman Croly, the managing editor of the Democratic newspaper *The New York World* (1860–1931), published an anonymous booklet claiming to be the product of an Abolitionist. He entitled his work, *Miscegenation: The Theory of the Blending of the Races, Applied to the American White Man and Negro*.[2] Croly's objective was to turn voters against Abraham Lincoln by convincing them his reelection would lead to the legalization of intermarriage.[3]

---

1. Except in quotations, this study employs contemporary ethnic identifiers.

2. Croly, *Miscegenation*, 1–72.

3. Ibid., 49. Croly declared, "When the President proclaimed Emancipation he proclaimed also the mingling of the races."

EQUALLY YOKED

The first paragraph of the treatise appealed in part to Scripture for its feigned support of intermarriage: "The teachings of physiology as well as the inspiration of Christianity settle the question that all the tribes which inhabit the earth were originally derived from one type [of human being]."[4] Next, the manuscript predicted, "The perfect type of the future will be that of the blended races, with the sunny hues of the South tinging the colorless complexion of the icy north."[5] Finally, the author ultimately appealed to Acts 17:26 as justification for a claim that scandalized the majority of his contemporary readers:

> You may build cisterns, and canals, and levees; but some time, the water that you seek will find its level again. Not the less so with the blood of man. As God made of one blood all nations of the earth, and as all are brothers from Adam; so, whatever artificial distinctions and barriers men may raise, the blood of humanity will at the end find its certain level.[6]

Croly's scheme to remove Lincoln from office was unsuccessful, but he cited a Bible verse Christian defenders of slavery often felt compelled to address.

For example, seven years earlier Reverend James A. Sloan, a Presbyterian minister from Mississippi, argued slavery was an acceptable practice for Christians. He was disturbed by the way abolitionists used Acts 17:26 to demonstrate God's disapproval of slavery:

> The passage from Acts 17:26 that is quoted to sustain the position that "the Gospel makes no distinction between men on the ground of color, or race," has no application to the point. That passage simply proves that all men of all nations are descended from the same original stock, or what is usually called "the unity of the race." This we have admitted, and are prepared to sustain. But the unity and equality of races is a distinction with a difference, and that difference has been made by the Creator himself.... Sin has disturbed this equality, while it has not interfered with its unity.[7]

Sloan then traced the so-called inequality of African Americans to their ancestor Ham. He insisted Noah had cursed this branch of his family tree, bestowing on it a life of servitude.[8] The implication of the pastor's argument

---

4. Ibid., 3.
5. Ibid., 27.
6. Ibid., 54.
7. Sloan, *The Question Answered*, 189–90.
8. This faulty interpretation of Gen 9:20-27 was popular among Christian

for the inequality of African Americans and Anglos was their unsuitability for intermarriage.

These examples establish that, at times, a significant percentage of the North American population has argued the New Testament prohibits at least certain forms of multiethnic marriage. While it is true the New Testament contains few explicit references to marriages between people who derive from diverse heritages, this portion of Scripture reveals much about the manner in which Christian representatives of different people groups should interact. These teachings are applicable to the topic of multiethnic marriage.

NEW TESTAMENT TEACHINGS REGARDING ETHNICITY

The Samaritans (John 4:1–42)

In 722 BC, the Assyrians conquered the northern kingdom of Israel after capturing Samaria, its capital city (2 Kgs 17:6). The policy of Israel's oppressors was to exile a portion of the population of each country it controlled and to settle foreigners in their place. The short-term purpose of this forced colonization was to erode any potential resistance against Assyria by intermingling groups that did not trust each other. The long-term result of this program was the emergence of the Samaritans, a polytheistic ethnic group that possessed both Israelite and Gentile ancestry.[9]

The enmity between the Jews and the Samaritans was well established by Jesus' day. The feud appears to have stemmed from an episode that occurred when the first group of exiles returned from captivity and began to rebuild the Jerusalem Temple (ca. 538 BC). Soon thereafter, the Samaritans offered to assist them in this important religious task.

In response, the Jewish governor Zerubbabel and the high priest Jeshua rejected the offer because of the Samaritans' syncretistic approach to religion (cf. Ezra 4:1–3; cf. 2 Kgs 17:24–41).[10] As a result, they revealed their true intentions by attempting to derail the Temple project (Ezra 4:4–6). Later, they also ridiculed Nehemiah's restoration of Jerusalem's wall (Neh 4:2).

---

slaveholders in the nineteenth century. For a discussion of the history of this tragic misuse of Scripture, see Botham, *Almighty God*, 96–111.

9. Morris, *The Gospel according to John*, 226–27.
10. Breneman, *Ezra, Nehemiah, Esther*, 97.

An event that occurred one hundred and fifty years before the dawn of the New Testament era damaged relations even further. According to Josephus, the Maccabean leader John Hyrcanus destroyed the Samaritan temple on Mount Gerizim because of its pagan associations.[11] The loss of their worship site intensified the resentment the Samaritans had for the Jews.[12] Perhaps in remembrance of Hyrcanus's provocative deed, over a century later,[13] a group of Samaritans infiltrated the Jewish Temple. They scattered human bones in the porticoes and the courtyard during the Passover celebration so as to render the area unclean.[14] This act prompted the Jewish religious leaders to ban all Samaritans from the Temple complex, setting the tone for the remainder of the first century.

Considering these troubled relations, Jesus' interaction with the Samaritan woman at Sychar was atypical (cf. John 4:1–42). Their midday conversation about religion not only broke the gender barrier and the moral barrier (because of her sinful lifestyle), but also the ethnic barrier.[15] The woman expressed disbelief when Jesus approached her: "How is it that you, being a Jew, ask me for a drink since I am a Samaritan woman?" (John 4:9a). Jesus' disciples also were astonished by his actions (John 4:27). John provided his readers with a contextual clue that explains their bewilderment: "For Jews have no dealings with Samaritans" (John 4:9b).

The content of Jesus' dialogue is remarkable for at least two other reasons. First, after telling the woman that the Samaritans worshiped God imperfectly (John 4:22),[16] He unexpectedly refused to take sides in the ongoing argument of whether Mount Gerizim or Jerusalem was the proper place to revere God (John 4:20). After emphasizing salvation truly was of the Jews, Jesus explained one's physical location was not as important as worshiping the Lord in spirit and in truth (John 4:22–23).

In other words, the Jewish religion as expressed in the Old Testament was the only system of faith acceptable to God. Jesus revealed, however, that countless believers soon would originate from outside the geographic and ethnic bounds of Israel. This international recognition of Yahweh as

---

11. Josephus, *New Complete Works*, 438.
12. Crown, "Redating the Schism," 30.
13. Whitacre, *John*, 101–2.
14. Josephus, *New Complete Works*, 588.
15. Keener, *The Gospel of John*, 1:585.
16. Morris, *The Gospel according to John*, 238. The Samaritans rejected all Old Testament books except the five Moses penned.

the only true God was a feature of the messianic age (e.g., Isa 49:6; 52:10), and Jesus invited the ethnically mixed Samaritans to take part in the movement. As a result of the Samaritan woman's testimony, many other residents of Sychar believed Jesus' message. They began to refer to him as "the Savior of the world" (John 4:42).

Second, interpreters sometimes overlook the fact that Jesus' appeal for the disciples to realize the fields were ready to harvest is a reference to the residents of Sychar (cf. John 4:35). Undoubtedly, his disciples, along with most Jews, "regarded [the Samaritans] as despised half-breeds,"[17] but Jesus saw them differently. He taught one's commitment to him was more important than one's ancestry, which is why John 3:1–21 and John 4:44 contrast unbelieving Jews with the repentant Samaritans whom God supposedly abhorred.[18]

Interestingly, John 4:1–42 contains the only preserved account of extensive contact between Jesus and the Samaritans. The reason for this intermittent interaction likely was his directive to the disciples not to enter the cities of the Samaritans and Gentiles during his earthly ministry because he desired to provide the house of Israel an opportunity to hear his message first (cf. Matt 10:5–6). However, the general tenor of Jesus' teachings reveals his indifference to the Samaritans' non-Jewish roots.[19]

For example, of the ten lepers whom Jesus healed, the only one who returned to thank him was a Samaritan (Luke 17:11–19). Additionally, in his lesson concerning what constitutes a neighborly attitude, Jesus depicted a priest and a Levite as self-absorbed and callous. A Samaritan, on the other hand, served as the protagonist of the story because he stopped to help the traveler whom robbers had beaten (Luke 10:30–37). Finally, the resurrected Jesus instructed his representatives to preach the gospel in Judea (i.e., to the people of Israel) before moving on to Samaria (i.e., Israelite–Gentile descendants) and then to the rest of the world (Acts 1:8).[20] In obedience to this command, Philip, a deacon, journeyed to the region of Samaria to proclaim Christ and enjoyed an overwhelmingly positive response (Acts 8:4–24).

---

17. Borchert, *John 1–11*, 199–200.
18. Kysar, *John*, 52.
19. Ibid., 71.
20. Marsh, *Saint John*, 204. Marsh correctly surmised the significance of Acts 1:8: "Samaria had some special category in the theology of missions in the early Church."

Jesus' teachings challenged the enduring resentment Jews and Samaritans had for one another. His loving attitude toward an ethnically amalgamated people also set the tone for the early church's outreach to non-Jews. By extension, Jesus implied multiethnic relations should not be a point of contention for his followers.

No Respecter of Persons (Acts 10:1–48)

Acts 8 records the evangelistic efforts of Philip among the Samaritans (Acts 8:4–24), as well as his personal meeting with the Ethiopian eunuch (Acts 8:25–40). These encounters set the stage for the book's first explicit reference to the place of half-Jews and Gentiles within Christendom. In Acts 10, readers learn of Cornelius, a centurion of the Italian cohort who was a God-fearer (Acts 10:2). This quality prompted the Lord to send an angel to speak to him. The heavenly messenger directed Cornelius to send for Simon Peter because he would reveal God's Word to him (Acts 10:3–8).

In the city of Joppa, the Apostle Peter received his own heavenly vision. Three times he observed an object resembling a great sheet, filled with all manner of unclean animals.[21] This recurring presentation served the dual purpose of affirming the vision's divine origin and establishing its importance.[22] A voice thrice encouraged Peter to kill and eat, but he refused to do so because he had never consumed any non-kosher food. In response, the Lord cautioned him not to consider unholy that which God had cleansed (Acts 10:9–16).

At that moment Cornelius's messengers arrived, and they invited Peter to accompany them so that he might speak to their master. Immediately, the Apostle began to understand the significance of his vision. He eagerly accepted their invitation and exclaimed to Cornelius and his household upon meeting them: "Certainty I understand God does not show favoritism, but in every nation the one who fears Him and does what is right is acceptable to Him" (Acts 10:34–35).

Peter's choice of the prepositional phrase *ep alētheias* (translated here *certainly*) is significant. Mikeal Parsons claimed each of the expression's five

---

21. Some New Testament scholars insist the force of the word *all* in verse 12 is such that the sheet contained not only unclean animals, but clean creatures as well. For a discussion of this interpretation as well as the manner in which unclean food could contaminate kosher food, see Keener, *Acts*, 2:488.

22. Kurz, *Acts of the Apostles*, 171.

occurrences in Luke–Acts asserts "the truthfulness (theological or historical) of the statement that follows.[23] In other words, in Acts 10 the Apostle insisted his teaching regarding ethnicity was not merely speculation on his part, but God's view of the matter. The modern reader might take for granted Peter's short proclamation because the teaching is widely accepted in the twenty-first century, but his declaration represents a profound break from the standard Jewish appraisal of Gentiles in the first century.[24]

Several observations are in order. First, although this revelation did not abolish the covenant the Lord had made with Abraham and his descendants, it did establish that the Jews were not the only people whom God loved. To limit him to a single ethnic group was in essence to relegate him to the status of a "tribal deity,"[25] a woefully insufficient description of the Creator whom the highest heavens could not contain (cf. 1 Kgs 8:27). God's estimation of humans had nothing to do with their bloodline because he shows no partiality (cf. Rom 2:11; Gal 2:6; Eph 6:9; Col 3:25). Peter's message intimates none of Christ's followers must allow prejudiced notions regarding ethnicity to cloud their judgment.[26]

Second, of interest also is the usage of the phrase "in every nation" (*en panti ethnei*) in Acts 10:35. Contrary to the modern notion of *nation*, the word "refers not simply to nation-states but also to any racial, ethnic, or cultural grouping by which humans distinguish themselves."[27] *Ethnicity* or *ethnic group*, English derivatives of the Greek term *ethnos*, are more appropriate renderings of the concept.[28] Furthermore, the expression *en panti ethnei* mirrors Jesus' Great Commission charge to disciple "all ethnic groups" in Matt 28:19 (*panta ta ethnē*; cf. Acts 1:8).

This description of believing Gentiles as benefactors of the Abrahamic covenant was not merely a New Testament notion. It also found root in God's declaration that he will bless all the peoples of the earth through

23. Parsons, *Acts*, 151. For other examples of the prepositional phrase *ep alētheias* in Luke–Acts see Luke 4:25; 20:21; 22:59; Acts 4:27.

24. Bond, "Acts 10:34–43," 225.

25. Lotz, "Peter's Wider Understanding," 201.

26. Pelikan, *Acts*, 131.

27. Larkin, *Acts*, 163.

28. Prior to this paragraph, the author followed the traditional English convention of translating the Greek word *ethnos* as *nation*. Now that this section of the study has established *ethnicity* and *ethnic group* are superior renderings of *ethnos*, the author will employ these translation choices in subsequent discussions of Matt 28:19, Acts 10:35, and any other passages in which the term appears within the Greek New Testament.

Jesus Christ, Abraham's seed (Gen 22:18; cf. Gal 3:16). This concept also addresses God's invitation to foreigners to worship him alongside the covenant people on his holy mountain (Isa 56:6–8). Yahweh's reminder to the Israelites of their status as descendants of an Amorite father and a Hittite mother (cf. Ezek 16:3) also stressed that the covenant people did not stem from a superior genetic stock, but a common lineage they shared with all Gentiles. Members of any ethnic group can find refuge with Jesus because he is the propitiation for the sins of the entire world instead of a select faction of humanity (cf. 1 John 2:2).

Third, the soteriological restrictions Peter placed on Gentiles were analogous to the limitations Jews already experienced. To put it another way, God did not embrace Gentiles because of their ancestral roots anymore than he welcomed representatives of the covenant people based merely on their pedigree.[29] Rather, Gentiles were to fear the Lord and obey his commandments in order for God to welcome them (cf. John 14:15; Exod 20:6; 1 Sam 15:22).

The comparison of Peter's speech to Old Testament passages that address the issue of multiethnic marriage provides helpful insight. Although some writers regard the invitation in the New Testament for Gentiles to embrace the God of Israel as "uncharted territory,"[30] the depiction is not entirely accurate. Granted, from the standpoint of first-century Jews, the notion of Gentile believers being on equal footing certainly would have been a shocking concept. This interpretation, however, developed because the Jews overlooked numerous Old Testament passages that recount the interweaving of non-Israelite believers into the covenant body.[31]

Further, Craig Keener astutely remarked: "Peter learned newly ... that he cannot presume uncircumcised Gentiles to be impure or treat this as a barrier to fellowship with them."[32] Since non-Jewish Christians were clean, and God set forth no fellowship restrictions between believing Jews and Gentiles, the implication of this solidarity appears to extend to the institution of marriage as well. Since God-fearing men and women who derived from diverse ethnic backgrounds were members of the same body, intermarriage is a natural extension of the principle of unity (cf. Rom 12:5).

---

29. Schnabel, *Acts*, 499.

30. Nguyen, "Crossing Cultural Boundaries," 462.

31. For a thorough discussion of this topic, see the section of chapter 2 that examines positive Old Testament examples of marriages between Israelites and non-Israelites.

32. Keener, *Acts*. 2:1796.

Multiethnic Marriage in the New Testament

Many Nations, One Common Ancestor (Acts 17:16–31)

During the Apostle Paul's second missionary journey, he visited the city of Athens and was greatly disturbed by the idolatry he found there. As was his custom, he proclaimed the gospel in the local synagogue before delivering the same message to the Gentile population in the market place. When the Epicureans and the Stoic philosophers questioned the doctrine of Jesus' resurrection, they brought Paul to the Areopagus (their standard location for holding debates) and invited him to articulate his teachings in front of a large crowd (Acts 17:16–21).

The resulting discourse, commonly called "the Sermon on Mars Hill," contextualized the Christian message for people who hailed from pagan backgrounds (Acts 17:22–31). One of the points Paul developed was the common ancestry of mankind: "And from one[33] he made all of the nations of mankind to inhabit the entire face of the earth" (Acts 17:26a). In addition to colliding with the standard Athenian view concerning the origin of humans, the statement also had ramifications for the way in which Christians should understand the subject of ethnicity.

The residents of Athens, like most Greeks, proudly considered themselves to be superior to other peoples.[34] They believed their creation to be autochthonous in nature,[35] meaning they supposed their forefathers to have originated in the region of Attica rather than having migrated from elsewhere. They pictured their ancestors as springing from the fertile soil on which Athens stood,[36] while teaching other humans consisted of materials of lesser quality.

Paul defied this opinion, insisting different civilizations were not the products of distinct acts of creation. Rather, all people groups (*pan ethnos*

---

33. Instead of reading "from one" (*ex henos*), certain Greek manuscripts contain the phrase "from one blood" (*ex henos haimatos*). Ultimately, the editorial committee of the United Bible Societies' Greek New Testament gave the first option a {B} rating because they held *haimatos* to be one of the "typical expansion[s]" they believed were characteristic of Western Greek texts. See Metzger, *A Textual Commentary*, 404–5.

34. Peterson, *The Acts of the Apostles*, 496–97. Centuries later, some writers of European descent continued to regard the Greeks in this manner. For example, in *The Descent of Man, and Selection in Relation to Sex*, Charles Darwin wrote: "[T]he old Greeks . . . stood some grades higher in intellect than any race that has ever existed." See Darwin, *Evolutionary Writings*, 264.

35. Bruce, *Book of Acts*, 357.

36. Gangel, *Acts*, 290. For a helpful summary of other Greek creation accounts see Keener, *Acts*, 3:2645.

anthrōpōn) stemmed from one source. The Apostle's usage of the word *one* in this verse refers not to God in his role as Creator, but rather to his creation of Adam, the first man.[37] Paul's sermon appealed to the book of Genesis and the historical Adam as witnesses to the unity of mankind.

Whereas Peter's speech in Acts 10 explained Jews were not superior to Gentiles, Paul's discourse in Acts 17 affirmed Athenian Greeks were not superior to Jews and other Gentile groups. Furthermore, since representatives from every ethnic group descended from Adam and were biologically unified, one Man (Jesus Christ) could judge the entire world because God the Father had raised him from the dead (Acts 17:30–31).[38] Likewise, through one man (the first Adam) sin entered the world, but through one Man (Jesus Christ, the last Adam) salvation became available to all (Rom 5:12, 15–17; cf. 1 Cor 15:45). Paul's description of hamartiology and soteriology in this section is dependent on the oneness of mankind.

This non-contestable unity means authors of the past who used God's Word to perpetuate the institution of slavery and the inequality of diverse ethnic groups[39] perverted the Bible's clear meaning. Keener, a New Testament scholar of Anglo extraction who married an African woman from the Congo, noted the irony of their eisegetical practices: "Those earlier, popular theological interpreters, especially in South Africa and North America, who exploited [Acts 17] to justify ethnic separatism not only missed its point but succumbed to its negative verdict."[40] In other words, to misread Scripture on this point is to misconstrue a major tenet of Scripture.

The anthropological consequence of mankind's oneness is such that it is erroneous to refer to multiple races of humans. Because of this inherent unity, Western naturalists and anthropologists found it difficult to define the word *race*,[41] tending to employ the terminology of zoology to categorize humans.[42] This unorthodox approach resulted in "a general hierarchy"[43] similar to the Athenians' estimation of diverse people groups. Only recently have geneticists and anthropologists begun to "agree with the

---

37. Litwak, "Israel's Prophets," 207.

38. Johnson, "Paul in Athens," 41.

39. E.g., Sloan, *The Question Answered*, 189–90. Accordingly, Sloan missed the entire point of Acts 17 when he argued, "Sin has disturbed [racial] equality."

40. Keener, *Acts*, 3:2651.

41. Romano, *Race Mixing*, 10.

42. Farber, *Mixing Races*, 30.

43. Ibid., 31.

idea that human races, in any kind of biological sense, do not really exist,"[44] a point Paul established two millennia ago.

The implication of humanity's ancestral oneness is significant. Since multiple races do not exist, the phrase *interracial marriage* is a misnomer. More appropriate is the term *multiethnic marriage*, since people stem from a large assortment of cultures, worldviews, and language groups rather than unrelated genetic stock. Accordingly, except in quotations, this author generally avoids using the terms *race* and *interracial marriage* throughout this study.

No Difference Between Jew and Greek (Rom 10:1–13)

The Apostle Paul also touched upon the subject of ethnicity in the book of Romans. In chapter 10, he fleshed out the concept of redemption for his audience, explaining how salvation pertained to both Jews and Gentiles. Previous to the composition of Acts, the early church grappled with what non-Jews must do to become true followers of Christ. At the Jerusalem Council the apostles, with James serving as their spokesmen, determined the grace of Jesus Christ—rather than the keeping of the Mosaic law—was the source of salvation (Acts 15:1–31). Paul expanded on this subject in Rom 9–10.

The Apostle Paul rejoiced because countless Gentiles had recognized Jesus as Lord. At the same time he expressed great sorrow and continual grief because the majority of Jews had rejected their Messiah (Rom 9:1–5).[45] The prophets Hosea and Isaiah had foretold that the Jews and Gentiles would react thusly to the gospel (cf. Hos 2:23; Isa 8:14; 28:16). Paul saw the fulfillment of these prophesies during his missionary journeys. This resistance to Christ prompted the Apostle and his associates to shake off the dust from their feet and shake out their garments as a visible testimony when their Jewish audiences intentionally spurned the gospel (Acts 13:51; 18:6; cf. Matt 10:14).

Ironically, the Gentiles, who had not pursued righteousness, attained the righteousness of faith through Christ. The Jews, on the other hand, had pursued the law of righteousness, but accomplished nothing because their

---

44. Smedley and Smedley, *Race in North America*, 300. Scientific research has proven "there are no genetic traits that are exclusive to one race."

45. Black, *Romans*, 137. The Apostle Paul's grief at his kinsmen's rejection of the Messiah is a major theme of Rom 9–10.

faith was misplaced (Rom 9:30–33). The Old Testament Law emphasized the importance of faith, but most Jews had misread Scripture. Instead, they trusted in their relationship to Abraham and their own works to obtain salvation.[46]

In Rom 10:1–4 Paul continued the discourse he began in 9:30, articulating his desire for all Israelites to be saved. Unfortunately, their zeal for God, which should have led them to embrace his Messiah, caused them to stumble; they had confused their concept of religion with God's righteousness.[47] They forgot that Moses himself, the giver of the Law, wrote on behalf of Yahweh: "The word is near you, in your mouth and in your heart" (Rom 10:8; cf. Deut 30:14). The reception of this word of faith (cf. Rom 10:8b) had nothing to do with one's ethnic heritage, and everything to do with one's confession of Jesus as Lord, to the glory of God the Father (Rom 10:9–10; 14:11; Phil 2:11).

The climax of the Apostle's dual discussion of ethnicity and salvation appears in Rom 10:11–13: "For Scripture says: 'Everyone who believes in Him will not be put to shame.' For there is no difference between a Jew and a Greek, for the same Lord of all is rich to all who call upon Him. For whoever should call upon the name of the Lord will be saved." The Roman Christians would have found the soteriological teaching of this pericope to be as revolutionary as Peter's message to the house of Cornelius in Acts 10:1–48.

In Rom 10:11–13, Paul made three declarations regarding ethnicity. First, he demonstrated his assessment of different people groups was not a personal opinion, but derived from Old Testament teachings.[48] In verse 11, the Apostle reminded his readers God had made justice his measuring line, so everyone could believe in him regardless of their ethnic associations (cf. Isa 28:16–17). Furthermore, in verse 13 Paul reiterated this multiethnic deliverance would originate "in Mount Zion, even in Jerusalem" (cf. Joel 2:32), a reference to the sacrificial atonement of Jesus Christ.

Second, the significance of the Old Testament's teachings regarding ethnicity asserted no difference existed between Jews and Greeks (Rom 10:12). In this section, Paul returned to a theme to which he had alluded earlier in the book: "Or is He God only of the Jews? Is He not also God of the Gentiles? Yes, also of the Gentiles, because there is only one God who

---

46. Best, *The Letter of Paul to the Romans*, 117.
47. Achtemeier, *Romans*, 167; Harrisville, *Romans*, 161.
48. Del Agua Pérez, "El 'Derás' Cristológico," 211–12.

will justify the circumcised by faith and the uncircumcised through faith " (Rom 3:29–30). In other words, "les promesses de Dieu faites au peuple ... étaient inconditionnées."[49] Because of his impartiality, God was no respecter of persons (cf. Acts 10:34; Rom 2:11).

Third, God's objectivity regarding one's ethnic heritage meant anyone who confessed Jesus as Lord would receive salvation (Rom 10:13). The Apostle's triple usage of the adjective *all* in verses 11–13,[50] a term that always "indicate[s] the universal extension of salvation through faith" in Romans 10,[51] reinforces this point.[52] In short, one's ancestry held no salvific merit.

While Rom 10:13 refers specifically to the realm of soteriology, the repercussions of the equality of Jews and Gentiles are far-reaching. One tenet of Paul's discussion in Rom 9–10 is the Lord recognizes no quantitative or qualitative differences between members of distinct ethnic groups. Christians, therefore, should not live as if such disparities existed. Regardless of people's bloodlines, they can become children of God through repentance and faith in his Son Jesus. Consequently, followers of Christ from sundry ancestral backgrounds have more in common with each other than unbelievers who possess similar genetic affiliations because Christians have become fellow partakers of the gospel (cf. Eph 3:6).

Unequally Yoked (2 Cor 6:11–18)

Although, as George Yancey noted, "little contemporary Christian literature ... overtly opposes interracial marriage,"[53] such was not the case fifty years ago. In his 1958 work *Stride Toward Freedom*, Martin Luther King Jr. observed that many Christians[54] were concerned desegregation would lead to comingling:

49. Lyonnet, *Etudes sur L'Epître aux Romains*, 265.

50. The adjective's forms in Rom 10:11–13 are as follows: *pas* (*everyone*, v. 11); *pántōn* (*all*, v. 12); *pas* (*whoever*, v. 13).

51. Belli, *Argumentation*, 303.

52. Rowe, "Romans 10:13," 140.

53. Yancey, "Unequally Yoked," 66. One should note this statement pertains only to written prohibitions against multiethnic marriage. A cursory Internet search quickly reveals that North American pastors, particularly from extreme fundamentalist backgrounds, continue to oppose this type of marriage. See Elias, "Tennessee Pastors."

54. According to a 1958 Gallup poll, Americans of every ethnicity found multiethnic marriages problematic. Only 4 percent of Americans approved of black-white

EQUALLY YOKED

> The church can . . . help by mitigating the prevailing and irrational fears concerning intermarriage. It can say to men that marriage is an individual matter that must be decided on the merits of individual cases. Properly speaking, races do not marry; individuals marry. Marriage is a condition which requires the voluntary consent of two contracting parties, and either side can always say no. The church can reveal that the continual outcry concerning intermarriage is a distortion of the real issue. It can point out that the Negro's primary aim is to be the white man's brother, not his brother-in-law.[55]

Christian detractors argued the government should leave segregation laws alone, because their dissolution necessarily would lead to intermarriage of the races.[56] They opposed this practice at least in part due to their faulty interpretation of Paul's prohibition in 2 Cor 6:14.

This verse is part of a pericope (2 Cor 6:11—7:4) in which the Apostle exclaimed the Corinthian Christians' affections for him had grown cold.[57] After inviting them to embrace him and his associates once more, he offered them a warning: "Do not be unevenly yoked with unbelievers" (2 Cor 6:14a). Paul's pairing of the present active participial form of *heterozugeō* with the negative particle *mē* probably signifies he prohibited an action some Corinthian believers already were committing.[58]

The verb *heterozugeō* is associative in nature[59] and compound in form. *Heteros* is a common adjective that usually carries the idea of "another of a different kind." *Zugos* can mean either "a frame used to control working animals" (i.e., *yoke*), or "an instrument for determining weight" (i.e., *scale*).[60] In 2 Cor 6:14, the first definition of *heterozugeō* is appropriate to the context because Paul alluded to Old Testament legislation prohibiting Israelites

---

unions. See Newport, "In U.S., 87% Approve of Black–White Marriage vs. 4% in 1958."

55. King, *A Testament of Hope*, 478.

56. The tendency to couple the specter of miscegenation to issues such as desegregation and ethnic equality already was well established when King wrote *Stride Toward Freedom*. For an excellent history of the development of the pairing of these concepts in the nineteenth century see Kaplan, "The Miscegenation Issue," 274–343.

57. Barnett, *The Second Epistle to the Corinthians*, 339; Harris, *The Second Epistle to the Corinthians*, 497.

58. Belleville, *2 Corinthians*, 176.

59. Wallace, *Greek Grammar Beyond the Basics*, 159.

60. Danker, *A Greek–English Lexicon*, 429.

from "plow[ing] with an ox and a donkey together"[61] (cf. Deut 22:10). The Apostle employed this agricultural illustration to alert Corinthian believers to the importance of restricting their associations with unbelievers.

In order to emphasize his point, Paul provided five rhetorical questions requiring a negative answer:[62] 1) "What partnership does righteousness have with unrighteousness?" (2 Cor 6:14b); 2) "What fellowship does light have with darkness?" (6:14c); 3) "What harmony does Christ have with Belial?" (6:15a); 4) "What portion does a believer have with an unbeliever?" (6:15b); 5) "What agreement does the law of God have with idols?" (6:16a). He then reminded readers they were the temple of the living God (6:16b), alluding to numerous Old Testament passages[63] to corroborate this conclusion. Finally, the Apostle Paul encouraged his audience to cleanse themselves from any defilement of the flesh or spirit so they might perfect "holiness in the fear of God" (7:1).

Scholars have speculated concerning the specific type of mismatching some of the Apostle's Corinthian readers practiced.[64] Paul's reasoning in 2 Cor 6:15—7:1 argues any spiritual contaminate is a source of concern for the believer.[65] For example, interpreters can apply the passage to the Christian's selection of an appropriate marriage partner, but this concern is not the thrust of 2 Cor 6:14.

Furthermore, contra nineteenth-century reasoning, no reference to the subject of ethnicity appears in the entire pericope. In fact, the only mention of diverse people groups in the surrounding context is collective in nature, revealing God reconciled the world to himself through Jesus Christ (2 Cor 5:17-19). Therefore, appealing to 2 Cor 6:14 in order to denounce intermarriage is spurious.

Only two groups of people appear in 2 Cor 6:14—7:1, and neither are ethnic designations. The first assembly consists of believers who have confessed Jesus as Lord, while the second includes unbelievers. In other words, Christianity is incompatible with all other religious teachings, so Christ's

---

61. McDougall, "Unequally Yoked," 127.

62. Bruce, *1 and 2 Corinthians*, 214.

63. Cf. Exod 25:8; Lev 26:12; 2 Sam 7:8, 14; Isa 43:6; 52:11; Jer 31:9; 32:38; Ezek 20:34, 41; 37:27; Amos 3:13; 4:13.

64. For a detailed discussion of the most likely mismatches Paul restricted, see Webb, "What is the Unequal Yoke," 162-79.

65. Hafemann, *2 Corinthians*, 278.

followers must resist any pressure to "espouse values, beliefs, and practices that are antithetical to the Christian faith."[66]

Believers who originate from diverse ethnic backgrounds are not biologically different from one another because of their mutual relationship to Adam. Furthermore, they are not spiritually dissimilar because of their love for Christ. On the other hand, believers and unbelievers are completely different breeds in a spiritual sense.[67] These principles led Yancey to make the following insightful observation: "Our identity in Christ is far more important than our skin color. Our relationship should be based on faith, not race. Christians of any color should have freedom in Christ to date and marry. They do not have the freedom to enter such a relationship with unbelievers."[68]

One in Christ Jesus (Gal 3:28)

During Paul's lifetime, Jewish society tended to place differing values on people because of their ethnicity, gender, and social standing. For example, in the Mishnah, a collection of ancient Jewish oral laws that rabbis eventually codified in the third century AD, readers find the following discussion:

> R[abbi] Judah used to say, a man is bound to say the following three blessings daily: "[Blessed art thou . . .] who hast not made me a heathen," ". . . who hast not made me a woman," and ". . . who hast not made me a brutish man." R[abbi] Aha b[en] Jacob once overhea[r]d his son saying "[Blessed are thou . . .] who hast not made me a brutish man," whereupon he said to him, "And this too!" Said the other, "Then what blessing should I say instead? " [He replied], ". . . who has not made me a slave." And is not that the same as a woman? A slave is more contemptible.[69]

The Greeks apparently had a similar philosophy. Diogenis Laërtius (ca. third cent. AD), in his work *Lives and Opinions of Eminent Philosophers*, noted that Thales mentioned some ancient writers had credited Hermippus—and others Socrates—with thankfulness for being "a man and not a beast, a male and not a female, [as well as] a Greek and not a Barbarian."[70]

66. Garland, *2 Corinthians*, 332.
67. Barnett, *The Second Epistle to the Corinthians*, 344.
68. Yancey, "Unequally Yoked," 74–75.
69. *Menachoth 43b*.
70. Laërtius, *Lives and Opinions*, book 1, sec. 33–34. The above quotation is the

Paul, on the other hand, declared the conventional Jewish and Greek sociological constructs of his day did not pertain to the realm of Christianity: "For all of you are sons of God through faith in Jesus Christ. For as many of you as were baptized into Christ have put on Christ. There is no Jew or Greek, neither is there slave or free, or male and female; for all of you are one in Christ Jesus" (Gal 3:26–28; cf. 1 Cor 12:13). Reading this pericope in the light of the *Menachoth* and the writings of Laërtius indicates the Apostle probably chose his three antithetical categories of people in order to counter the viewpoints of Galatian believers who did not yet understand their new identity in Christ.[71]

Another potent adversary at work in Galatia was a group whom the Apostle called the Judaizers.[72] This faction embraced certain aspects of Christianity but insisted Gentiles believers must keep the Law of Moses in order to receive salvation (cf. Acts 15:1). Accordingly, the Judaizers demanded non-Jewish males undergo the rite of circumcision in order to experience full instatement into the body of Christ.

Their influence was so powerful at Antioch that they convinced Peter and Barnabas to withdraw from fellowshipping with Christian Gentiles until Paul rebuked the church leaders for their hypocrisy (Gal 2:11–13). In his writings, the Apostle often disputed this fallacious reasoning (e.g., Rom 2:25—3:8; 1 Cor 7:19). For example, he addressed the controversy concerning circumcision frequently in the epistle to the Galatians (cf. Gal 5:1–15; 6:15). Paul insisted Gentiles did not become believers by means of keeping the Mosaic law, but through the blood of Jesus Christ (Eph 2:13).

This redemption meant, on a fundamental level, the Galatian believers no longer were the same beings they once had been. As a result of their regeneration, they were new creations who operated under a new economy (cf. 2 Cor 5:17). Henceforth, they all were sons of God (Gal 3:26) who equally had become the true heirs of the Abrahamic covenant[73] (Gal 3:29; cf. Gen 22:15–18). In spite of their diverse backgrounds, their common spiritual bond had unified them because they had become "one in Christ" (Gal 3:28).

Modern reaction to the Apostle's three antithetical categories proves his teaching is as controversial today as it was two thousand years ago. On

---

author's translation of the Greek text.

71. Fung, *The Epistle to the Galatians*, 175; Martin, "The Situational Antithesis," 112.
72. Adelakun, "Complementarians Versus Egalitarians," 77.
73. Shreiner, *Galatians*, 258.

the one hand, some interpreters make the message of Gal 3:28 more universal than Paul intended it to be. For example, Robert Mesle lamented, "Christians have rarely been able to extend this principle [of unity] beyond the boundaries of Christianity."[74] The biblical text teaches nothing concerning religious ecumenism. Rather, people can attain unity only by means of Christ[75] (i.e., *en Christō Iesoû*). No other method of harmony is available.

Furthermore, some theologians misread Paul by abolishing the categories of ethnicity, gender, and social standing altogether.[76] These understandings of Gal 3:28 were not the Apostle's intention. As far as bloodlines were concerned, Jews remained Jews and Greeks did not cease being Greeks. Genetically, the categories of male and female persisted. Sociologically, Romans continued to view their slaves as a different class than themselves.[77] Paul's declaration meant only one means of salvation existed,[78] but also no believer was superior to any other in the family of Christ.[79] Charles Cousar noted, "Being in Christ d[id] not do away with Jew or Greek, male or female, even slave or free, but it ma[de] the differences before God irrelevant."[80]

On the other hand, some modern day Christians and churches have not incorporated the teachings of Gal 3:28 in such a way that their lives reflect the oneness believers enjoy in Christ Jesus.[81] For this reason, on August 9, 1953 at Ebenezer Baptist Church in Atlanta, Martin Luther King Jr. reminded his congregation Christian unity should be a present reality instead of an eschatological platitude:

---

74. Mesle, *Process Theology*, 89.

75. Walden, "Galatians 3:28," 48.

76. E.g., Pitta, *Disposizione e Messaggio*, 117; Rastoin, *Tarse et Jérusalem*, 223; Ruether, "Feminism and the Future," 11.

77. Anders, *Galatians, Ephesians*, 40.

78. Ibid., 39.

79. Williams, *Galatians*, 106–7. Lamentably, Williams noted these types of divisions "still characterize the institutions of 'the present evil age.'"

80. Cousar, *Galatians*, 85–86.

81. William Hendrickson's negative comments in his 1979 commentary on Galatians and Ephesians serve as a case in point: "Are there not some people today who, in their mania for unity and equality, have left common sense and genuinely scriptural teaching far behind? Is it not absurd, for example, in the interest of 'integration' to force into the fourth grade children, of whatever race, who cannot do fourth grade work?" (Hendrickson, *Galatians, Ephesians*, 150).

Multiethnic Marriage in the New Testament

> Slavery could not have existed in America for more than two hundred and fifty years if the Church had not sanctioned it. Segregation and discrimination could not exist in America today without the Church. I am ashame[d] and appalled at the fact that eleven o'clock on Sunday morning is the most segregated hour in Christian America ... When religion becomes [so] involved in a future good "over yonder" that it forgets the present evils "over here" it is a dry as dust religion and needs to be condemned.[82]

King's sermon was a plea to American churches to do more than merely identify themselves as followers of Christ. He urged them to make their Lord's teachings regarding Christian brotherhood a part of the fabric of their everyday lives.

This message is still of importance over sixty years after King delivered it. As Samuel M. Ngewa remarked, "Race, tribe social status, and gender still divide us today."[83] Certainly, this estimation of the situation does not apply to all North American believers, but an indeterminate percentage of Christians in this region of the world (like all other continents) appear not to have assimilated the groundbreaking contents of Gal 3:28.

For instance, in 2012, the same year the Southern Baptist Convention elected Fred Luter Jr. as its first African American president, First Baptist Church of Crystal Springs, Mississippi, failed to consider Paul's teachings. The Anglo congregation required a black couple to withdraw plans to hold their wedding service on church property when some of its members protested because of the couple's ethnicity.[84] Additionally, in spite of the incremental escalation of marriages between different people groups, "currently only 2.5 percent of American churches are multiethnic."[85] As more congregations adopt a manner of thinking consistent with Gal 3:28, travesties such as what occurred in Crystal Springs will continue to diminish. Churches that purposefully seek to become multiethnic in nature will multiply and flourish.

A careful consideration of Gal 3:28 has shown the text to be one of the most developed New Testament arguments for multiethnic Christian unity. The verse implies if no substantive differences exist between Jews and Greeks whose allegiance belongs to Christ, each would make a suitable

---

82. King, "Communism's Challenge."
83. Ngewa, *Galatians*, 118.
84. "Church Refuses to Marry Black Couple in Mississippi."
85. Loritts, *Right Color, Wrong Culture*, 208.

marriage partner for the other if they choose to wed. By extension, this inference relates to any other people group as well. Multiethnic Christian marriages are one manifestation of the teaching that believers are one in Jesus Christ.

No Distinction in Christ (Col 3:9–11)

In the epistle to the Colossians, Paul once again addressed the issue of ethnicity from a Christian perspective. He explained why believers should set their minds on the things of Christ and cease to perform the wicked acts characteristic of unbelievers (Col 3:1–7). After listing a number of sins they must avoid (Col 3:8–9a),[86] Paul placed a special emphasis on abstaining from falsehoods.[87] He most likely considered the matter of truthfulness because Colossian believers had difficulty with this aspect of Christian living.

The Apostle turned this focus on speaking truthfully into an opportunity to instruct his audience concerning the Christian's new identity in Jesus. He wrote, "Do not lie to each other; you have put off the old man with his deeds. And you have put on the new, which is renewed to knowledge according to the image of the One who created him, where there is no Greek and Jew, circumcision and uncircumcision, Barbarian, Scythian, slave, free; but Christ is all and in all" (Col 3:9–11).

Whereas in Gal 3:28 the Apostle listed three antithetical categories of people in order to make his point, here he made use of four seemingly dissimilar pairs. While one group related to the keeping of the Mosaic law (circumcision–uncircumcision), and another pertained to diametrically opposed social classes (slave–free), the other two enumerated ethnic classifications (Greek–Jew; Barbarian–Scythian).

Because the author thoroughly examined the pairing of the words *Greek* and *Jew* in a previous section of this study,[88] he need not repeat the research here. In the present context of Col 3, the coupling "indicates a Jewish perspective" of ethnicity.[89] Only descendants of Abraham placed

---

86. John MacArthur insightfully noted while Col 3:5–9a "tells believers what to put off . . . 3:12–17 . . . [instructs] them what to put on" in sin's place (MacArthur, *Colossians and Philemon*, 148).

87. Talbert, *Ephesians and Colossians*, 228.

88. See the section in this chapter that examines Rom 10:1–13.

89. Dunn, *The Epistles to the Colossians and to Philemon*, 224.

Multiethnic Marriage in the New Testament

themselves in a grouping separate from all others people, hence the delineation between Greeks and Jews in this text. Conversely, the juxtaposition of the terms *Barbarian* and *Scythian* appears to betray a Greek assessment of human taxonomy.

Maurus Servius Honoratus (ca. fourth–fifth cent. AD), a celebrated grammarian and scholar, recorded the common Greek opinion of the era. In his commentary on the *Aeneid* by Virgil (70–19 BC), he noted the Greeks considered *pas mē Hellēn Barbaros*[90] (i.e., "everyone who is not a Greek is a Barbarian"). The term *barbarian* was onomatopoetic in nature, referring to the unintelligible *bar-bar* sound Greeks heard when Barbarians spoke their tribal languages.[91] Furthermore, the word *barbarian* carried the conspicuously derogatory significance of being uncivilized.[92] In essence, the Barbarians were to the Greeks what the Greeks were to the Jews.

From a Greek perspective, the Scythians also would have fallen into the Barbarian category, but in Col 3:11 the Apostle Paul contrasted the groups.[93] Edwin Yamauchi argued that the word *Scythian* "designate[d] a number of nomadic tribes from the Russian steppes."[94] Their very name had stricken fear in the hearts of the inhabitants of the Fertile Crescent and the Mediterranean world since their brutal raids of these lands in the seventh century BC.[95] The Greek historian Herodotus (ca. 484–425 BC) painted a gruesome portrait of the fearless warriors in book IV, sections 64–65 of *The Histories*:

> When a Scythian has slain his first man, he drinks some of his blood: and of all those whom he slays in the battle he bears the heads to the king; for if he has brought a head he shares in the spoil which they have taken, but otherwise not. And he takes off the skin of the head by cutting it round about the ears and then

---

90. Honoratus, *Commentary on the Aeneid of Vergil*, line 504.
91. Harris, *Colossians & Philemon*, 154.
92. Dunn, *Colossians and Philemon*, 225.
93. Certain scholars insist the Barbarian–Scythian pairing is not one of contrast like the categories of Greek–Jew, circumcision–uncircumcision, and slave–free. This scholarly difference of opinion, however, falls without the confines of the present research because it does not affect one's interpretation of Paul's discussion of ethnicity in Col 3:11. For the argument that the terms *Barbarian* and *Scythian* complement each other, see Martin, "The Scythian Perspective," 249; Melick, *Colossians, Philemon*, 298; Simpson and Bruce, *The Epistles to the Ephesians and Colossians*, 276.
94. Yamauchi, "The Scythians," 90.
95. Hendriksen, *Philippians, Colossians, Philemon*, 153.

taking hold of the scalp and shaking it off; afterwards he scrapes off the flesh with the rib of an ox, and works the skin about with his hands; and when he has tempered it, he keeps it as a napkin to wipe the hands upon, and hangs it from the bridle of the horse on which he himself rides, and takes pride in it; for whosoever has the greatest number of skins to wipe the hands upon, he is judged to be the bravest man . . . and to the skulls themselves, not all but of their greatest enemies, they do thus . . . they make use of [them] as a drinking-cup.[96]

Whether or not Herodotus's depiction of the Scythians exaggerated their war practices, his portrayal mirrors the standard assessment Greeks had of their bitter enemies in Paul's day.

Frequently, the Greeks employed the term *barbarian* to refer to any population they considered uncouth. This designation easily could apply to the Scythians in most contexts. The pairing of Barbarians and Scythians in Col 3:11 does not suggest qualitative differences, but most likely either geographical extremities or intensification for rhetorical purposes.

On the one hand, while the Scythians originated from the frozen wastelands of the north, the Greeks were particularly fond of using the appellation *barbarian* for peoples who lived to their south.[97] If this option is at work in Col 3:11, Paul's desire was to "contrast the northern and southern reaches of the [known] world."[98] On the other hand, inhabitants of civilized lands often regarded the Scythians to be some of the most dangerous and undesirable representatives of the nomadic lifestyle (i.e., the Barbarian's Barbarian).[99] In this case, the Apostle would be reinforcing his message of Christian unity by visualizing followers of Jesus whom both Jews and Greeks would have difficulty accepting. Despite their descent from an especially feared and despised tribe of people, Scythian believers were Christians nonetheless.

In either scenario, however, by means of using diametrically opposed classifications, Paul emphasized all believers have the same Savior and possess a brotherly bond that transcends societal barriers. Scholars refer to

---

96. Herodotus, *The Histories* 4.64–65.

97. For example, the Romans referred to the North African people group who now call themselves the i-Mazigh-en as Berbers. This designation derived from the term *barbaria*, the Latin cognate of the Greek word βαρβαρία.

98. Sumney, *Colossians*, 206.

99. For example, in ca. AD 400, Synesius used the term *Scythian* as a byword for evil and reckless activity. See Heather, "The Anti-Scythian Tirade," 152–54, 159–60.

this literary device as *merismus*, the allusion to the outermost boundaries of a given category "in order to portray it as a totality—that is, those opposites and everything in between them."[100] In other words, taken together, Barbarians and Scythians represented all ethnic groups Jews and Greeks considered uncivilized. Consequently, the four ethnic designations in Col 3:11—Jews, Greeks, Barbarians, and Scythians—represented every culture on earth.

Similar to Gal 3:28 and 1 Cor 12:13, Paul's purpose in Col 3:11 was not to demolish the sundry ethnic backgrounds of Christians. To the contrary, the diversity of each distinct people group remains intact under the New Covenant, "contribut[ing] to the living variety of the people of Christ."[101] Rather, Christ's followers experience a reversal of Babel (cf. Gen 11:1–9; Acts 2:1–11) in the sense that any notion of racial superiority necessarily evaporates in the light of the oneness the Son of God brings about through his redemption.[102] The alternative position—continued prejudice in spite of spiritual renewal—amounts to "a denial of our justification through faith."[103]

From a human perspective, the integration of completely dissimilar populations such as Greeks, Jews, Barbarians, and Scythians seemed unachievable,[104] but with God all things are possible (cf. Matt 19:26). The Lord concerns himself not with one's ethnic makeup, but instead one's spiritual union with his Son (2 Cor 5:17). Since Christ's bride (i.e., the church; cf. Rev 19:7–8) consists of redeemed individuals from every nation, tongue, tribe, and culture who enjoy uninhibited fellowship with each other, the implications are clear. When Christian men and women with disparate bloodlines seek to wed each other, ethnicity is not a legitimate barrier to their marriage.

Timothy's Multiethnic Background (Acts 16:1–3; 1–2 Tim)

A cursory reading of the book of Acts and the Pauline Epistles reveals that Timothy was one of Paul's most dependable associates. In addition to being

---

100. Klein et al, *Introduction to Biblical Interpretation*, 302.

101. Bruce, *The Epistles to the Colossian*, 149.

102. Dunn, *Colossians and Philemon*, 226.

103. Garland, *Colossians and Philemon*, 231.

104. MacArthur, *Colossians and Philemon*, 152; Zeitlin, "Judaism as a Religion," 222–23.

the Apostle's "true child in faith" (cf. 1 Tim 1:2),[105] a familial expression that refers to his mentorship,[106] Timothy often served as Paul's trusted emissary. Often, he himself could not visit the churches he had established on his missionary journeys (cf. 1 Cor 4:17; Phil 2:19–24). Moreover, Timothy was the addressee of two Pauline letters preserved in the New Testament. Besides Theophilus (cf. Luke 1:1–4; Acts 1:1–2), no other individual possesses the distinction of being the recipient of more than one book of the Bible.

Acts 16:1–2 reveals Timothy possessed a dual ethnic heritage: "But [Paul] came also to Derbe and to Lystra. And behold a certain disciple was there named Timothy, the son of a Jewish woman of faith—but his father was a Greek—who was spoken well of by the brothers who were in Lystra and Iconium." New Testament scholars who are interested in the topic of multiethnicity have found Timothy to be a particularly intriguing character because of his prominence and his diverse ancestry. As a result, they have examined the literature and the practices of the first century world in order to determine whether or not the Israelites would have considered Timothy to be a Jew, a Greek, or both.

While matrilineal descent was not unheard of in the New Testament era,[107] most researchers agree the Jews probably would have viewed Timothy as a Gentile.[108] His uncircumcised state at the beginning of Acts 16 raises the probability of this conclusion. Despite this modern supposition, Scripture neglects to categorize Timothy according to his ethnicity. The likely reason for this omission was his identity in Christ. While Timothy's heritage did not disappear, it no longer served as a legitimate source of division. Whether civilization identified Timothy as a Jew, a Greek, or a hybrid of the two people groups, he was first and foremost a Christian.

Unfortunately, some first century believers had failed to understand their new identity in Christ. Apparently, they had ignored the Jerusalem

---

105. Paul also considered Titus his "true child according to common faith" (Titus 1:4).

106. Larson, *1 and 2 Thessalonians*, 144.

107. God stated in the Torah inheritance rights could pass through daughters if no male heirs existed. (Num 27:7). In *Kiddushin* 68b the Talmud taught: "R. Johanan said on the authority of R. Simeon b. Yohai, Because Scripture saith, For he will turn away thy son from following me: thy son by an Israelite woman is called thy son, but thy son by a heathen is not called a son. Rabina said: This proves that thy daughter's son by a heathen is called thy son" (*Mas. Kiddushin* 68b).

108. E.g., Bryan, "A Further Look," 292–94; Cohen, "Was Timothy Jewish," 251–68; Schnabel, *Acts*, 664.

Multiethnic Marriage in the New Testament

Council's ruling that Gentile Christians did not have to keep the Mosaic dietary law or receive circumcision in order to become believers (cf. Acts 15:1–29). Accordingly, when "Paul desired [Timothy] to go with him [on his missionary journey] . . . he took and circumcised him because of the Jews who were in those parts. For they knew his father was a Greek" (Acts 16:3).

On first reading, Paul's actions may seem hypocritical at worst, and inconsistent at best, because the Apostle to the Gentiles insisted in over half of his epistles circumcision had no inherent value as far as one's relationship with Christ was concerned.[109] He even criticized the Apostle Peter for allowing members of the circumcision party to shame him into refusing to fellowship with the Gentiles as he formerly did (Gal 2:11–14). Why, then, did Paul require Timothy to undergo circumcision in order to accompany him on his missionary journey? The answer to this important question relates to critics' estimation of Timothy's ethnicity.

While Paul had no problem laboring alongside Jewish, Greek, and multiethnic believers, others were not so enlightened when it came to the matter of one's heritage. One may surmise from the standard Jewish antipathy toward Samaritans[110] that Timothy faced similar obstacles because his bloodline was not thoroughly Jewish.[111] His circumcision would protect him from unnecessary stigmatization while, at the same time, open a doorway to share the gospel with legalistic Jews who may not have given him a hearing otherwise.

Paul did not violate his teachings regarding circumcision and uncircumcision when it came to Timothy, but operated under the principle of not insulting others with one's personal freedom. Elsewhere he cautioned, "Do not give offense to Jews and Greeks and the church of God, just as I also in all things please all men, not seeking my own benefit but that of many, so they might be saved" (1 Cor 10:32–33). Timothy could do little to appease individuals who despised him because of his dual ancestry, but he could mute their criticism that he was a breaker of the Law.

Timothy's contribution to the New Testament concept of multiethnicity is twofold. First, because neither Paul (his mentor) nor Luke (the author of the book of Acts) attempted to identify Timothy's pedigree (i.e., Jew

---

109. E.g., Rom 2:25–29; 3:1; 4:9–12; 1 Cor 7:19; Gal 2:11–14; 5:1–6; 6:15; Eph 2:11–22; Phil 3:1–6; Col 2:8–15; 4:10–12; Titus 1:10–16.

110. Borchert, *John 1–11*, 199–200.

111. Bruce, *The Book of Acts*, 322.

or Greek? Both or neither?), their lack of interest implies the answer was unimportant from a Christocentric standpoint. Paul's "personal and filial language"[112] regarding Timothy meant he deemed the young man to be a true son in the faith regardless of his ancestral background.

Second, the fact Timothy played an important role in the early church is significant. In other words, his ancestry was not a barrier to meaningful service in the body of Christ. All that really mattered to the Apostle and like-minded Christians was Timothy's commitment to Jesus and his godly testimony.[113] These qualities also mattered to God. Acts 16:1–3 and 1–2 Tim portray multiethnic believers positively, and, by extension, multiethnic Christian marriages as well.

A Multiethnic Multitude (Rev 7:9)

For over nineteen centuries, the book of Revelation has served the purpose of comforting believers who suffer. It also has encouraged all followers of Christ to conduct their earthly affairs in the light of the imminent appearance of the messianic kingdom.[114] The final New Testament book prophesies not only the defeat of wickedness (e.g., Rev 14:8; 18:1–2), but also the creation of a new Heaven and a new earth (Rev 21:1–4). At some point prior to this glorious event, Rev 7 depicts a diverse multitude standing before God's throne. Their express purpose is to worship God the Father as well as the Lamb—an allusion to his Son (Rev 7:10)—alongside the angels, twenty-four elders, and the four living creatures (Rev 7:11–12).

In reality, this chapter makes reference to two separate assemblies that ultimately merge to form one massive collection of believers.[115] The first gathering of people (Rev 7:4–8) numbers 144,000 and represents the remnant of the tribes of Israel[116] that has come to recognize Jesus as their promised Messiah. This congregation consists of twelve thousand "from

---

112. Johnson, "First Timothy 1,1–20," 25.

113. Hendriksen, *Thessalonians, Timothy, Titus*, 41.

114. Frank Macchia noted, "Though the Apocalypse assumes wrath for those who ultimately blaspheme God, there is also great confidence that multitudes will be redeemed by the blood of the Lamb." This message has brought great hope to Christians of every era. See Macchia, "The Covenant of the Lamb's Bride," 15.

115. Court, *Revelation*, 119.

116. Other explanations regarding the identity of the 144,000 exist, but the group's identification with Israel is the most straightforward reading of the text. For other interpretational possibilities, see Patterson, *Revelation*, 193–99.

Multiethnic Marriage in the New Testament

every tribe of the sons of Israel" who experience the Lord's salvation (Rev 7:4).

The second assembly includes the first alongside a countless number of Christians "from all ethnic groups,[117] and tribes, and peoples, and tongues. They stood before the throne and before the Lamb, clothed in white robes, and palm branches were in their hands" (Rev 7:9). The four descriptors that pertain to this congregation emphasize "the universality of the multitude."[118] In other words, while not every human who has ever existed will be a part of this future heavenly scene (cf. Rev 20:11–15; 21:8), the point is no ethnic group will be missing from God's throne room. All peoples become one in Christ.[119]

This passage portrays the ultimate fulfillment of Yahweh's messianic promise to Abraham:[120] "And by means of your seed all peoples[121] of the earth will be blessed, because you have obeyed My voice" (Gen 22:18). Previously the Old Testament had anticipated this multiethnic unification (e.g., Isa 11:10; 42:6–7; 49:6; 52:15; Jer 3:17). Paul had proclaimed repeatedly ethnicity should not be a barrier to fellowship because it had no soteriological significance (e.g., Gal 2:11–14; 5:1–6; 6:15). In Rev 7:9, the concept reaches its zenith as representatives of all people groups sing together about the Lord's great salvation.

This passage speaks both to the diversity and the unity of all Christians. On the one hand, when the Apostle John beheld the incalculable multitude that stood before God's throne, the people's cultural backgrounds and languages were discernible to him. In other words, even in Heaven markers such as ethnicity continue to function as tangible realities.

Although one's new identity in Christ signifies one's Adamic sin nature has "passed away" (cf. 2 Cor 5:17), it does not suggest union with the Son of God negate one's ancestral heritage. This feature of humanity is an

---

117. Often, English versions of the Bible render the Greek term *ethnos* as *nation*, but this translation can be deceptive because *ethnos* does not carry the idea of a sovereign nation-state as many Westerners assume. Consequently, this study translates the term as *ethnicity* or *ethnic group* in order to emphasize the idea inherent in *ethnos*.

118. Mounce, *The Book of Revelation*, 162.

119. Kelly, "Revelation 7:9–17," 292.

120. Easley, *Revelation*, 128.

121. The Hebrew word *gôyim* (i.e., *Gentiles, peoples*) is the Hebrew equivalent of the Greek word *ethnos*. In fact, the LXX renders the phrase *kōl gôyê hāareṣ* as *panta ta ethnē*, the same phrase Jesus used to instruct His followers to go to "all ethnic groups" and make disciples (Matt 28:19).

EQUALLY YOKED

indispensible part of one's contributory makeup. Accordingly, John's Jewish readers remained Jews, just as his Gentile readers remained Gentiles, and neither classification was inferior to the other.

On the other hand, the ethnically diverse mass in John's vision harmoniously testifies to God's greatness and his ability to heal the racial dissonance that often exists on earth. The ultimate purpose of Rev 7:9 is not only to show believers how Heaven will operate in the future, but to strive toward ethnic harmony under the banner of Christ in the present era. Multiethnic marriages in which both partners are followers of Jesus are one manifestation of the unity the Son of God produces.

IMPLICATIONS FOR PREMARITAL COUNSELING

The New Testament contains no explicit information regarding multiethnic marriage apart from the references to the Samaritans' Jewish-Gentile background (e.g., John 4:1–42) and Timothy's parentage (Acts 16:1–3). Nevertheless, the New Testament's overall message concerning the equality of various ethnic groups implies a permissive regard for the practice whenever potential husbands and wives are both believers. In cases in which one of the individuals is a Christian and the other is not, Paul's illustration of the uneven yoke applies (cf. 2 Cor 6:11–18). Consequently, the New Testament reinforces the Old Testament teaching that marriage is not a biblical option for spiritually disparate couples.

The preceding examination of New Testament passages that touch upon the issue of ethnicity has proven fruitful. Once again, Paul's assurance rings true that Scripture provides guidance for every aspect of believers' lives (cf. 2 Tim 3:16–17). Careful consideration of the above texts reveals a number of guidelines that assist biblical counselors in the task of providing relevant premarital counsel for multiethnic Christian couples.

First, all human beings descend from one common ancestor (Acts 17:16–31). Although ethnic differences abound, multiple species of people do not. Every person is a member of the same human race. Counselors would do well to emphasize to counselees the dual realities of racial solidarity and ethnic diversity. Misunderstandings regarding mankind's shared parentage lead to unbiblical views of anthropology. Ignorance of the existence of different values and cultural practices sets the stage for inevitable marital conflict.[122]

---

122. For a thorough examination of challenges that multiethnic couples often

Second, in a salvific sense, Jews have no soteriological advantage over other people groups because God is no respecter of persons (Acts 10:1–48). Rather, his desire is for all representatives of every ethnic group to repent and confess that Jesus, his resurrected Son, is Lord over all creation (cf. 2 Pet 3:9). As a consequence of salvation, Jews, Greeks, Barbarians, and Scythians experience oneness in Christ (Rom 10:1–13; Gal 3:28; Col 3:9–11). Counselors should explain to counselees that in spite of possible worldview differences, all Christians possess a common spiritual heritage. This unity provides multiethnic couples with a solid foundation on which to build lasting, Christ-honoring marriages.

Third, in the future, all Christians of every era will gather around God's throne to worship him and his Son (Rev 7:9). While the ethnic identity and language of each individual is detectable in this heavenly scene, these differences are not divisive. Rather, they underscore the accord ethnically diverse believers attain by means of union with Christ. Counselors must teach their counselees that the bonds of matrimony do not dissolve ethnic distinctions. Rather, just as individual chords blend together to produce musical harmony, Christian couples from dissimilar backgrounds can achieve consonance in their relationships.

Fourth, Paul equipped Timothy to minister successfully to multiple people groups by helping him to bridge cultural gaps. In other words, Timothy's mentor caused him to realize some aspects of his cultural identity (e.g., uncircumcision) impeded the effectiveness of his work among the Jews. By removing controversial barriers, Timothy increased his ability to operate in multiple ethnic contexts. This cultural malleability serves as a helpful analogue for the flexibility multiethnic couples should exhibit in their marriages.

While Christians do not have the liberty to violate biblical principles, certain cultural practices are ambiguous in nature.[123] Premarital counseling sessions offer an exceptional venue for sensitizing multiethnic couples to ways in which they can bridge their respective cultural gaps. Like Paul, counselors serve as mentors who help to pinpoint harmful obstructions to healthy marriages. Additionally, they offer biblically informed solutions that promote marital harmony.

In summary, cultural differences do not necessarily lead to divisiveness. Similarly, ethnic distinctions are not a foregone threat to marital

---

experience, see chapter 5.

123. For a discussion of ambiguous cultural practices, see chapters 5 and 6.

compatibility. Multiethnic Christian couples are one in Christ. Despite their diversity, genuine unity is achievable because they possess an unfaltering foundation that binds them together. Biblical counselors bear the responsibility of revealing how this mutual underpinning is capable of transforming spouses' distinct cultural voices into a Christ-honoring harmony.

4

A Historical Survey of Attitudes Toward Multiethnic Relationships in North America

INTRODUCTION

THE PRACTICE OF MULTIETHNIC marriage in the Western Hemisphere is not a recent development. Shortly after Christopher Columbus inadvertently reached the New World in 1492, Native American, African, and European peoples began to comingle. This intermixture initiated the period archaeologists and sociologists often refer to as the Homogenocene Era.[1] Other civilizations eventually intermingled with the above three populations, and further amalgamation occurred.

Two factors guide the contents of this chapter. First, not every multiethnic pairing in the Americas occurred within the context of the marriage covenant. A significant number of unions were transitory liaisons, while others were not consensual in nature.[2] This section of the study focuses on

---

1. Mann, *1493*, 17–19, 24–26.

2. One of the appalling consequences of institutional slavery in the Americas was that numerous slaveholders violated their female African slaves, producing multiethnic children that often experienced lives of servitude like their mothers. For a discussion of this practice in the United States see Meacham, *Thomas Jefferson*, 55.

neither of these aspects of ethnic admixture unless they help to explicate the milieu in which they occurred.

Second, the limitations of this project prohibit a historical survey of the practice of multiethnic marriage throughout the entire Western hemisphere. Consequently, the two emphases of this chapter are intermarriage within North America and society's reactions to the practice. While the primary focus of the research is the region now known as the United States, the author also briefly examines Mexico and Canada.

THE COLONIAL ERA

Initial Contact

In 1519, the conquistadors set their sights on the land of Mexico. Their hope was to acquire the nation's magnificent treasures and to present the territory to the Spanish Crown for colonization. After feigning goodwill upon initial contact with the native population, Hernán Cortés and his company of soldiers revealed their true intentions when they marched upon Tenochtitlan, the capital city of King Moteuczoma II.[3] In their company was a young female interpreter of Nahua descent named Malinalli, or alternately, Malintzin. The Spaniards had obtained her, along with a number of other female slaves, from indigenous peoples whom they had met in Tabasco.[4]

Malinalli is one of the most controversial individuals in the annals of Mexico's history. On the one hand, Mexicans often despise her because of her traitorous role in the Spanish occupation of Moteuczoma's empire. On the other hand, they recognize her conversion to Catholicism (and her subsequent reception of the Christian name Marina) as an integral part of their nation's religious heritage.[5]

In 1522, Malinalli gave birth to Cortés' son, naming the infant Martín. Historians consider this child to be "the first mestizo, origin of the Mexican

---

3. Later Spanish writers erroneously rendered the ruler's name as *Montezuma*, but this spelling was the result of unfamiliarity with the intricacies of the Nahuatl language. *Mot'ucz°ma* most certainly is the proper transliteration of the Aztec king's name, which linguists often Anglicize as *Moteuczoma*. For a discussion of Moteuczoma's name, see Launey, *An Introduction to Classical Nahuatl*, loc. 6769–77.

4. Thomas, *Conquest*, 171–72.

5. Eakin, *The History of Latin America*, 66. A variant of this appellation is Doña Marina, *doña* being a Spanish honorific that translates as *madam*. Mexicans often attribute to her son the masculine form of this title, referring to him as Don Martín.

A Historical Survey of Attitudes Toward Multiethnic Relationships

nation, the union of the Amerindian and European."[6] After this initial intermingling of the Old and New Worlds, amalgamation soon became widespread. As a result, at present nearly two thirds of Mexican citizens are mestizos.[7] Mexico set the precedent for intermarriage in mainland North America, with the pattern repeating itself in Spanish, French, and British Colonies in the following centuries.

The Spanish Colonies (1519–1821)

Native Americans and Europeans readily intermarried in the Spanish settlements. The importation of 5.7 million Africans to Spanish and Portuguese colonies also contributed to this ethnic mingling.[8] Native Americans and Africans, as well as Europeans and Africans, also produced offspring that, in turn, married representatives of the three major ethnic groups, as well as each other.

As intermarriage increased and compounded, the Spaniards became obsessed with labeling the resulting progeny. They finally settled on a system of sixteen classifications intended to demarcate the numerous possible combinations that occurred when multiethnic women bore the children of multiethnic men:

1. Spaniard with an Indian woman is a Mestizo;
2. Mestizo woman with a Spaniard is a Castizo;
3. Castizo man with a Spanish woman is a Spaniard;
4. Spaniard man with a Black woman is a Mulatto;
5. Mulatto woman with a Spaniard is a Morisco;
6. Morisco man with a Spanish woman is a Chino;
7. Chino man with an Indian woman is a Step Backward;
8. A Step Backward man with a Mulatto woman is a Wolf;
9. A Wolf man with a Chino woman is a Gibaro;
10. A Gibaro man with a Mulatto woman is a Leper;

---

6. Cypess, *La Malinche*, 9.

7. "North America: Mexico."

8. Andrews, *Afro-Latin America, 1800–2000*, 3. Andrews noted, "[T]en times as many Africans came to Spanish and Portuguese America . . . as to the United States."

11. A Leper man with a Black woman is a Cambujo (very dark);

12. A Cambujo man with an Indian woman is a Zambaigo;

13. A Zambaigo man with a Wolf woman is a Calpa Mulatto;

14. A Calpa Mulatto man with a Cambujo woman is a Stay in the Air;

15. A Stay in the Air man with a Mulatto woman is an I Don't Understand Thee;

16. An I Don't Understand Thee man with an Indian woman is a Step Backward.[9]

The Spaniards knew their peculiar taxonomy made little genealogical sense, but it ensured their continued dominance in the New World.

The arbitrarily derived list served the purpose of maintaining "social control, since it created status differences between groups . . . who might otherwise have united against their oppressors."[10] In essence, this strategy pitted the resulting classes against each other in such a way that the formation of an anti-Spanish coalition proved impossible. Because this artificially imposed caste system worked to the Spaniards' advantage, they chose not to illegalize multiethnic marriages.

The French Colonies (1605–1803)

Within France's colonial holdings and the surrounding territories, fur traders were the first Europeans to intermarry. As more Frenchmen entered the profession and natural resources became more difficult to acquire, trappers soon learned profitability necessitated close relations with Native American tribes. In fact, indigenous "communities insisted on [Native-French] marriage[s] because [they] created the assurance of mutuality and reciprocal obligations between the spouses' families. If a man refused to take a wife who had kinship ties to the community with which he wanted to do business, he was not trusted."[11]

One factor that contributed to the practice of intermarriage was the lack of European women in the French colonies.[12] Some men, however,

---

9. Cottrol, "The Long, Lingering Shadow," 443. One should note that a number of these categories dehumanized multiethnic people by comparing them to animals.

10. Cope, *The Limits of Racial Domination*, 4.

11. Murphy, *Gathering of Rivers*, 85.

12. Lansing, "Plains Indian Women," 419.

A Historical Survey of Attitudes Toward Multiethnic Relationships

married Native women from each tribe with which they interacted, in addition to maintaining Caucasian wives and families in French settlements.[13] Toussaint Charbonneau (1767–1843), the fur trapper and trader Meriwether Lewis and William Clark hired to accompanying them on their historic expedition, was a product of this custom.

Charbonneau was a descendant of both French and Native peoples. Throughout his life, he also married multiple Native American women to improve his business relations.[14] His most famous wife was Sacagawea, a Shoshone who helped to bridge the cultural and linguistic gap between the members of the Lewis and Clark Expedition and Native American tribes they encountered. During their journeys, she and Charbonneau became the parents of a son whom they named Jean Baptiste.

As their numbers soared, French-Native offspring acquired the appellative *métis*,[15] the French cognate of the Spanish word *mestizo*. Detractors refused to use this term, however, referring derogatorily to the children as "half-breeds."[16] The categorization of French-Native Canadians as Métis persists in the twenty-first century.[17]

Acceptance of French-Native marriages was by no means universal. A number of European descendants (among them the clergy) frowned upon the unions because they tended to promote polygamy. An additional concern was that participants did not seek official sanction from the Catholic Church.[18]

As previously mentioned, Native American peoples generally encouraged the unions, but some grew concerned because of the frequency with which they began to take place. One Arikara leader remarked to Henry Brackenridge, an American writer and politician, "Why is it that your people are so fond of our women, one might suppose they had never seen any before?"[19] Despite these misgivings, the Canadian government did not outlaw intermarriage, but the Métis regularly experienced discrimination.[20]

---

13. Sleeper-Smith, *Indian Women*, 24.

14. Anderson and Clark, "Probing the Riddle," 5; Jackson, *Children of the Fur Trade*, 233.

15. Douaud, "Canadian Metis Identity," 71–72.

16. Jackson, *Children of the Fur Trade*, 215–17.

17. Sawchuk, "Negotiating an Identity," 73–92.

18. Sleeper-Smith, *Indian Women*, 19.

19. Brackenridge, *Journal of a Voyage*, loc. 1064–68.

20. Jackson, *Children of the Fur Trade*, 227–28.

EQUALLY YOKED

The British Colonies (1607–1776)

Initial Ambivalence

The establishment of Jamestown (originally James Fort) in 1607 by the Virginia Company of London marked the beginning of permanent English settlements in the New World. Colonists built this outpost (in what is modern-day Virginia) in the midst of land the Powhatan Confederacy inhabited. Wahunsonacock, the paramount chief of this coalition of Native Americans, was the father of a young girl who would become a participant in "America's first interracial love story."[21]

Pocahontas (also known as Matoaka) first appeared in an account Captain John Smith published in 1608. Although only a child at the time,[22] Smith was impressed by her intelligence and comportment. Smith estimated her to be "tenne [sic] years old: which not only for feature, countenance, and proportion, much exceedeth any of the rest of [her father's] people: but for wit and spirit, the only Nonpareil of his Country."[23]

In an attempt to coerce her father to return the English goods he had confiscated when relations between the Powhatans and the colonists soured, the Europeans abducted Pocahontas and held her for ransom. In spite of his daughter's status as an abductee, Wahunsonacock refused to acquiesce to English demands, and she remained a prisoner. Because of her father's apparent apathy for her well-being, Pocahontas eventually elected to remain with the English. She converted to Christianity and received the Christian name Rebecca. Planter John Rolfe wedded her in 1613, and she gave birth to their son Thomas the following year. This union was the first intermarriage in the English colonies.[24]

The British Crown initially found this development worrisome because of Pocahontas's Native American heritage. Garrett Epps explained, "King James of England sought to prosecute Rolfe for high treason for the marriage, but his wrath subsided when the Privy Council assured him that

---

21. Edwards, "The United Colors," 148.

22. Ibid., 150. In her article, Edwards corrected a common misconception: "Pocahontas was a child at the time . . . the myth of a romance between [her and John Smith] was created and popularized in the nineteenth century."

23. Smith, *A True Relation*, loc. 655–71. For the sake of historical accuracy, quotations from this era retain their original spelling.

24. Smith, *The Generall Historie of Virginia*.

A Historical Survey of Attitudes Toward Multiethnic Relationships

Rebecca's issue would not be heirs to England's holdings in Virginia."[25] In 1624, the king changed his mind after John Smith identified Rolfe's wedding as the key to renewed relations with the Powhatans: "The bruite [rumor] of this . . . marriage came soone [sic] to [Wahunsonacock's] knowledge, a thing acceptable to him, as he appeared by his sudden consent thereunto."[26]

For a time, the marriage had the desired effect of reestablishing peace between the Powhatans and the English colonists, but the goodwill did not persist for long. After having visited London, Pocahontas died in 1617 as her ship began its return voyage to Virginia. John Rolfe expired five years later, possibly as a result of an assault his wife's uncle Opechancanough led against the colony in 1622.[27]

British Historian John Oldmixon noted that after the promising start to more amiable multiethnic interactions, few marriages like Rolfe's followed: "The English were not fond of taking the Indian women to their beds as their wives. Whether it was on account of their being pagans or barbarians we cannot decide; or whether that nicety was not very unseasonable in the infancy of the settlement."[28] The recurrent skirmishes between the Powhatans and the English also minimized the incidence of intermarriage. Xenophobic attitudes among both populations were the result of these conflicts.

An analysis of the earliest era of British colonial history indicates intermarriage between Native Americans and Europeans did not meet with either widespread or enthusiastic approval. Guarded permissiveness for expediency's sake appears to have been the general reaction to any such unions. Because of their indifference, the colonists did not create legal obstructions to prevent the two people groups from intermingling. Such marriages remained possible, though uncommon, in Jamestown and subsequent Virginian settlements.

---

25. Epps, "What's Loving," 482.
26. Smith, *A True Discourse*, n.p.
27. Nash, "The Hidden History," 941–43; cf. Fausz, "An 'Abundance,'" 3–56.
28. Oldmixon, *The British Empire*, 232. For the sake of readability, the author has taken the liberty of modernizing the tendency to render the letter *s* as *f* in this stage of the English language (e.g., *Englifh* instead of *English*; *unfeafonable* instead of *unseasonable*).

EQUALLY YOKED

Commencement of Restrictions

Africans arrived in the New World a little over a decade after the Englishmen built their first permanent settlements. Due in large part to the Virginian colonists' fondness for growing tobacco, and their perception that too few Europeans resided in the colony to sustain the burgeoning enterprise, they began to import slaves in 1619 to perform the backbreaking work of plantation life.[29] The introduction of yet another ethnic group to the region had the predictable result of further admixture.

Natives often welcomed escaped Africans into their villages, oftentimes intermarrying with them.[30] If any Europeans and Africans exchanged wedding vows in this period, the records are lost to history. At best, the practice would have been rare. A record from September 17, 1630 suggests such marriages virtually were nonexistent: "Hugh Davis to be soundly whipped, before an assembly of Negroes and others for abusing himself to the dishonoring of God and shame of Christians, by defiling his body in lying with a negro; which fault he is to acknowledge next Sabbath day."[31]

Potential African-European marriages faced an almost insurmountable obstacle. Intimate associations between the two ethnic groups threatened the perpetuation of slavery, so the colonies fought vociferously against this threat to the status quo. The question also arose as to whether the children of multiethnic marriages should be slaves or free. Virginian lawmakers addressed this matter on December 14, 1662:

> Whereas some doubts have arisen whether children got by any Englishman upon a negro woman should be slave or ffree, Be it therefore enacted and declared by this present grand assembly, that all children borne in this country shalbe held bond or free only according to the condition of the mother, And that if any christian shall committ ffornication with a negro man or woman, hee or shee soe offending shall pay double the ffines imposed by this former act.[32]

---

29. Wadlington, "The Loving Case," 1191.

30. Nash, "Hidden History," 947. Nash explained that this intermingling of Native Americans and Africans occurred throughout the colonial era, as well as during the early years of United States history: "In every part of eastern North America from the 1600s to the 1800s, escaping African slaves sought refuge among Native Americans. . . . The Africans took Indian spouses, produced children of mixed blood, and contributed to Afro-Indian transculturation."

31. Hening, *Statutes at Large*, 1:146.

32. Hening, *Statutes at Large of Virginia*, 2:170; spelling is sic.

A Historical Survey of Attitudes Toward Multiethnic Relationships

Historians recognize this legislative edict as the "first law prohibiting intermarriages" in the British colonies.[33]

The parlance of the ruling indicates two factors about multiethnic relations in Virginia during the 1600s. First, European men tended to cohabitate or intermarry with African women at a greater rate than European women with African men. This disparity largely was the result of some slaveholders forcing themselves upon their unwilling female slaves. Second, the decision discouraged multiethnic marriages, while at the same time minimizing the necessity of importing new slaves from Africa.[34] In other words, the offspring of slave women always would be slaves regardless of the heritage of their fathers, thus preventing a decline in the slave population in the colonies.

The colony of Maryland also grappled with the issue of intermarriage, but records demonstrate their concerns were somewhat different than Virginia's. In September 1664, the General Assembly of Maryland issued "an act concerning Negroes & other Slaves":

> All Negroes or other slaves already within the Province And all Negroes and other slaves to bee hereafter imported into the Province shall serve Durante Vita [i.e., for life] And all Children born of any Negro or other slave shall be Slaves as their ffathers were for the terme of their lives And forasmuch as divers freeborne English women forgettfull of their free Condicōn and to the disgrace of our Nation doe intermarry with Negro Slaves by which alsoe diverssuites may arise touching the Issue of such woemen and a great damage doth befall the Masters of such Negros for prevention whereof for deterring such freeborne women for such shamefull Matches Bee itt further Enacted by the Authority advice and Consent aforesaid That whatsoever free borne woman shall inter marry with any slave from and after the Last day of this present Assembly shall Serve the master of such slave dureingthe life of her husband And that all the Issue of such freeborne woemen soe marryed shall be Slave as their fathers were And Bee itt further Enacted that all the Issues of English or other freeborne woemen

---

33. Johnston, *Race Relations*, 166.

34. Sohoni, "Anti-Miscegenation Laws," 594. According to Sohoni, in the colonial era another reason British inhabitants of Virginia disapproved of multiethnic marriages was their socioeconomic impact: "Racial mixing would undermine the distribution of economic and social privileges in a race-based stratification system."

> that have marryed Negroes shall serve the Masters of Their Parents till they be Thirty yeares of age and noe longer.[35]

While Maryland did not make intermarriage illegal, the colony did everything in its power to prevent the crossing of ethnic boundaries by English females, an issue that especially concerned its European inhabitants.[36]

In addition to shaming women who desired to enter such unions, the law required them to become slaves alongside their African husbands and surrender their children to servitude for the first thirty years of their lives. The threat of enduring bondage successfully curtailed instances of intermarriage, but the practice did not disappear altogether. Ultimately, these "attempts to patch holes in the fabric of the [legal] system"[37] failed in both Maryland and Virginia. They did, however, lay the foundation for American marriage restrictions that endured for over three centuries.[38]

Further Restrictions

On April 3, 1691, the Virginia legislature once more saw the need to revisit the issue of intermarriage:

> And for prevention of the abominable mixture and spurious issue which hereafter may encrease in this dominion as well by negroes, mulattoes, and Indians intermarrying with English, or other white women, as by their unlawfull accompanying with one another, Be it enacted by the authoritie aforesaid, and it is hereby enacted, That for the time to come, whatsoever English or other white man or woman being free shall within three months after such marriage be banished and removed from this dominion forever, and that the justices of each respective countie within the dominion make it their perticular care, that this act be put in effectuall execution.[39]

The wording of this law provides revealing information concerning the issue of multiethnic marriage in the late 1600s.

---

35. Browne, *Archives of Maryland*, 533–34.

36. Jacobs, "The Eastmans," 31. Jacobs observed, "[W]hite Americans were much more threatened by interracial sex and marriage that involved white women and non-white men. Where there was a higher incidence of such liaisons . . . colonies and states were much more likely to pass laws against interracial marriages."

37. Higginbotham and Kopytoff, "Racial Purity," 84.

38. Pascoe, "Miscegenation Law," 48–49.

39. Hening, *Statutes at Large of Virginia*, 3:86–87.

A Historical Survey of Attitudes Toward Multiethnic Relationships

First, while earlier efforts to inhibit multiethnic marriages focused primarily on English women and African slaves, new legislation targeted English men as well. Almost eight decades of institutional slavery in the Americas had hardened ethnic lines considerably.[40] The offspring of Anglo[41] men and African women were slaves like their mothers. Virginia then defined any intimate contact with Africans as abominable, whether the Anglo participant was male or female.

Second, Native Americans now appeared in the list of forbidden marriages as well. Due to periodic skirmishes with the settlers, significant cultural differences, and non-Christian practices, "the image of Indians as fearsome, brutish, and depraved . . . persisted in many English minds."[42] These factors prompted the legislature to ban Native-Anglo marriages.

Third, Virginian law also condemned marriages between Anglos and a group known as the mulattoes. Contrary to later usage, the word *mulatto*[43] originally referred to individuals with any degree of hybridity rather than one specific type of admixture. For example, on October 4, 1705, Virginia defined the term as "the child of an Indian and the child, grand child, or great grand child [sic], of a negro."[44] Eventually other ethnic designations developed as mulattoes intermarried with each other and their parent populations.[45]

The very existence of mulattoes within the colonies suggests previous legislative efforts to keep Anglos, Africans, and Native Americans separate were unsuccessful. This visible reminder of amalgamation impelled the framers of the 1691 law to prevent intermarriage from becoming more prevalent in the future. Their primary strategy was to urge negligent

---

40. Nash, "Hidden History," 941.

41. Because British colonies in the New World were over ninety years old in 1691, many of the inhabitants of the settlements had been born in the Americas. The author describes native-born colonists from this era as Anglos in order to recognize their British ancestry, while emphasizing their distinctiveness as Americans. The term *Caucasian* did not appear in literature until 1781. See Sohoni, "Anti-Miscegenation Laws," 602.

42. Smedley and Smedley, *Race in North America*, 77.

43. According to etymologists, the term *mulatto* probably originates from one of two linguistic sources: Spanish (*mulo*, i.e. mule, the offspring of a male donkey and a female horse), or Arabic (*muwallad*, i.e., mestizo). See Sollors, "'Never was Born,'" 310.

44. Hening, *Statutes at Large of Virginia*, 3:252.

45. Eventually *mulatto* came to refer to half-African and half-Anglo individuals. *Quadroon* often designated people who were one-quarter African, while *octoroon* identified individuals who were one-eighth African. The children of Native Americans and Africans, or Anglos and Africans, were *mustees*. See Williamson, *New People*, xii–xiii.

authorities to do a better job of policing ethnic boundaries. As a last resort, they sent offenders into exile so their daily presence within the colony would not tempt others to follow the same path.

Early Eighteenth-Century Legislation

In the first quarter of the 1700s, other colonies joined Virginia and Maryland's lead by producing marriage acts of their own. Prohibitions in this period typically did not discriminate against Native Americans, but focused exclusively on Africans and mulattoes. Because the latter class of people defied conventional ethnic taxonomies, many colonists feared that, left unchecked, miscegenation would eradicate the Anglo race.

A generation after this new round of legislation appeared, Maryland performed a census that included demographic information pertaining to ethnicity. Estimates placed the number of mulattoes at about 2.4 percent of the population.[46] Since many mulatto children came into existence outside the bonds of matrimony,[47] the actual number of multiethnic marriages in the colonies must have been negligible in the early eighteenth century.

In spite of the relatively rare occurrence of intermarriage, the colony of Massachusetts passed its first anti-marriage regulation on October 24, 1705:

> And be it further declared and enacted by the authority aforesaid, (Sect. 4) That none of her majesty's English or Scottish subjects, nor of any other Christian nation within this province, shall contract matrimony with any negro or molatto; nor shall any person duely authorized for solemnize marriages presume to joyn any such marriage, on pain of forfeiting the sum of fifty pounds, one moiety [i.e., half] thereof to her majesty for and towards the support of the government within this province, and the other moiety to him or them that shall inform and sue for the same in any of her majesty's courts of record within the province, by bill, plaint or information.[48]

This law, which in certain matters echoed Virginia's earlier rulings,[49] was innovative in other respects.

46. Ibid., 13.
47. Woodson, "The Beginnings of Miscegenation," 44–45.
48. *Acts and Resolves*, 578.
49. Wallenstein, *Tell the Court*, 42.

A Historical Survey of Attitudes Toward Multiethnic Relationships

Instead of concentrating exclusively on multiethnic couples who desired to wed, Massachusetts employed a secondary stratum of regulations that targeted ministers and justices of the peace. Marriages could not take place without their cooperation, and any officiators who dared to join Anglos and Africans in holy matrimony would pay the substantial penalty of fifty pounds. Because informants pocketed half of this fine when they reported such infractions to the authorities, proponents of intermarriage could not be certain who might expose their unauthorized activities. Other colonies soon adopted Massachusetts's new tactic.

In 1715, the North Carolina General Assembly passed an anti-miscegenistic law in order "to prevent Illegal & Unlawfull Marriages not allowable by the Church of England."[50] In this instance, the new law served as a restatement of a preexisting code of conduct:

> [No one] shall presume to join together in Marriage any persons whatsoever contrary to the Table of Marriages which the Church-Wardens & Vestry are hereby to cause to set up in all Churches & Chappells under the Penalty of Five Pounds: Nor shall any persons forbidden to intermarry by such Table of Marriages presume to be joined together in Marriage under the like Penalty of Five Pounds.[51]

The emphasis on the banning of unions that already were forbidden implies some ministers and officials had been ignoring the Church of England's official stance on multiethnic marriage. Although the fine of five pounds was significantly less than the penalty Massachusetts required, the sum was by no means a pittance for eighteenth century colonists.

In addition to collecting a fine of ten pounds from Anglo females who chose to marry African or mulatto husbands, Delaware also applied corporal punishment to offenders in its 1721 resolution. These women could expect the humiliation of a severe public whipping alongside their spouses, so as to discourage others from following in their footsteps. Furthermore, any offspring the multiethnic couple produced must become slaves, serving in this capacity until the age of thirty-one.[52]

This last stipulation unfairly punished children for the actions of their parents, but the law served two purposes. First, it portrayed mulattos and quadroons as substantially different than Anglos, thus reinforcing

---

50. Saunders, *Colonial Records*, 2:212.
51. Ibid., 212–13.
52. *Laws of the State of Delaware*, 108–9.

EQUALLY YOKED

the ethnic boundaries Delaware lawmakers had established. Second, the legislation discouraged multiethnic spouses from reproducing, for they knew the dreadful fate that awaited any potential progeny. Essentially, the measure served as a sort of eugenics program that diminished categories of people whom the colony deemed unfit.

On March 5, 1725 Pennsylvania produced a thorough injunction against multiethnic marriages. The colony incorporated material from the laws of each settlement that heretofore had addressed the issue:

> (Section VII.) And be it further enacted by the authority aforesaid, That no minister, pastor or magistrate or other person whatsoever who according to the laws of this province usually (join) people in marriage shall upon any pretense whatsoever join in marriage any negro with any white person on the penalty of one hundred pounds. (Section VIII.) And be it further enacted by the authority aforesaid, That if any white man or woman shall cohabit or dwell with any negro under pretense of being married, such white man or woman shall forfeit and pay the sum of thirty pounds or be sold for a servant not exceeding seven years by the justices of the respective county court, and the child or children of such white man or woman shall be put out to service as above directed until they come to the age of thirty-one years; and if any free negro man or woman shall intermarry with a white woman or man, such negro shall become slave during life, to be sold by order of the justices of the quarter-sessions of the respective county...[53]

One might expect the southern colonies to possess harsher legislation regarding multiethnic marriage because they retained the institution of slavery longer than their northern counterparts. Such was not the case, however, because Pennsylvania, a Mid-Atlantic settlement, issued the strictest pronouncements of the era.

Like North Carolina, Pennsylvania sought to castigate ministers and government officials who dared to officiate at intermarriages. Any infraction garnered a fine of one hundred pounds, the largest penalty of any colony to date. Furthermore, Anglo males and females that intermarried risked the punishment of seven years of slavery. On the other hand, free Africans who did likewise would become slaves for life.

This decree indicates that the maintenance of existing social classes no longer was the primary concern of lawmakers. In large part, colonists had begun to divide their society along racial lines. Granted, "wide variance

---

53. Mitchell and Flanders, *Statutes at Large*, 62–63.

A Historical Survey of Attitudes Toward Multiethnic Relationships

in . . . attitudes"[54] toward intermarriage existed in the earliest days of the British colonies. As time passed, however, each governing body gradually developed a general distaste for any intermingling whatsoever between Anglos and African descendants. By 1725, colonial law had developed into a mechanism for preserving Anglo racial purity.

Ramifications of Anti-Miscegenistic Laws

Early British America's increasingly strict intermarriage laws provide a glimpse of the desperation colonial governments experienced as they attempted to curtail a practice they found reprehensible. These legislative efforts proved to be influential because they set the course for the remainder of the colonial period. Nevertheless, colonial restrictions ultimately proved unsuccessful at halting the occurrence of miscegenation.

Multiethnic couples who wished to marry found ways to circumvent government bans. For example, within the colonies some people secretly married with the assistance of supportive ministers. Historical records reveal that the clandestine ceremonies sometimes came to light, incurring the wrath of officials who punished husband, wife, and minister alike.[55]

Other individuals fled from oppressive marriage laws. Groups such as the Melungeons established isolated communities in western Virginia, the Carolinas, and eventually eastern Tennessee. They and their descendants insisted they were the descendants of Portuguese or Mediterranean voyagers[56] who arrived in North America in the mid-1500s, but recent genetic studies have uncovered their true story.

In reality, the Melungeons were "the offspring of sub-Saharan African men . . . white women of northern central European origin,"[57] and Native Americans.[58] Their assertion that they were Anglos with no admixture was nothing more than a means to protect them from societies who would despise their very existence had they known the truth. Numerous generations of Melungeon descendants were ignorant of their ancestry until science shed light on their actual heritage.

---

54. Mills, "Miscegenation," 18.
55. E.g., Saunders, *Colonial Records*, 2:591.
56. Kennedy and Kennedy, *The Melungeons*, xiii.
57. Loller, "Melungeon."
58. DeMarce, "Looking at Legends," 37.

EQUALLY YOKED

THE LATE EIGHTEENTH AND NINETEENTH CENTURIES (1776-1900)

Antebellum Attitudes

Native American Acceptance

After the War for Independence, the newly formed United States of America retained much of the anti-miscegenistic sentiment that existed in the colonial era. One exception to the legislation of the 1600s was that the earlier aversion to intermarrying with Native Americans softened considerably. As a result, "in 1784, Patrick Henry nearly pushed through the Virginia legislature a law offering bounties for white-Indian marriages and free public education for interracial children."[59] Similarly, Thomas Jefferson noted approvingly in 1783 that indigenous women who wedded themselves to "white traders [could expect their husbands to] feed them and their children plentifully and regularly [and] exempt them from excessive drudgery."[60] The frequency with which these types of unions began to occur earned states such as Connecticut "the land of intermarriages."[61]

At times, the acceptance of Native American and Anglo unions was not altogether altruistic. For example, on December 21, 1808, President Jefferson encouraged a delegation of Miami, Potawatomi, Delaware, and Chippewa chiefs "to join us in our government, to mix with us in society, and your blood and ours united will spread again over the great island [of America]."[62] In Jefferson's mind, the absorption of Native Americans into United States society would remove a major obstacle to the Anglo settlement of the entire continent.[63]

Continued African American Rejection

Intermarriages between Anglos and African Americans continued to engender as much animosity as ever in this era. Despite this stance, society often ignored adulterous liaisons between Anglo men and African American women. Alexis de Tocqueville, an influential French political thinker,

59. Nash, "Hidden History," 943.
60. Jefferson, *Writings*, 186.
61. Gaul, *To Marry an Indian*, 89–90.
62. Jefferson, *Writings of Thomas Jefferson*, 439.
63. Berger, "After Pocahontas," 73.

A Historical Survey of Attitudes Toward Multiethnic Relationships

ironically observed in 1840, "To corrupt a colored girl scarcely harms an American's reputation; marrying her dishonors him."[64]

This hypocritical approach to multiethnic relations was not a new development in de Tocqueville's time, but as old as the United States itself. When the travel writer Fortescue Cuming visited Natchez in the early 1800s, he noted "the great mixture of colour of the people in the streets,"[65] yet said nothing concerning the existence of intermarriage in the city. In his novel *Redburn* (1849), Herman Melville suggested, "You cannot spill a drop of American blood without spilling the blood of the whole world."[66]

By the 1820s, commentators who addressed the topic of marriage between African Americans and Anglos began to refer to the practice as *amalgamation*. They borrowed this term from the field of metallurgy, which used the expression to describe the process of blending different metals together.[67] Amalgamation almost always had a negative connotation, with the children of such unions receiving the epithets *mixed-blood* and *half-breed*.[68]

Early American Legislation

In the early American period, states continued to observe colonial regulations that forbade intermarriage between African Americans and Anglos. States also instituted a new round of legislation that strengthened existing legislation. The majority of these laws came into being in the 1830s and 1840s. During these decades, the nation began to grapple with the morality of slavery.

On December 22, 1836, nine years before Texas became a state, the Republic of Texas passed a law that rendered minorities second-class citizens. The statute barred "negroes, mulattoes, Indians, and all other persons of mixed blood descended from negro or Indian ancestors, to the third generation inclusive, though one ancestor of each generation may have been a white person," from serving as witnesses when Anglos were on trial.[69] Less than six months later, on June 5, 1837, lawmakers isolated non-Anglos even further by placing restrictions on intermarriage:

64. Tocqueville, *Democracy in America*, 717.
65. Cumings, *Early Western Travels*, 320.
66. Melville, *Redburn*, loc. 2681.
67. Pérez-Torres, "Miscegenation Now," 378.
68. Smithers, "The 'Pursuits,'" 260.
69. Gammel, *The Laws of Texas*, 1:205–6.

> Be it further enacted, That it shall not be lawful for any person of European blood or their descendants, to intermarry with Africans, or the descendants of Africans; and should any person as aforesaid violate the provisions of this section such marriage shall be null and void, and the parties on conviction shall be deemed guilty of a high misdemeanor and punished as such.[70]

After this law went into affect, Anglo and African American couples had little recourse but to leave the territory if they wished to avoid stiff penalties. When Texas entered the Union in 1845, the new state continued to operate under this statute.

In its second year of existence as a state, Arkansas passed a bill similar to that of Texas. Once again, the law, which came into effect in October 1837, focused exclusively on African Americans and their descendants: "All marriages of white persons with negroes or mulattoes are declared to be illegal or void."[71] In other words, the Arkansas legislature gave itself the authority to dissolve ethnically diverse marital unions, even if intermarried husbands and wives objected to the measure.

In 1849, Virginia revised its existing law codes. One of the subjects upon which the General Assembly touched was the issue of multiethnic marriages. Repeating the decisions of Texas and Arkansas before it, Virginia declared, "All marriages between a white person and a negro . . . shall be absolutely void, without any decree of divorce, or other legal process."[72]

Like Massachusetts, North Carolina, and Pennsylvania over a century earlier, Alabama thought it best to avert intermarriages by focusing its attention on ministers. In 1852, the state established a fine for clergymen who failed to observe Alabama's statutes: "Any person solemnizing the rites of matrimony with the knowledge that . . . one of the parties is a negro and the other a white person, is guilty of a misdemeanor, and on conviction, must be fined not less than one thousand dollars."[73] For its day, this monetary penalty was exorbitant.

Of interest is the General Assembly's concession that a pastor unintentionally might perform a wedding ceremony in which one of the

---

70. Ibid., 234–35.

71. Ball and Roane, *Revised Statutes*, 536.

72. *The Code of Virginia*, 471.

73. Ormond et al, *The Code of Alabama*, 377. This fine also applied to ministers who knowingly performed weddings when one participant had not attained the age of consent.

A Historical Survey of Attitudes Toward Multiethnic Relationships

participants was African American. Well before this period of American history, intermixture had occurred over so many generations that some slaves virtually were indistinguishable from Anglos. At times, slave owners placed advertisements in their local newspapers, imploring readers to help them locate escaped mulattos with "sandy hair, blue eyes, [and] ruddy complexion[s]."[74]

In 1861, three years before attaining statehood, the Territory of Nevada passed the first anti-miscegenistic law specifically targeting Asians.[75] In her article regarding the history of marriage in Nevada, Rachel Anderson provided a photocopy of the page on which the *Laws of the Territory of Nevada* prohibited such unions: "If any white man or woman intermarry with any black person, mulatto, Indian, or Chinese, the parties to such marriage shall be deemed guilty of a misdemeanor, and, on conviction thereof, be imprisoned in the territorial prison, for a term not less than one year, nor more than two years."[76] In this period of time, the term *Chinese* was interchangeable with *Mongolian*, often referring to people who originated from any part of Asia.[77]

Because Nevada's proximity to the Pacific coast (the main entry point for people fleeing Asia) meant numerous Asians found their way into the territory, Anglos in the region worried the new immigrants would steal their jobs. American citizens became convinced "economic competition, created by the importation of exploitable laborers without political rights," would cause them and their families to starve.[78] This fear soon devolved into a general xenophobia that extended to Anglo-Asian intermarriages.

Multiethnic Marriage and the Lincoln–Douglas Debates

In 1858, Republican Abraham Lincoln and Democrat Stephen A. Douglas agreed to a series of seven debates. Both men were candidates for the Illinois Senate seat, and they held strikingly different views regarding the issue of slavery. Their differences encapsulated the conflicting attitudes Americans expressed in the years leading up to the Civil War. Their speeches

---

74. Spickard, *Mixed Blood*, 251.
75. Sohoni, "Anti-Miscegenation Laws," 587.
76. Anderson, "African-American History in Nevada (1861–2011)."
77. Volpp, "American Mestizo," 86.
78. Ibid.

also demonstrate that many voters believed the abolition of slavery necessarily would lead to widespread marriages between Anglos and African Americans.

Like many of his comrades in the Democratic Party, Douglas accused Republicans who fought for the abolitionist cause with secretly approving of intermarriage.[79] In response to this charge, Lincoln said in Charleston, Illinois on September 18, "I am not, nor ever have been in favor of making voters of the negroes, or jurors, or qualifying them to hold office, or having them to marry with white people."[80] In an earlier debate, Lincoln had made his point more forcefully: "But Judge Douglas is especially horrified at the thought of the mixing blood by the white and black races: agreed for once—a thousand times agreed."[81]

On October 7, 1858, Douglas scoffed at this response in his Galesburg, Illinois speech. He accused Lincoln of being a closet amalgamationist who knew how to conceal his true feelings in order to obtain more voter support: "He is voted for in the South as being a Pro-Slavery man; he is to be voted for in the North as being an Abolitionist . . . Up here, he thinks it is all nonsense to talk about different races."[82] The notion that Anglos and African Americans belonged to the same race was an inflammatory statement in the 1860s, and Douglas's unremitting insinuations led many to believe Lincoln really was a proponent of intermarriage.

Almost a year later, Lincoln still was seeking to undo the political damage Douglas' allegations had created. In a speech he gave in Columbus, Ohio on September 16, 1859, Lincoln spoke more forcefully on the subject:

> I have never had the least apprehension that I or my friends would marry negroes, if there was no law to keep them from it; but as Judge Douglas and his friends seem to be in great apprehension that they might, if there were no law to keep them from it, I give him the most solemn pledge that I will to the very last stand by the law of the State, which forbids the marriage of white people with negroes.[83]

79. Paulin, *Imperfect Unions*, xxi.
80. Holzer, *The Lincoln-Douglas Debates*, 189.
81. Lincoln, *Speeches and Writings, 1832-1858*, 400.
82. Holzer, *Lincoln-Douglas Debates*, 246.

83. Lincoln, *Speeches and Writings, 1859-1865*, 33. In an era when many believed the Federal government was growing too powerful, Lincoln's argument also served the purpose of assuring hearers he was a firm believer in States' rights.

These pronouncements did little to calm the fears of anti-miscegenists, who throughout the Civil War maintained the end of slavery would lead to rampant intermarriage between Anglos and African Americans.[84]

Post–Civil War Attitudes

Reconstruction Era

After the Emancipation Proclamation (1863) eradicated slavery, and the North's decisive victory over the South (1865) ensured slave states must observe the declaration, relations between Anglos and African Americans worsened.[85] Julie Novkov explained that during the Reconstruction Era (1865–1877), "both whiteness and blackness had to be renegotiated and reconstructed, since slavery was no longer a yardstick."[86] Numerous states redoubled their efforts to keep Anglos and African Americans separate by enacting a new round of anti-miscegenistic legislation.[87]

Additionally, Congress regularly broached the issue: "Whenever any [Congressman] proposed measures for the protection of Negro rights, the cry 'Do you want your daughter to marry a Negro?' was raised."[88] At times, congressional opponents of intermarriage invoked religion to support their position. For example, on February 8, 1868, Senator James R. Doolittle of Wisconsin insisted miscegenation was an affront to God himself. He asserted, "It is the fiat of the Almighty which is stamped upon this very idea of forcing an amalgamation of the races against nature and against the laws of God. Those who attempt to do it are warring against all history and warring against the laws of Him that made history and made the races of men."[89]

Not all arguments against intermarriage arose from Anglo circles. Research suggests that, after the Civil War, the majority of African Americans shunned intermarriage, as did their Anglo counterparts.[90] On February 5, 1868, at the Arkansas Constitutional Convention, African American

---

84. Kaplan, "The Miscegenation Issue," 276, 314.
85. Brattain, "Miscegenation," 630.
86. Novkov, "Racial Constructions," 227.
87. Holder, "What's Sex," 154.
88. Avins, "Anti-Miscegenation Laws," 1227.
89. *Congressional Globe*, 1010.
90. Leon, "Tensions," 30.

Representative William Gray of Phillips County voiced the objection many of his constituents held:

> As far as the intercourse between the races is concerned, there is no gentleman, here, whatever may be his opinions, that objects to it more strenuously than I . . . In regard to laying down the line of demarcation, as proposed in the resolution offered by the gentleman from Pulaski (Mr. Hinds), expressing our disapproval of miscegenation, and declaring that the Legislature here assembled after the ratification of the Constitution, shall make such laws as they see necessary, for its prevention, be it legitimate or illegitimate, I am willing that such should be the case. But I am utterly opposed to the insertion, into the Constitution, of any piece of prejudice that shall give evidence that men have not outgrown their swaddling clothes.[91]

In a period of American history when people regularly conflated the issues of ethnic equality and intermarriage, Gray reminded his colleagues the government could extend to African Americans equal rights and representation without supporting marriages between them and Anglos.

Lawsuits that challenged the legality of anti-miscegenation statutes also were a feature of this era. Multiple states heard cases in which individuals challenged the injunctions against intermarriage. Regardless of the arguments proponents of multiethnic marriage employed, "judges declared that the laws were constitutional because they covered all racial groups 'equally.'"[92] Where intermarriage persisted in spite of strict prohibitions, states prosecuted citizens who intermarried.[93]

In order to sidestep incarceration, multiethnic spouses such as Pinkney Ross, an African American, and his Anglo wife, Sarah, learned to move from state to state frequently in order to remain one step ahead of the authorities.[94] This strategy was little more than a temporary measure because intermarried couples' dissimilar physical appearances prevented them from blending into society. In addition to the threat of imprisonment, citizens often took the law into their own hands by beating—and sometimes killing—people who married across ethnic lines.[95]

91. Pomeroy, *Debates and Proceedings*, 492.

92. Pascoe, "Miscegenation Law,'" 50; cf. Robinson, "Legislated Love," 75.

93. For a helpful list of state court cases that occurred during the Reconstruction Era, see Phillips, "Miscegenation," 135.

94. Jones and Wertheimer, "Pinkney and Sarah Ross," 330.

95. Ibid.

A Historical Survey of Attitudes Toward Multiethnic Relationships

The Late Nineteenth Century

Pace v. Alabama (1883) was the first major incident in the late nineteenth century that addressed the issue of multiethnic marriage. Because Tony Pace, an African American, could not legally marry Mary Cox, an Anglo woman, the couple decided to live together instead. The police arrested Pace and Cox in 1881, and they both received a prison term of two years in the state penitentiary. The court's decision reinforced the state law code, promising punishment for "any white person and any negro, or the descendant of any negro to the third generation, inclusive, though one ancestor of each generation was a white person, [who] intermarr[ies] or live[s] in adultery or fornication with each other."[96]

One Supreme Court case that reinforced—and essentially strengthened—anti-miscegenistic laws was *Plessy v. Ferguson* (1896). Four years earlier, Louisiana resident Homer Plessy, an octoroon who was indistinguishable from full-blooded Anglos,[97] had purchased a train ticket in New Orleans for a railroad car the East Louisiana Railroad had reserved exclusively for Anglos. Upon taking his seat, authorities who were aware of his heritage promptly arrested him because he had violated segregation laws. At his state trial, Judge John Ferguson ruled Louisiana was well within its rights to separate railroad cars according to ethnicity. Plessy contested the ruling, and the case ultimately appeared before the Supreme Court.

In a 7–1 decision, the justices upheld Judge Ferguson's original ruling. The court argued prior federal legislation, such as the Fourteenth Amendment, did not prohibit segregation:

> The object of the [fourteenth] amendment was undoubtedly to enforce the absolute equality of the two races before the law, but in the nature of things, it could not have been intended to abolish distinctions based upon color, or to enforce social as distinguished from political, equality, or a commingling of the two races upon terms unsatisfactory to each other.[98]

---

96. *Pace v. Alabama* 106 U.S. 583 (1883).

97. In the nineteenth century, the term *octoroon* referred to individuals who were seven-eighths Anglo and one-eighth African American. Because of prodigious ethnic comingling in the state, countless octoroons resided in Louisiana.

98. *Plessy v. Ferguson* 163 U.S. 537 (1896).

This ruling had ramifications for multiethnic marriages because it reinforced the states' ability to implement anti-miscegenistic laws.[99]

In spite of the Supreme Court's support of anti-miscegenistic state laws, marriages between Anglos and African Americans continued to be a major concern of Americans in the late nineteenth century. This anxiety manifested itself in period art, drama, and literature, which represented intermarriage as repulsive and inevitably disastrous for both the couple and society.[100] Authors of fiction also bemoaned the plight of multiethnic children, as the themes of "the tragic mulatto,"[101] "the tragic quadroon,"[102] and even the "tragic octoroon"[103] became standard fare.

THE TWENTIETH CENTURY PRIOR TO LOVING V. VIRGINIA (1901–1966)

The Rise of Scientific Racism

In the early twentieth century, the field of science reflected society's disdain for intermarriage. This scholarly disapproval of intermixture was not new, but in the past scientists had ignored the subject altogether. For example, in *The Descent of Man* (1871), Charles Darwin refused to believe mulattos were the offspring of Anglos and African Americans.

Darwin regarded mulattos' relatively lighter skin as the result of evolutionary mechanisms: "There is . . . a considerable body of evidence shewing [sic] that in the Southern States the house-slaves of the third generation present a markedly different appearance from the field-slaves."[104] His writings also perpetuated the opinion that non-Anglos were less than human. He observed, "The resemblance of *Pithecia satanas* [a South American monkey] with his jet black skin, white rolling eyeballs, and hair parted on the top of the head, to a negro in miniature is almost ludicrous."[105]

99. Elliott, "Telling the Difference," 116.

100. For a survey of anti-miscegenistic trends in American literature during the late nineteenth century, see Paulin, *Imperfect Unions*, 51–97.

101. Chadwick, "Forbidden Thoughts," 87.

102. Kaplan, "The Miscegenation Issue," 306.

103. Judith Wilson, "Optical Illusions," 88, 105.

104. Darwin, *Evolutionary Writings*," 254, 286. At least in part because Darwin was European, he deemed the Greeks and their intellectual successors to be superior to other ethnic groups.

105. Ibid., 316.

A Historical Survey of Attitudes Toward Multiethnic Relationships

The beginning of the twentieth century also was momentous because it "saw the rise to prominence of a new form of scientific racism based in genetics."[106] While in previous centuries proponents of anti-miscegenation often presented social arguments against the practice of intermarriage, they now couched such sentiments in scientific jargon. Furthermore, scientists described Anglos, African Americans, and other people groups as wholly distinct from one another. Accordingly, *race*, a term that often described different classifications of animals,[107] became a technical descriptor for human beings.

Advocates of eugenics programs, such as Margaret Sanger, the founder of Planned Parenthood, seized upon prevailing scientific opinions to argue that Anglos should employ birth control "to create a race of thoroughbreds."[108] Her plan required the elimination of other ethnicities so as to prevent intermixing. In a letter she addressed to birth control advocate C. J. Gamble on December 10, 1939, she suggested using African American ministers to persuade their communities that Sanger and her associates bore them no ill will: "We do not want word to go out that we want to exterminate the Negro population and the minister is the man who can straighten out that idea if it ever occurs to any of their more rebellious members."[109]

The field of science gradually shifted away from its discriminatory tendencies after World War I,[110] but not before influencing an entire generation's view of intermarriage. Consequently, the early twentieth century became one of the most anti-miscegenistic periods in United States history. As a result of this mindset, "groups were dichotomized into White and non-White categories . . . This [second] category included Hispanics, Asian Pacific Islanders, and Native Americans."[111]

---

106. Novkov, "Racial Constructions," 273.

107. Farber, *Mixing Races*, 26.

108. Sanger, "Unity," 3.

109. Sanger, "Letter from Margaret Sanger."

110. For a survey of the scientific community's shifting views during this era, see Barkan, *Retreat*, 279–340.

111. Lewis and Ford-Robinson, "Understanding the Occurrence," 412.

EQUALLY YOKED

Anglo and African American Objections

The majority of Anglos and African Americans in the early twentieth century objected to intermarriage. For example, in his book *The Leopard's Spots*, a manuscript that countered *Uncle Tom's Cabin*, Southern Baptist minister Thomas Dixon Jr. expressed the contempt many Anglos had for multiethnic marriages. He placed his personal sentiments in the mouth of the novel's minister:

> Nationality demands solidarity. And you can never get solidarity in a nation of equal rights out of two hostile races that do not intermarry. In a Democracy you can not [sic] build a nation inside of a nation of two antagonistic races, and therefore the future American must be either an Anglo Saxon or a Mulatto. And if a Mulatto, will the future be worth discussing?[112]

This telling paragraph reveals that Anglos who supported anti-miscegenation often desired to retain racial purity.

African Americans who demurred intermarriage often did so for other reasons. For many, the desire to obtain an Anglo spouse implied a rejection of one's one people in favor of their oppressors.[113] African American sociologist W. E. B. Du Bois articulated the disgust numerous descendants of slaves felt for the way in which slave owners had mistreated African women: "[W]e are determined that white men shall let our sisters alone."[114]

Intensification of Anti-Miscegenation Laws

Nineteenth-century legislation focused primarily on intermarriage between Anglos and African Americans, and to a lesser extent Anglo-Asian marriages. In the twentieth century, states modified their statutes in order to prohibit Anglos from marrying other people groups as well. In 1951, James Browning provided a helpful survey of states that outlawed intermarriage:

> [T]wenty-nine states . . . have taken steps to prevent miscegenation . . . All these states prohibit Negro-white marriages. Fourteen states, chiefly west of the Mississippi, forbid intermarriages of white and Mongoloid persons. Three states, Louisiana, North

---

112. Dixon, *The Leopard's Spots*, loc. 10287–10290.

113. Schoff, "Deciding on Doctrine," 282.

114. Du Bois, "Intermarriage," 180–81. Du Bois noted, "both races are practically in complete agreement [against intermarriage]."

Carolina, and Oklahoma prohibit Negro-Indian marriages. Four states forbid Indian-white marriages. Six states consider racial intermarriage with such abhorrence that its prohibition is provided for in their Constitutions.[115]

In every region of the nation, the majority of states, along with the preponderance of their citizens, thought intermarriage to be an atrocious concept.

One concession to the ban on intermarriage appeared in Virginia's statutes in 1924. Because some of John Rolfe and Pocahontas' descendants had become prominent Virginians, the state instituted the Pocahontas exception. This edict permitted Anglos who possessed one sixteenth or less of Native American blood to identify as white.[116]

Demise of Anti-Miscegenation Laws

In 1964, President Lyndon B. Johnson signed into law the Civil Rights Act, which illegalized "discrimination or segregation of any kind on the ground of race, color, religion, or national origin."[117] Three years later, the Supreme Court agreed to hear Richard and Mildred Loving's case against the Commonwealth of Virginia.[118] In the fifteen years prior to *Loving v. Virginia* (1967), the Supreme Court had avoided such cases three times,[119] but the passing of the Civil Rights Act had brought into question anti-miscegenistic state laws. Some lawyers insisted, "[T]he fourteenth amendment does not forbid state laws preventing interracial marriage or extra-marital sexual relations."[120] Proponents of intermarriage countered that states should not discriminate against multiethnic couples that desired to marry.

On June 12, 1967, the Supreme Court ruled in favor of the Lovings, declaring that states could not prohibit marriages solely because husbands and wives were ethnically diverse:

---

115. Browning, "Anti-Miscegenation Laws," 31.

116. Wadlington, "The Loving Case," 1202.

117. "Transcript of Civil Rights Act."

118. See chapter 1 of this study for background information concerning the Lovings' case.

119. Wadlington, "The Loving Case," 1212–13.

120. Avins, "Anti-Miscegenation," 1255. Alfred Avins, Professor of Law at Memphis State University Law School argued in 1966 that a Supreme Court decision to strike down anti-miscegenation laws would be an attack on the Constitution of the United States as well as state sovereignty.

Marriage is one of the "basic civil rights of man," fundamental to our very existence and survival. *Skinner v. Oklahoma*, 316 U.S. 535, 316 U.S. 541 (1942). See also *Maynard v. Hill*, 125 U.S. 190 (1888). To deny this fundamental freedom on so unsupportable a basis as the racial classifications embodied in these statutes, classifications so directly subversive of the principle of equality at the heart of the Fourteenth Amendment, is surely to deprive all the State's citizens of liberty without due process of law. The Fourteenth Amendment requires that the freedom of choice to marry not be restricted by invidious racial discriminations. Under our Constitution, the freedom to marry, or not to marry, a person of another race resides with the individual, and cannot be infringed by the State.[121]

Instantly, the ruling caused over three centuries of colonial and United States laws forbidding intermarriage to crumble, allowing ethnically diverse couples from every corner of the nation to marry indiscriminately for the first time in American history.

NORTH AMERICAN ATTITUDES AFTER LOVING V. VIRGINIA (1967–PRESENT)

Late Twentieth-Century Sentiments

While legal objections to multiethnic marriage dissolved overnight, public sentiment changed at a slower rate. Opponents of intermarriage stubbornly bemoaned the Supreme Court's role in the dismantlement of state laws, but research demonstrates "racial and ethnic boundaries appear to have become less important during the time frame between 1970 and 1986."[122] As intermarriages became more commonplace, totaling roughly 3 percent of all marriages by 1980,[123] public opinion gradually softened.

One variety of intermarriage that gained acceptance at a more sluggish pace than other types of multiethnic marriage was African American and Anglo pairings.[124] Centuries of poor relations between the two groups continued to affect attitudes on both sides. Outmoded beliefs often found their way into contemporary discussions of intermarriage.

---

121. *Loving v. Virginia*, 388 U.S. 1 (1967).

122. Lewis and Ford-Robinson, "Occurrence of Interracial Marriage," 411.

123. Ibid., 414. By 2000, the number of multiethnic marriages had risen to over 5 percent of the national average.

124. Foeman and Nance, "From Miscegenation," 541.

A Historical Survey of Attitudes Toward Multiethnic Relationships

Television producer Norman Lear captured the *zeitgeist* of the era in two popular television shows that examined the issue from the perspective of both ethnicities. On the show *All in the Family* (1971–79), an Anglo named Archie Bunker regularly criticized both non-whites and intermarriage. On *The Jeffersons* (1975–85), African American George Jefferson ridiculed his multiethnic neighbors Tom Willis (an Anglo) and his wife Helen (an African American). He also grumbled because the Willis' mixed ancestry daughter married his son.[125] As the programs progressed and the main characters interacted with people from a variety of ethnic backgrounds, their negative views of other cultures relaxed in much the same way North Americans were changing their minds about interethnic relations.

Early Twenty-First-Century Sentiments

By the turn of the century, multiethnic marriage essentially had become a mainstream practice in North America,[126] although resistance had not faded away completely. This disparity is discernible in the rate at which intermarriage occurred in various regions of the United States: "[I]n 2000, the western United States had the highest occurrences of interracial marriages, with these unions making up nearly 10% of all marriages. The smallest percentages of interracial marriages were found in the Midwest (4%) and the Northeast (4%)."[127] Despite the uneven distribution of multiethnic marriages in the United States, by the year 2000 these unions had produced sufficient offspring to require a change in the United States census. For the first time, participants could "check more than one race at a time."[128]

Perhaps the strongest evidence Americans as a whole have come to accept the practice of intermarriage is observable in the results of the presidential election of 2008. Barack Obama, forty-fourth president of the United States, is the offspring of an African father from Kenya and an Anglo mother from Kansas. A 2014 poll that surveyed Americans' estimation of President Obama's ethnicity revealed 52 percent of responders consider him to be a mixed race individual.[129] Considering that such a high number of voters deem the Commander in Chief to belong equally to both of his

---

125. Cadet, "The Jeffersons."
126. Qian, "Breaking the Racial Barriers," 263.
127. Lewis and Ford-Robinson, "Occurrence of Interracial Marriage," 414.
128. Brunsma, "Interracial Families," 1131.
129. Cillizza, "Is Barack Obama 'Black'?"

parents' ethnic groups, the implication is that multiethnic marriage is more accepted in the second decade of the twenty-first century than in any other period of United States history.

IMPLICATIONS FOR PREMARITAL COUNSELING

The inhabitants of North America have wrestled with the issue of multiethnic marriage over the past four centuries. In the colonial era, Native Americans, Africans, and Europeans intermarried intermittently, and public opinion of the practice varied greatly. As time passed and Europeans sought to maintain the distinction between themselves and African slaves, the colonies introduced progressively stricter legislation in order to prohibit intermarriage.

This anti-miscegenistic trend continued throughout United States history until the Supreme Court ruled in 1967 that the Fourteenth Amendment forbade states from denying marriage licenses to couples based on their diverse heritage. Since then, citizens of the United States have grown more accepting of intermarriage, even electing a multiethnic president in 2008. Although Americans by no means unanimously approve of intermarriage, the practice is more acceptable in the second decade of the twenty-first century than at any other time.

North America's shifting attitudes serve as a warning for counselors and counselees alike. Too often, current public opinions influence believers' views of certain subjects. This unfortunate propensity is true of the topic of intermarriage. Since the 1600s, churches frequently have followed society's lead rather than observing Old and New Testament teachings that imply Christian men and women from diverse ethnic backgrounds can marry each other. Biblical counselors must not make this same mistake in the counseling room.

Peter assured readers of his epistle that Scripture is a dependable prophetic word because of its divine origin (2 Pet 1:19–21). Paul insisted, "All Scripture is inspired and is useful for instruction, for reproof, for correction, for instruction in righteousness" (2 Tim 3:16). Jesus quoted the Torah to demonstrate its authoritative nature: "Man shall not live merely by means of bread, but by every word that comes out of God's mouth" (Matt 4:4; cf. Deut 8:3).

These texts indicate that the Bible is not a book of recommendations. Rather, God's Word is free from error and applicable to any situation in

A Historical Survey of Attitudes Toward Multiethnic Relationships

which believers find themselves. Counselors are not at the mercy of shifting community beliefs when it comes to the topic of multiethnic marriage. Scripture provides an unchanging standard by which to evaluate the practice, and to instruct counselees who choose to marry across ethnic lines. With confidence, counselors can prepare multiethnic Christian couples for intermarriage when they use the Bible as their guide because "the word of the Lord endures forever" (1 Pet 1:25).

5

Challenges of Multiethnic Couples

INTRODUCTION

EVERY MARRIAGE EXPERIENCES CHALLENGES and adjustments for which engaged couples must prepare themselves. In addition to the standard difficulties all couples should learn to negotiate, Christian men and women who enter multiethnic marriage covenants need to understand they will encounter additional pressures that relate to their interethnic status.[1] Some of these trials, such as the potential for familial or societal ostracism, are external in nature. Others arise from cultural dissimilarities such as worldview, communication, and day-to-day issues.

The purpose of this chapter is twofold. First, the following investigation will assist multiethnic couples to think deeply about the distinctive complications they likely will experience. Second, the research will help biblical counselors to provide relevant premarital counseling for multiethnic Christians who decide to marry.

---

1. Foeman and Nance, "From Miscegenation," 540.

Challenges of Multiethnic Couples

ACCEPTANCE

Familial Acceptance

One of the greatest potential impediments multiethnic couples often encounter is denunciation by parents or other family members who are troubled by the relationship. While some relatives may express outright prejudicial inclinations because of differences in skin color, cultural practices, or national origin, others sincerely may believe they have their relatives' best interest at heart. Additionally, Christian family members who misunderstand scriptural teachings regarding multiethnic marriage may object to the union on biblical grounds.[2]

Past and present difficulties in the realm of North American race relations also may influence family members' objections. For example, one American Anglo who excitedly reported to his parents his intentions to propose to a Nigerian woman was flabbergasted when he heard the following response: "We're not racists . . . but with all the problems there are in a marriage between two people, you have no business adding another dimension."[3] Research indicates this tentativeness is not the exclusive purview of Anglo fathers and mothers. Minority parents who have experienced racial injustice may perceive their child's choice of a spouse as ethnic betrayal, or a case of "dominant-group men exploiting subordinate group women."[4]

While some parents ultimately grow accustomed to their children's intermarriage, even learning to love and accept their offspring's spouse, others never acclimate to the multiethnic aspect of the relationship. Renee Romano noted, "strained relations with their families"[5] might persist for several years, or, in extreme cases, permanently. Endorsement or denunciation at the familial level is important. Studies show "social acceptance of the couple is, to some extent, dependent on how easily the couple is accepted into primary relationships."[6]

---

2. Botham, *Almighty God*," 110. Chapters 2 and 3 of this study established that Scripture permits multiethnic marriage as long as both partners are Christians.
3. Romano, *Intercultural Marriage*, 91.
4. Spickard, *Mixed Blood*, 364.
5. Romano, *Race Mixing*, 70.
6. Lewis and Ford-Robinson, "Understanding the Occurrence," 410.

EQUALLY YOKED
Societal Acceptance

Judy Scales-Trent, an African American woman whom strangers often mistake for an Anglo because of her relatively light skin and European features, observed that for some, "my very existence unsettles expectations of 'race.'"[7] The same statement holds true for multiethnic couples. Because intermarriage bridges a so-called racial gap (that in reality is a "social construct with no natural or biological quality"),[8] society has at times viewed ethnic intermingling as a threat to the status quo and/or racial purity.[9]

As a whole, American culture has grown more supportive of intermarriage.[10] Individuals, however, do not always adhere to current societal practices of acceptability. As a result, multiethnic couples should expect a variety of reactions from people in their day-to-day encounters. These responses often are directly proportionate to the degree of dissimilarity between spouses' physical appearances.[11]

Research indicates Anglo-American society usually is more accepting of relationships in which Anglo men wed non-Anglo women, than instances in which Anglo women wed non-Anglo men.[12] The reverse is true in non-Anglo cultures. They might perceive marital unions in which women from their particular ethnic group outmarry as a rejection of cultural standards of attractiveness in favor of whiteness (i.e., betrayal).[13] Non-Anglo men also might find outmarrying as a threat to their own marital prospects. One Salvadoran man expressed to the author, "Why do so many gringos (i.e., Anglo Americans) like you marry Salvadoran women? If this trend continues, there will be no women left for us to marry."

Strangers serve as another potential source of consternation. People in stores and restaurants often stare at intermarried couples out of sheer curiosity, unaware their inquisitiveness causes discomfort. Husbands and wives

---

7. Scales-Trent, *Notes of a White Black Woman*, 7.
8. Pérez-Torres, "Miscegenation Now," 373.
9. Arendt, "Reflections on Little Rock," 499.
10. Johnson, "A Mixed Race Society," 469.
11. Spickard, *Mixed Blood*, 363–64; Nash, "The Hidden History," 948. Nash explained that as early as World War I, in the United States diverse ethnic groups such as Punjabis and Mexicans often experienced little discrimination because their skin color often possessed a similar tone. Husbands and wives whose skin tone is markedly different from one another do not possess this type of camouflage.
12. Wilson, "Optical Illusions," 101; Cf. Jacobs, "The Eastmans," 31.
13. Romano, *Race Mixing*, 219–21.

will have to endure the knowledge that a whispered conversation nearby may relate to their multiethnic status. Occasionally, angry glares or comments from people who disapprove of intermarriage may sour an outing.

WORLDVIEW

Much like missionaries who labor cross-culturally experience some degree of culture shock, multiethnic couples will encounter significant cultural differences within the marriage covenant. Regardless of how long husbands and wives have been acquainted with each other prior to their wedding, routine interactions inevitably will reveal innumerable cultural practices of which they were unaware. Committed Christians possess a spiritual kinship and a theological system of belief that is common to them, but the way in which representatives of unrelated cultures approach certain matters may be worlds apart.

Missiologists, anthropologists, and theologians refer to this phenomenon as worldview. Apologist James Sire provided an excellent definition of this important concept:

> A worldview is a commitment, a fundamental orientation of the heart, that can be expressed as a story or in a set of presuppositions (assumptions which may be true, partially true or entirely false) which we hold (consciously or subconsciously, consistently or inconsistently) about the basic constitution of reality, and that provides the foundation on which we live and move and have our being.[14]

Multiethnic couples cannot prepare themselves for every conceivable cultural difference that awaits them within the bonds of matrimony, but they can enter their marriage with the knowledge that worldview disparities will arise. This portion of the chapter will examine common worldview variances such as identity, values, concept of time, and male and female roles.

Identity

Christians find their identity "in Christ"[15] as they crucify their old sinful way of life and "put on the new man" (Eph 4:24; cf. Rom 6:6; Gal 2:20). In

---

14. Sire, *The Universe Next Door*, 17.
15. E.g., Rom 3:24; 6:3, 11, 23; 8:1, 2; 8:39; 12:5; 15:17; 16:7; 1 Cor 1:30; 4:15.

the context of this treatise, however, the term *identity* refers to the manner in which members of a culture interrelate to one another. Each population effectively defines the nature of its members' associations from birth onward. Because participants consequently pay little conscious attention to the manner in which they interact with each other,[16] this aspect of worldview functions as "the silent language of culture."[17]

Depending on their cultural background, people may belong to individualistic societies, community-based societies, or fall somewhere between these extreme positions. Western civilization is an excellent example of a culture in which "excessive individualism" exists.[18] In addition to displaying a strong sense of autonomy that rejects any perceived personal intrusions, adherents run the unbiblical risk of exhibiting narcissistic tendencies. They often quantify their sense of worth in terms of their personal achievements.[19] Consequently, commodities such as one's occupation and net worth become intertwined with one's identity.

Community-based societies (Latin America being a prime example), on the other hand, "view themselves as part of a group, which usually is their family, tribe or community. People in these cultures [are] . . . part of a greater whole."[20] Ethnic groups who subscribe to this worldview value family and social connections greatly,[21] with the practical result that people tend not to make significant decisions apart from the collective influence of their society.

Marriages in which husbands and wives originate from opposite ends of the identity spectrum must overcome considerable and persistent challenges. Spouses who operate individualistically may become irritated by what they perceive as unnecessary intrusions and meddling by their partners' immediate family. Conversely, spouses who originate from community-based societies may agonize over their companions' apparent disregard of their families' good-natured interactions. In either case, multiethnic couples must learn to come to terms with each other's respective cultures[22] according to scriptural mandates.

16. Klingbeil, "Between 'I' and 'We,'" 322.
17. Lingenfelter and Mayers, *Ministering Cross-Culturally*, 27.
18. Rah, *Many Colors*, 32.
19. Hierbet, *Anthropological Insights*, 123.
20. Lane, *A Beginner's Guide*, 87.
21. Garrison, *Church Planting Movements*, 37.
22. Bystydzienski, *Intercultural Couples*, 79. While Bystydzienski correctly identified

Challenges of Multiethnic Couples

An honest examination of both spouses' belief sets likely will reveal areas that are in accordance with Scripture. Other practices (e.g., worldview, values, gender roles, communication) will not be compatible with biblical teachings. Husbands and wives from disparate worldview systems will have to manufacture a hybrid system of identity that does not violate the precepts of God's Word.

Values

As the name of this category suggests, the concept of values as it pertains to ethnic groups[23] refers to that which a society cherishes or considers a core tenet of its ideological makeup.[24] Admittedly, this element of culture is somewhat elusive because every member of a specific people group does not necessarily assess all commodities equally.[25] This segment of the study need not examine all possible permutations of a particular culture's value because its primary purpose is to make biblical counselors and multiethnic couples aware of potential value differences.

The two fundamental types of capital are material and nonmaterial assets.[26] Each culture regards one of these resources as more important than the other. For example, citizens of the United States normally focus heavily on the conversion of time into income.

Because residents of Mexico do not devote the same amount of energy to this goal as their northern neighbors, Mexican satirists sometimes ridicule the intensity with which Americans pursue this objective. One immensely popular comedic television show of the 1970s and 1980s, *Chapulin Colorado*, featured an American superhero whose name was Super Sam. This riches-obsessed champion wore a Superman costume that sported a dollar sign as a chest insignia, but his hat and goatee mimicked Uncle Sam's iconic appearance. Super Sam's catchphrase was the clichéd expression,

---

the intermarried couple's need to understand each other's cultural background, from a biblical perspective her discussion did not consider Scripture's role in negotiating differences.

23. One should note in a business context the phrase *cultural values* commonly refers to the economic affinities that a people group exhibits. For this application of the concept, see Choi et al, "Assessing Cultural Values," 312.

24. Malina, *Christian Origins*, 115.

25. Henry, "Family Structure," 293–94.

26. Nida, *Customs and Cultures*, 42.

EQUALLY YOKED

"Time is money!" The program's titular character, Chapulin Colorado, always bested his American counterpart because many Mexicans believed their approach to life was superior to the materialistic philosophy of the United States.[27]

The concept of freedom is a suitable illustration of an intangible value sundry people groups visualize differently. Everett Rogers and Thomas Steinfatt highlighted this principle by relating the story of an individual who lived in a communistic country: "An old woman in Saigon told one of the authors that she felt that she could not tolerate the lack of freedom in the United States. In Vietnam she was free to sell her vegetables on the sidewalk without being hassled by police or city authorities."[28] While an American doubtlessly would lament the elderly Vietnamese woman's lack of political freedom, she bemoaned the inability of Americans to participate in sidewalk business ventures at will.

Perceptions of directness contrast greatly as well. While certain cultures value blunt honesty, others seek to appease their hearers at the cost of truthfulness. For example, a man might agree to meet a friend at a designated hour without intending to keep the appointment. For him, his well-intentioned lie is preferable to frankness.

Without question, values are one of the most difficult subjects to reconcile in a cross-cultural context.[29] To exacerbate matters, ethnically diverse spouses may not be able to anticipate areas in which challenges will arise until the dissimilarities emerge in everyday situations or conversations. Intermarried couples will need to remember love is patient as they sort out their distinct cultural values in a way that glorifies God and contributes positively to their status as one flesh (1 Cor 13:4; Mark 10:8).

---

27. "El Chapulin Colorado 1978." Roberto Gómez Bolaños and Ramón Valdés, the actors who portrayed Chapulin Colorado and Super Sam respectively, are two of the most recognizable comedians in Mexico. Over three decades after their program originally aired, the television show remains popular throughout Latin America and portions of the United States in which Spanish speakers reside.

28. Rogers and Steinfatt, *Intercultural Communication*, 84.

29. Bradshaw, *Change Across Cultures*, 232.

Challenges of Multiethnic Couples

Concept of Time

People's concepts of time vary appreciably depending on the worldviews they inherit from their parents and society.[30] Cultural anthropologist Paul Hiebert remarked that in a missiological context "cultural differences can lead to humorous situations."[31] In the bonds of matrimony, however, conflicting perceptions of time can be a source of irritation. Multiethnic couples may find themselves grappling with two issues pertaining to time: time-orientation versus event-orientation, and opposing notions of punctuality.

Time-oriented cultures, to which Anglo societies chiefly belong, structure their lives according to their clocks.[32] Additionally, they place high premiums on qualities such as organization and preparation. Adherents to this way of thinking spend much time planning for the future,[33] sometimes to the detriment of focusing on the present.

The event-oriented mindset, to which much of the Third World adheres, focuses on the present as well as "the relationships between people and events."[34] In other words, the fact that an event occurs is more important than the time in which it occurs. Because devotees often think little about planning for the future, they may be unprepared when tomorrow arrives.

Because time-orientation and event-orientation are largely incompatible,[35] representative of either position frequently will exasperate adherents of the opposite philosophy. For example, at the author's wedding, his Anglo family and his bride's Salvadoran family converged for the ceremony in Houston. When the wedding did not begin at the scheduled hour because few attendees had arrived, some of the author's relatives despaired because of the delayed proceedings. This anxious reaction was a curiosity to the bride's family. As far as they were concerned, these activities fit the characteristic pattern of a Latin American wedding ceremony. An hour later, with a full auditorium, the service began and the tensions of the

---

30. Brown and Segal, "Ethnic Differences," 350–51.
31. Hiebert, *Anthropological Insights*, 63.
32. Kane, *Life and Work*, 101.
33. Breckenridge and Breckenridge, *What Color is Your God*, 140.
34. Hiebert and Meneses, *Incarnational Ministry*, 131.
35. For an excellent resource that highlights the differences between time-orientation and event-orientation, see Kraft, *Worldview for Christian Witness*, 233.

time-oriented and the event-oriented societies momentarily dissolved as two cultures became intertwined in marriage.

One's perception of promptness also is a subjective function of worldview. Sherwood Lingenfelter and Marvin Mayers provided helpful insight regarding varying approaches to this matter:

> Americans and Germans . . . have a very short time-fuse and experience anxiety when there is a delay of five or more minutes. The concept of being late varies significantly from one culture to the next and from one individual to the next . . . Most North Americans will begin to experience tension when others are fifteen minutes late; most Latin Americans will have tension when others are more than one hour late, whereas Yapese [a Micronesian people group] will not experience tension until the expected party is about three hours late.[36]

Since punctuality (or the lack thereof) touches upon nearly every aspect of one's day-to-day routine, multiethnic couples who do not share a corresponding pattern of timeliness will discover this contrast early in their relationship.

In their courtship phase, couples' timekeeping routines already begin to emerge. Boyfriends and girlfriends, however, usually overlook behavior that is eccentric from their standpoint more readily than do husbands and wives.[37] When the demands and adjustments of abiding together on a permanent basis begin to materialize, and spouses persistently insist their activities conform to their personal concept of time, clashes inevitably will occur. Husbands and wives will have to learn how to address the conflict in a Christlike manner that pays particular attention to the attitudinal tone they express toward one another.[38]

Male and Female Roles

Before surveying this topic, a qualification about male and female roles is necessary. In Western culture, the matter has garnered much interest and generated countless volumes that examine the subject from every conceivable angle. Often, these discussions unfairly accuse Christianity of

---

36. Lingenfelter and Mayers, *Ministering Cross-Culturally*, 38.

37. Eyrich, *Three to Get Ready*, 84. Eyrich rightly noted that engaged couples tend to think in terms of romantic feelings rather than the concrete realities of married life.

38. Adams, *Christian Living*, 39.

Challenges of Multiethnic Couples

demeaning women by regarding them as inferior to men.[39] For evangelical Christians who believe in the verbal plenary inspiration of the Bible, this depiction is unacceptable (e.g., Joel 2:29; Gal 3:28).[40] Rather, "Scripture is the final judge of all cultural forms,"[41] including the subject of male and female roles within the context of marriage.

Nevertheless, certain roles are ambiguous as far as Scripture is concerned, varying greatly depending on one's cultural heritage. In some societies, only women prepare food, while in other locales both men and women share the burden interchangeably.[42] In certain contexts, society considers agrarian endeavors like gardening and agriculture to be the work of females, whereas in other regions males exclusively engage in these activities.[43] The question of whether women should work outside of the home is perhaps one of the most culturally divisive issues, and distinct people groups provide dissimilar answers.

Multiethnic couples who find themselves in disagreement over gender roles will need to perform two tasks. First, they must examine Scripture in order to determine whether either of the spouses have beliefs that are incompatible with God's Word. Second, if this investigation reveals any unbiblical attitudes regarding the responsibilities of husbands and wives, spouses must amend their views in order to reflect scriptural teachings. In the event that couples discover areas of divergence that are culturally (rather than biblically) derived, they will need to agree on a resolution that is: 1) consistent with scriptural standards, 2) satisfactory to both the husband and wife, and 3) conducive to producing the marital harmony Christian spouses should enjoy.

COMMUNICATION

In its most basic sense, "communication is the transmission of information from a 'sender' to a 'receiver.' It may occur between humans, animals, and

---

39. Freedman, *No Turning Back*, 274–75; cf. Schussler Fiorenza "Public Discourse," 1077–1101; Ruether, "The Theological Vision," 22; Trible, *Texts of Terror*, 28–29.

40. For an excellent rejoinder to this unwarranted portrayal, see Patterson, "The High Calling," 364–77.

41. Elmer, *Cross-Cultural Conflict*, 181.

42. Bystydzienski, *Intercultural Couples*, 98.

43. Grunlan and Mayers, *Cultural Anthropology*, 130.

even machines."⁴⁴ In the context of this chapter, the primary focus is upon the manner in which people exchange their thoughts and ideas with one another in a multiethnic relationship. Other types of discourse fall without the bounds of this examination. Interpersonal communication consists of two components that help to express one's thoughts and emotional state: verbal interchange and nonverbal signals.

Verbal Communication

Spoken language naturally is an indispensable feature of the communicative process, but it is not the only component at work within a given oral transaction. For example, diverse ethnic groups possess differing standards of acceptability in regards to the tone of voice suitable to a particular type of conversation.⁴⁵ Consequently, when husbands and wives originate from dissimilar backgrounds, their standards of appropriateness may or may not correspond to their spouses' notion of proper and improper etiquette.

Gail Benjamin conducted an experimental study comparing the perception of tone by Japanese and American subjects. Participants listened to prerecorded Japanese audio exchanges that did not include a visual representation of the orator. Not surprisingly, the findings indicated Japanese speakers accurately recognized the significance of tonal quality more readily than their American counterparts.⁴⁶ This high prediction rate was the result of the Japanese language's heavy emphasis on timbre, as well as the Japanese participants' familiarity with these unwritten rules. The study's predictable results draw attention to the role cultural competency plays in the accurate interpretation of clues accompanying verbal communication.

Two other facets of oral communication that may prove to be sources of bewilderment in multiethnic marriage situations are ironical statements and idiomatic expressions. Verbal irony refers to utterances meaning "the opposite of [their] literal form[s]."⁴⁷ Studies show that as much as 8 percent of interactions between friends contain ironical observations, which even

---

44. Hiebert, *Anthropological Insights*, 142; cf. Hiebert, *Cultural Anthropology*, 122–25.

45. Sperling et al, "Voice in the Context," 74. The major thrust of this article was the voice as it pertains to literacy research, but the authors also emphasized the culturally derived concept of intonation.

46. Benjamin, "Tone of Voice," 11.

47. Clift, "Irony in Conversation," 524.

in this familiar setting may cause confusion because of their ambiguous nature.[48] One should expect a similar reaction within the bonds of marriage, especially when conflicting worldviews are at play.

Idiomatic expressions are unique figures of speech in that "their meanings cannot be predicted from the literal meaning of their parts and the choice of component lexical items is largely a matter of convention."[49] Because idioms are an outgrowth of culture and worldview,[50] they make little sense to outsiders. Spanish speakers are fond of the phrase, "las palabras se las lleva el viento." The expression's literal translation, "words are taken away by the wind," does not convey the actual spirit of the saying. Only an individual versed in Spanish and English realizes the adage actually means, "Actions speak louder than words."

Tone, irony, and idioms are but a few of the instruments of verbal communication with which multiethnic couples often contend. Knowing of their problematic nature beforehand will help intermarried husbands and wives recognize miscommunication when it occurs and respond in a biblical manner instead of taking offense hastily. "A gentle answer turns away wrath" (Prov 15:1a), and Christian spouses who put this principle into practice in their marriages will disarm possible altercations before they escalate.

Nonverbal Communication

Nonverbal communication denotes "the process whereby a message is sent and received through any one of the senses without the use of language."[51] Eugene Nida explained that numerous speakers do not realize the influence their gesticulations have upon the messages they wish to relate:

> Their failure to understand what they really are communicating usually results from a misconception as to the true nature of communication. They presume that their words are the message, while in reality their words are only part of the message, in fact, a relatively small part. For along with the words, they are always

---

48. Pexman, "It's Fascinating Research," 286.
49. O'Grady, "The Syntax of Idioms," 280.
50. Leslau, "Harari Idioms," 150.
51. Grunlan and Mayers, *Cultural Anthropology*, 96.

transmitting another message, by tone of voice, gestures, stance, eye contact, and distance.[52]

In other words, nonverbal signals strongly influence the recipient's comprehension of the speech act. Communicators who desire to convey a particular thought unknowingly may impart another idea altogether if their gestures do not accord with the hearer's perception of these signs.

In a multiethnic context, one also must be aware that a harmless hand movement in one culture may be a vulgar insult to another people group. One example of this phenomenon is the use of one's hands to relay messages.[53] Stephen Grunlan and Marvin Meyers explained, "The hand motion with fingers extended down from the palm and moved in rhythm toward the speaker signifies 'goodby' [sic] to someone from the United States but means 'come here' to most Latin Americans."[54] One fascinating—and potentially mortifying—point the authors did not disclose, however, is that the gesture Americans use to call someone (the hand motion with fingers extended up from the palm) is inappropriate in a Latin American environment. Rather than serving as a suitable manner by which to request someone's attention, Hispanics use the gesticulation to call their dogs.

If intermarried husbands and wives are not aware every culture possesses unique nonverbal communication, they may inadvertently demean each other if they innocently make rude gestures that possesses no such stigma in their native society. Employed haphazardly, such signals are capable of causing great offense. A frank but courteous conversation about culturally unacceptable nonverbal signals, along with a measure of forbearance when the occasional faux pas occurs, will prevent this considerable challenge from becoming a source of contention.

DAY-TO-DAY ISSUES

Food

Sustenance is a universal requirement of humankind, but that which people consider palatable varies greatly from culture to culture. In his international travels, his gracious hosts have offered the author local delicacies such

---

52. Nida, "The Other Message," 110.

53. Another example of nonverbal communication is facial expressions. See Rogers and Steinfatt, *Intercultural Communication*, 163.

54. Grunlan and Mayers, *Cultural Anthropology*, 97.

Challenges of Multiethnic Couples

as toasted ants (Guatemala), guinea pig (Ecuador), boiled cow intestines (Peru), and chicken embryo (The Philippines). Undoubtedly, many Americans would find at least some of these items repulsive. Representatives of the above countries likewise would turn their noses at some examples of typical American cuisine. Because of the subjectivity of food preferences, one people group's banquet is another's garbage,[55] or in certain circumstances, a beloved pet.[56]

In addition to the exotic dishes a particular culture enjoys, multiethnic spouses may find other aspects of their mates' mealtime habits unfamiliar as they begin to establish a collaborative dining routine. Dugan Romano listed three other potential areas of discord: 1) the time of the main meal (breakfast, lunch, or supper); 2) the location of the meal (a table or a mat on the floor); and 3) the instrument one uses to place food in one's mouth (fingers, silverware, or chopsticks).[57] Individuals with limited cross-cultural experience are unlikely to anticipate all of these divergences without the assistance of a knowledgeable biblical counselor to guide them proactively through this assortment of items.

Two practical observations are worth noting. First, since New Testament dietary restrictions are almost nonexistent (cf. Acts 10:1–35), for the most part food preferences are culturally dictated and, hence, morally ambiguous.[58] Second, neither spouse should expect mealtime in a multiethnic house to reflect only one of the participant's cultures. Consequently, thoughtful, mutual compromise will help to develop a menu and a schedule with which both spouses are comfortable.

Finances

The manner in which couples manage their finances is a crucial feature of monocultural marriages,[59] and multiethnic unions are no different. Mul-

---

55. For a list of ethnic delicacies that some people groups find abhorrent, see Alupoaicei, *Your Intercultural Marriage*, 139–40. Some of the strangest foods (from a Western perspective) Alupoaicei itemized include owl soup, calf's head, fermented shark meat, monkey toes, and sheep brains.

56. Jandt, *Intercultural Communication*, 177.

57. Romano, *Intercultural Marriage*, 41.

58. Two exceptions would be the consumption of blood and strangled animals, prohibitions that the apostles placed on Jews and Gentiles alike (Acts 15:19–20; cf. 1 Cor 10:31–32).

59. Yodanis and Lauer, "Managing Money," 1307–8.

tiple studies suggest that "the number-one area of conflict in a marriage ... is money. How money is to be earned and spent, and by whom, and who manages it, are questions which every couple needs to ask."[60] Spouses who possess a similar cultural heritage bicker over finances because their ideologies do not always correspond. One should expect multiethnic couples to experience even greater trials when their worldviews do not align with one another.

In cultures in which participants plan for the future, a larger percentage of capital will find its way into savings and retirement accounts. Civilizations in which the present takes precedence over days to come will focus more on contemporary considerations. To presume all members of a particular ethnic group think analogously about a given subject is a gross simplification. To some extent, however, a population's predominant worldview influences decisions regarding the acquisition, investment, and expenditure of money.[61]

For example, one's financial commitment to family members other than spouses and children tends to vary according to ethnicity. In some cases, this obligation manifests itself in the form of sending a portion of one's earnings to relatives who reside outside of the United States.[62] Such remittances may be difficult for fledgling marriage partners to afford, and one spouse may question the practice of distributing their resources altogether.

Another financial responsibility that varies from culture to culture relates to the amount of in-house caregiving couples provide their elderly parents:

> A 2001 survey on multicultural boomers by AARP [The American Association of Retired Persons] found that Asians, Blacks, and Hispanics are more likely to have three generations under one roof or extended family living in the home than Whites. Furthermore, Asians (42%) were more likely to care for an older relative than Hispanics (34%), Blacks (28%) or Whites (19%).[63]

---

60. Shelling and Fraser-Smith, *In Love But Worlds Apart*, 89. Unfortunately, disagreements over money are a leading cause of divorce.

61. Julia, "The Need for Cultural Considerations," 18–19.

62. Cf. Johnson and Stoll, "Remittance Patterns," 431–43; Kapur and McHale, "Migration's New Payoff," 48–57; Nathan, "Sending Love and Money," 52–59; Semyonov, "Labor Migration," 45–68; Thai, "Money and Masculinity," 247–71.

63. Pandya, "Racial and Ethnic Differences."

One ramification of these statistics is that people who marry across ethnic lines are prone to deviate on the issue of how much caregiving is appropriate.

Furthermore, spouses may feel trapped between the expectations of aging parents and the desires of their marriage partners. In this case, couples will need to recall scriptural principles regarding the preeminence of the marital relationship (Gen 2:24; Matt 19:4–6). They cannot allow varying cultural norms to drive a wedge between them. Instead, they must apply biblical passages regarding finances and caring for the elderly (e.g., Luke 14:28; Mark 7:9–13; 1 Tim 5:8) to their situation so they can be certain the Bible directs their path.

Childrearing

Parenthood brings great changes to the lives of married couples. Intermarried spouses who have begun to grow accustomed to each other's idiosyncrasies should expect to revisit these distinctives as they prepare to bring a new life into the world. Issues to consider include the child's cultural identity (i.e., monocultural or bicultural),[64] language acquisition (i.e., monolingual or bilingual when parents speak multiple dialects),[65] and even the infant's official racial designation as recorded on the birth certificate. Couples should discuss these items thoroughly as they begin to think about raising a family.

In some cases, intermarried spouses also will need to ready their parents for the arrival of a multiethnic child. Marla Alupoaicei offered the following practical questions for consideration: "Are the grandparents and other family members prepared to accept a biracial, bicultural, and bilingual child? Do they understand that the child may not look like their side of the family?"[66] On a positive note, parents who have had difficulties accepting their child's multiethnic marriage often reconsider their reservations at the birth of their grandchild.[67]

Intermarried parents also must decide what type of training is necessary to help their offspring manage any insults others may direct toward them because of their multiethnic heritage. Terms such as *oreo* and *zebra*

---

64. Hiebert, *Anthropological Insights*, 242.
65. Alupoaicei, *Your Intercultural Marriage*, 170.
66. Ibid.
67. Lewis and Ford-Robinson, "Understanding the Occurrence," 410.

that were common derogatory remarks a generation ago[68] usually are not a part of an antagonist's vocabulary today, but other types of insults exist. For example, when former Shelby County, TN Commissioner Henri Brooks recently got into an altercation with a biracial individual in June 2014, witnesses reported that she exclaimed, "Do you think you're white or something?"[69] Multiethnic parents cannot shield their offspring from ridicule, but they can emphasize the advantages of belonging to dual heritages. Furthermore, they also can underscore the manner in which God employed multiethnic Christians such as Timothy to reach multiple people groups with the gospel.

Cultural Implementation

Missionaries who move to exotic environments struggle to adjust to unfamiliar languages, customs, and worldviews. Similarly, multiethnic couples will have to acclimate to mates whose cultural underpinnings are altogether strange from their perspective. The technical term for the frustration that accompanies this realization of dissimilarity is *culture shock*.

Louis Luzbetak aptly described culture shock as "the constant jolting and the consequent stress and fatigue associated with living in a society that has different ways and values from those that have become second nature to the outsider."[70] Mercifully, missionaries who undergo this type of tension find momentarily relief in the refuge of their homes. In the case of multiethnic marriage, however, no such haven exists because the home is the primary place in which culture shock occurs.

Many anthropologists and worldview experts doubt an outsider ever can become fully habituated to another set of cultural proclivities,[71] but familiarization and accommodation is possible for spouses who intermarry. Patty Lane reminded readers that the acculturation process certainly "impacts our application of God's truth, but does not change the absolute nature of God's truth."[72] In other words, believers must learn to jettison any cultural practices that contradict Scripture. Neutral behaviors and mindsets, however, are negotiable.

68. Foeman and Nance, "From Miscegenation," 548.
69. Kenney, "Commissioner Henri Brooks."
70. Luzbetak, *The Church and Cultures*, 204.
71. Lingenfelter and Mayers, *Ministering Cross-Culturally*, 121.
72. Lane, *A Beginner's Guide*, 137.

Challenges of Multiethnic Couples

If multiethnic spouses are to have joyous, Christ-honoring marriages, they must not allow differences to become causes of strife. They must learn to live with each other in an understanding way despite any cultural peculiarities (cf. 1 Pet 3:7a). While "adjusting one's lifestyle and thought patterns to fit a new culture is a . . . stressful experience,"[73] especially in the context of matrimony, participants who view the enterprise properly will not become exasperated. Couples can learn to appreciate—and even enjoy—the uniqueness that each mate has to offer.

G. Shelling and J. Fraser-Smith, the authors of a work that addressed the topic of multiethnic marriage, likened the assimilation that inevitably transpires within marriage to a masterpiece on which two artists collaborate: "Each partner brings a different set of tools to the task of creating an art piece. . . . Each partner learns to understand how the tastes and preferences of the other function, what good they can bring to the project, and how they can enrich the whole picture."[74] The consequence of this optimistic outlook is what missiologists refer to as "150 percent persons,"[75] that is, people who learn to operate in other cultures with a degree of ease.

As multiethnic couples cleave to one another and weave a new life together, they will learn not only to tolerate differences, but also to enjoy each other's food, customs, and unique contributions to the marriage covenant.[76] Apart from God and adherence to his biblical principles, this type of intimacy may be unobtainable for intermarried Christians. However, when couples remember that as believers they are one in Christ Jesus regardless of ethnic heritage, they will realize no cultural challenge is insurmountable if they follow the scriptural model of marriage.

---

73. Loss, *Culture Shock*, 47.
74. Shelling and Frayser-Smith, *In Love*, 53.
75. Lingenfelter and Mayers, *Ministering Cross-Culturally*, 124.
76. Hiebert, *Anthropological Insights*, 76.

6

Premarital Counseling Propositions for Multiethnic Couples

INTRODUCTION

PASTORS WHO PROVIDE COUNSELING for their church members often report "marriage and family problems outnumber all other counseling problems combined."[1] One of the evidences for this somber observation is that in the twenty-first century, the divorce rate stands at roughly 50 percent in the United States.[2] Lamentably, studies indicate marriages of multiethnic couples dissolve at an even higher rate than their monoethnic counterparts.[3]

According to experts such as F. Dean Lueking, one of the reasons divorce has reached epidemic proportions is because most couples engage in "little or no serious preparation for the high calling and hard work of

---

1. Adams, *Solving Marriage Problems*, 1.

2. Astle, "An Ounce of Prevention," 733; cf. Larson and Holman, "Premarital Predictors," 228.

3. Bratter and King, "'But Will it Last,'" 160. Bratter and King reported, "[A]lthough entering an interracial marriage tends to carry less social stigma [than in past decades of American history], these relationships are less likely to remain intact [than monoethnic unions]." M. D. Bramlett and W. D. Mosher, reporting for The National Center for Health Statistics, related that after ten years of marriage, intermarried couples had a 10 percent higher rate of divorce than couples originating from the same ethnic group. See Bramlett and Mosher, "Cohabitation," 19.

Premarital Counseling Propositions for Multiethnic Couples

marriage."[4] In cases where couples receive premarital counseling, statistics confirm a significant decrease in problems in the first few years of marriage.[5] Such unions also enjoy a long-term drop in the number of divorces that occur.[6] For these reasons, some states now encourage their residents to receive premarital counseling before exchanging vows to curtail the alarming number of divorces in their respective jurisdictions.[7]

These findings underscore the necessity of churches providing premarital counseling for their members. The fundamental role the institution of marriage plays in society also means pastors must prepare themselves to serve as knowledgeable counselors.[8] Because many clergymen report their training for the task of providing adequate premarital counseling is lacking,[9] the purpose of this chapter is to help equip them for this important task. Accordingly, the following investigation will outline premarital counseling propositions that pertain to multiethnic couples.

PRINCIPLES OF PREMARITAL COUNSELING

Preparation for Premarital Counseling

Before biblical counselors commence their first appointment with multiethnic couples, ample preparation is necessary. Any counseling session

---

4. Lueking, *Let's Talk Marriage*, 12–13.

5. Carroll and Doherty, "Evaluating the Effectiveness of Premarital Prevention Programs," 114–15. Page 114 of this study, which examined only monoethnic Anglo marriages, demonstrated husbands and wives who undergo some form of couples counseling prior to marriage enjoyed more fulfilling relationships "for at least six months to three years."

6. Amato and Furstenberg, "Strengthening Marriage," 953. Statistics gathered from Oklahoma, Texas, Kansas, and Arizona kept track of which spouses took advantage of counseling prior to their wedding ceremonies. In all four states, proactive preparation diminished instances of marital dissolution: "[C]ouples that participated in any type of premarital education had an 18 percent lower probability of divorce after twenty years, compared with other couples."

7. Astle, "An Ounce of Prevention," 736.

8. Oates, *Premarital Pastoral Care*, 6.

9. Firmin and Tedford, "An Assessment," 421. In addition to revealing the lack of formal training that countless pastors receive, Firmin and Tedford's article also provides an insightful glimpse at the number of counseling courses evangelical Baptist seminaries offer their pastoral students.

necessarily reflects the values of the person who conducts the meeting,[10] so counselors first should develop an epistemology regarding the practice of intermarriage. As God's infallible Word, Scripture is the believer's ultimate authority. Pastors should ascertain what the Bible teaches about intermarriage in a Christian context.

The contents of chapters 2 and 3 of this study will prove beneficial in this endeavor because they contain a comprehensive analysis of the teachings of the Old and New Testament as they pertain to multiethnic marriage. Additionally, chapter 5 will prove helpful since this section informs counselors about challenges spouses from different cultures likely will experience. This information will assist counselors in competently leading couples to think about their impending marriage in a realistic manner at a time when they are most willing to listen to godly counsel.[11] Disarming potential sources of contention before they erupt into more serious problems is a principal goal of premarital counseling. Counselors can accomplish this task by familiarizing themselves with the contents of this study.

Giving Hope

Discouragement or disbelief may be the first reaction multiethnic couples express when their counselor divulges the sheer quantity of challenges they may encounter as a result of intermarriage. The majority of ethnically diverse couples, however, likely will minimize the data. During the engagement stage of their relationship, couples often mistakenly reckon their bond robust enough to weather any potential conflicts that occur within marriage. The emotional excitement of their impending wedding, along with the prospect of their new life together, tends to overshadow the fact that all spouses experience conflicts.

In cases in which couples become discouraged by the challenges they might face, counselors should not dismiss the couple's disheartenment immediately. Their reaction may be an indication they have decided too hastily to marry. Directed questioning, as well as diligent observation of subsequent halo data,[12] will help counselors to decide whether couples

---

10. Worthington, *Counseling Before Marriage*, 8.

11. Mudd, *The Practice of Marriage Counseling*, 28; Hawkins, *A Pastor's Primer*, 18.

12. Mack, "Taking Counselee Inventory," 228–29. The term *halo data* refers to nonverbal cues such as facial expressions, gestures, and tone of voice. Mack wisely noted, "Never underestimate the importance of this kind of observation—it can provide as

Premarital Counseling Propositions for Multiethnic Couples

should reconsider their engagement status. On the other hand, when dismay stems merely from the realization of the quantity of challenges their marriage will endure, couples need hope.[13] The counselor's responsibility is to help them to understand their ethnic differences are not irreconcilable.

In an era of North American history when a significant number of spouses cite incompatibility as a primary reason for the dissolution of their marriage,[14] Christians would do well to recall the words of Jay Adams:

> Compatibility is not something which is native to two persons . . . There is no factor which is really essential for compatibility. Race, age, social status, everything else is secondary, although there may be desirable qualities within the one basic requirement of Scripture. Yet Scripture itself makes no such distinctions.[15]

In other words, regardless of whether couples choose to marry monoethnically or multiethnically, problems will arise because all husbands and wives possess a sin nature that complicates their relationship. The idea of compatibility is not consistent with scriptural teachings. Multiethnic couples should understand this important fact before exchanging their vows.

In cases in which couples disregard impending challenges, counselors labor to open their counselees' eyes to the unavoidable marital trials that await them in the future. This correction of erroneous notions is an essential aspect of premarital guidance.[16] The realization of the inevitability of marital conflict may occur gradually over the course of several sessions instead of immediately, so counselors must reiterate this point as necessary. Couples who doubt worldview disparities exist eventually will alter their opinions after troubles emerge in their lives. When reality sets in, they need hope to resolve difficulties in a biblical manner.

---

much information as merely concentrating on what the counselee says."

13. Adams, *Critical Stages*, 20–21; cf. Adams, *The Christian Counselor's Manual*, 39–48.

14. Rao and Sekhar, "Divorce," 554; Cleek and Pearson, "Perceived Causes of Divorce," 181.

15. Adams, *Competent to Counsel*, 249.

16. Rutledge, *Pre-Marital Counseling*, 86. Rutledge's observation is helpful, but his recommendation in the same paragraph that couples make use of Planned Parenthood's resources is problematic.

Proper Perspective

Multiethnic couples withstand hardships foreign to their monoethnic counterparts, but they need to learn that none of these stressors are unique to their particular relationships.[17] On the contrary, Eccl 1:9 affirms, "There is nothing new under the sun." One may apply this proverb to the realm of intermarriage as readily as to any other context. Countless intermarried Christians throughout the ages have overcome worldview and cultural differences. Additionally, they have weathered external pressures with resiliency and grace as they have adhered to scriptural mandates.

Multiethnic Christian couples can avoid despair by recalling an important aspect of their spiritual heritage. The Apostle Paul affirmed believers no longer know each other according to previous associations because they have become new creations in Christ (2 Cor 5:17). In other words, as coheirs with the Son of God, and by extension spiritual brothers and sisters (cf. Rom 8:17), intermarried believers have more in common with each other than they might expect. Their mutual union with Christ means no difficulty is too sizeable for them to overcome, as long as they apply biblical principles to their situation and learn to "serve one another in love" (Gal 5:13; cf. Rom 12:3–5; 1 Cor 13:1–13).

Sufficiency of Scripture

One crucial aim of any counseling session is to instruct counselees that Scripture is a God-given, infallible resource. As such, it conveys the proper course of action for any conceivable situation in which believers find themselves (cf. 2 Tim 3:16). In this regard, premarital counseling for multiethnic couples mirrors any other type of guidance counselors may provide. The long-term goal of this aspect of biblical counseling is to habituate counselees to the practice of finding in Scripture solutions to their inquiries.

Another reason this objective is central to the counseling process is an increasing number of Western theologians and denominations find biblical authority and absolute truth untenable beliefs. The popularization of the postmodern interpretational model has convinced proponents that "anything goes in the study of the Bible."[18] As a result, theological pluralism

---

17. Adams, *Competent to Counsel*, 213.
18. Barton, "Biblical Studies," 18–19.

reigns in these circles.[19] Often, the only system of theology that garners resistance is the one that teaches Scripture contains truth without any admixture of error. The Bible summarily rejects any notion of pluralism, but provides the standard by which to evaluate all situations.

Scripture is not a book of recommendations, or a work containing valuable "diamonds in a dunghill"[20] of inconsistent half-truths. Rather, God's Word is "the supreme standard by which all human conduct, creeds, and religious opinions should be tried."[21] Counselors can say with assurance, "Thus says the Lord," when they explain what the Bible requires of counselees.

Nature of Marriage

Another factor to emphasize in premarital counseling sessions is the nature of marriage. Christ's teachings provide an apt place to begin. In Matt 19:3–9, some of the Pharisees sought to test Jesus by asking him what constituted a legitimate divorce. The influential rabbis of the era (e.g., Shammai, Hillel, and Aqiba) held vastly different views. Mosaic experts vigorously debated the issue. By inviting Jesus to weigh in on the issue, the Pharisees sought to entrap Him. They also desired to erode his popularity with supporters who disagreed with whatever position he supported.

Rather than citing a rabbinical tradition as the basis for his authority, Jesus appealed to Scripture. He insisted one should root one's view regarding divorce, as well as the nature of marriage, in the initial chapters of Genesis instead of a faulty interpretation of Deut 24:1.[22] An accurate understanding of the original matrimonial bond was the key to understanding God's intention for marriage.

---

19. Zimmermann, *Incarnational Humanism*, 280–81; McLaren and Litfin, "Emergent Evangelism," 42–43. This philosophy contradicts Jesus' affirmation of scriptural reliability in Matt 4:4 (cf. Deut 8:3).

20. Jefferson, *Writings*, 1301. President Jefferson coined the above unorthodox phrase in a personal correspondence he addressed to John Adams on October 12, 1813. His erroneous view of Scripture anticipated the demythologizing movement that took root in the early twentieth century due in large part to the teachings of theologians such as Rudolph Bultmann. For more information on the emergence and popularization of this movement, see Grenz and Olson, *20th-Century Theology*, 89–90.

21. "The 2000 Baptist Faith and Message."

22. Keener, *Matthew*, 295.

Citing Gen 1:27 and 2:24, Jesus declared, "Have you not read that from the beginning that the Creator made them male and female and said, 'for this reason a man shall leave his father and mother and be joined to his wife, and that the two shall become one flesh'?" (Matt 19:4b–5). The Pharisees were guilty of selective reading, having overlooked the foundational Toranic passage regarding marriage. Because the Creator's intent was for marriage partners to become one flesh, "divorce contradicts God's original plan for humanity."[23] For this reason, no one must separate what God has joined together. As the originator of marriage, God has the right to define the boundaries of marriage (Matt 19:6).

When the Pharisees objected that Moses had ordered husbands to write out a certificate of divorce and send their wives away, Jesus corrected them. The giver of the law had not commanded divorce to take place, but had permitted it because of the hardness of the people's hearts.[24] Once more, Jesus repeated the counsel he gave in Matt 5:32, stating that husbands who divorce their wives for any other reason than sexual immorality cause them to commit adultery (Matt 19:9).

Premarital counseling sessions should make clear to multiethnic couples that biblical marriage is not a temporary convention. It is a permanent institution designed to endure, even when cross-cultural conflicts occur.[25] As a result of becoming one flesh, husbands and wives need to realize they are responsible for making decisions in their lives rather than relying on authority figures from their past.[26] When, for example, parents inadvertently or intentionally overstep their bounds by attempting to control aspects of their children's marriage, couples cannot allow this intrusiveness to drive a wedge between them. They have left their parents and ought to cleave to one another.

Adams explained that as Christian couples establish a home, optimally they will implement any godly aspects of their upbringings into their new family unit:

23. Polaski and Polaski, "Listening to a Conversation," 593.

24. France, *The Gospel of Matthew*, 720; Molldrem, "A Hermeneutic," 46.

25. Unfortunately, this view of marriage no longer reigns supreme in Western culture. Incidentally, counselors cannot assume their counselees understand the nature of the institution from a scriptural perspective. This type of premarital training is doubly important when one considers multiethnic couples may have differing, culturally informed views of marriage. For a summary of how the West's concept of marriage has changed in recent times, see Cunningham and Thornton, "The Influence," 660.

26. Powlison and Yenchko, *Pre-Engagement*, 19.

Premarital Counseling Propositions for Multiethnic Couples

> They cannot maintain intact all of the customs and habitual ways of living that each knew before. Neither one should expect the other to make all the changes, but both parties should together think through how they are going to create a new decision-making unit. In doing so they should consciously take the best (i.e., the Christian elements) from both of the backgrounds. In that way, their marriage will become a third, distinct thing, better than the home from which either came.[27]

Multiethnic spouses can learn to take the strengths of their respective heritages and synthesize them into an innovative model that reflects and celebrates both cultures in a balanced, Christ-honoring fashion.

Common Errors

An important responsibility of biblical counselors is to help couples anticipate types of problems common within marriage. Many of these complications are iterative in nature, reappearing at regular intervals. One category of difficulties stems from fallacious notions that lead to "sinful attitudes or practices" in marriage.[28] These defective ideas may manifest themselves in a variety of forms, including the following: 1) spurious interpretations regarding the biblical roles of husbands and wives; 2) unreasonable expectations husbands and wives place on one another; 3) the manner in which husbands and wives understand the biblical concept of love; and 4) giving more consideration to one's cultural norms than scriptural authority.

The solution to each of these presenting problems is identical, beginning with a scriptural examination of the institution of marriage. This investigation should be a standard component that counselors present to every couple they instruct. Once God's standard for matrimony is well defined, counselors impress upon them to enact "a biblical course of action"[29] whenever disagreements occur. Implementation of this practice will prompt spouses to evaluate their expectations and conduct on a biblical basis, instead of culturally. Additionally, they will learn how to replace sinful conduct with biblical patterns of behavior.[30]

---

27. Adams, *Competent to Counsel*, 251.
28. Adams, *Solving Marriage Problems*, 11.
29. Peace, *The Excellent Wife*, 35.
30. Viars, "'Brian,'" 79.

Another set of difficulties pertains to the couple's interactive skills. Two prevailing areas of discord are "poor communication... and poor conflict management. [By contrast] studies indicate that only twenty percent of marriages fail as a result of infidelity."[31] Intermarried couples certainly will experience their share of miscommunication because of their diverse heritages (and in some cases, their lack of a primary language).[32] Counselors, therefore, should emphasize the importance of communicating biblically.

Furthermore, counselors need to provide counselees with direction that will guide their relationship when, for example, they misread each other's tone or unintentionally express a culturally inappropriate level of public affection. Examples of concrete instruction include the following: 1) the command to be quick to hear, slow to speak, and slow to anger (Jas 1:19); 2) the need to respond to harsh words in a gentle manner (Prov 15:1); and 3) the warning not to sin when angry (Eph 4:26). These simple, yet profound directives will help spouses to shift their focus "from persons to problems"[33] when the frustrations of intercultural collision threaten their marital harmony.

PARADIGM

Effective premarital counseling is both systematic and flexible. On the one hand, counselors should develop a series of sessions that examine the institution of marriage from a biblical perspective. When couples are multiethnic, each session should relate somehow to this aspect of their relationship.[34] The following section of the chapter will focus primarily on this topic.

On the other hand, counselors also should pay close attention in each session to items such as halo data and counselees' questions. Additionally, a Personal Data Inventory (PDI) form[35] (completed prior to counseling),

---

31. Eyrich, *Three to Get Ready*, 63.

32. For helpful discussions of the challenges that are unique to intercultural communication and interactions, see Kang-Yum, "Cross-Cultural Miscommunication," 46; Olsina, "Managing Understanding," 37–57.

33. Adams, *Competent to Counsel*, 234.

34. For guidance in developing material that focuses on the intercultural dynamics of multiethnic marriages, see chapter 5 of this study.

35. For a digital example of a PDI form, see Adams, "Personal Data Inventory."

data gathering in the sessions,[36] and responses to homework assignments[37] will provide helpful information. These tools serve the purpose of more specifically pinpointing a couple's strengths and weaknesses, while revealing which topics require more attention. Information counselors glean from these vital sources of information will allow them the flexibility to shape each session as needed.

Structure of Counseling Sessions

Regardless of whether counselors interact with monoethnic or multiethnic couples, the configuration of their premarital counseling sessions will possess a similar structure. One fundamental aspect of premarital guidance is the number of meetings counselors will arrange with their counselees. Because of busyness, counselors often err by offering too few sessions. Limited commitment to premarital training, however, produces insufficient opportunities for the adequate training of couples.

Individuals typically approach counselors for assistance with a problem in their lives. In *Critical Stages of Biblical Counseling*, Adams suggested, "Ordinarily counseling [should take] . . . a maximum of twelve weeks."[38] Premarital counseling, however, is different from this type of guidance in that a particular difficulty usually is not the impetus for these sessions. Rather, premarital counseling is preventative, aiding couples to learn how to respond to marriage trials before they present themselves.

Howard Eyrich's experience as a biblical counselor led him to recommend seven sessions[39] as a sufficient number of meetings to lay an adequate preparatory foundation. Nevertheless, few couples likely will agree to attend this quantity of meetings. Counselors would do well to plan for three sessions, scheduling additional periods of instruction if the counselees require further training.

---

36. Data gathering is the indispensable "process [of] asking questions, listening carefully, and attempting to understand them." Counselors should take extensive notes during each session in order to remember essential information. See Peace, "'Ashley' and Anorexia," 144.

37. For helpful examples of homework, see Mack, *Homework Manual*, 2:1–32.

38. Adams, *Critical Stages*, 169. Adams sometimes officiated over more than twelve sessions for a given counselee, but only in extreme circumstances.

39. Eyrich, *Three to Get Ready*, 71.

Counselors likewise set the length of time each meeting will persist. A period of sixty minutes is a sensible minimum interval for conducting effective guidance. Ninety minutes is the maximum duration counselors should expend with couples.[40]

Content of Counseling Sessions

Multiethnicity is not the only topic with which counselors concern themselves when training couples who derive from diverse heritages. This theme should permeate each of the sessions because no area of life remains untouched when ethnically diverse couples marry. Counselors must contextualize[41] their premarital training in such a way that multiethnic couples readily grasp how biblical principles of marriage relate to their relationship.

For instance, certain cultures are reluctant to speak candidly if they fear the truth might offend their listeners. Other people groups have no problem communicating in a straightforward manner, but lack sensitivity. When representatives of these opposing philosophies marry, the potential for contention is prodigious. Jesus' admonition to express oneself honestly (cf. Matt 5:37) provides valuable counsel to advocates of the first position. Adherents of the second school of thought find a helpful counterbalance to their terseness in Paul's command to express the truth in love (Eph 4:15).

Another example of a subject that requires contextualization is food preferences. Since spouses who originate from dissimilar ethnic backgrounds usually have different tastes, their mealtime menus necessitate compromise. Paul wrote about the importance of giving God glory no matter what one eats (cf. 1 Cor 10:31). Implementation of this principle in a multicultural home requires that couples attempt to enjoy each other's favorite dishes. In the event that this type of accommodation is not possible, they should learn to appreciate each other's exotic preferences with a measure of forbearance.

Counselors should familiarize themselves with the material in this study in order to be cognizant of the needs of multiethnic couples. Next, they should develop each counseling session with this content in mind. The following list presents a suggested model that includes each of the

---

40. Hawkins, *Pastor's Primer*, 33; Eyrich, *Three to Get Ready*, 71.

41. *Contextualization* is the process by which communicators present a message in such a way that it "fit[s] into different contexts" without compromising its integrity. See Loum, "Diversity and Contextualization," 173.

Premarital Counseling Propositions for Multiethnic Couples

subjects the author examined in chapter 4 of this project: Session 1: Eligibility of couple for marriage; meaning of being equally yoked; overview of challenges multiethnic couples encounter; Session 2: Communication; male–female roles; biblical concept of love; finances; day-to-day issues; Session 3: Sex; family; childrearing; family worship; cultural implementation; ceremony and date.[42]

APPLICATION

Premarital counseling is largely ineffective when divorced from the realm of practicality. Application assists couples to put into practice what they have learned in their guidance sessions. Counselors ensure their training is useful by developing concrete exercises that gauge the couple's comprehension and implementation of the counseling material. An excellent tool that assists counselors in this important task is the dispensing of weekly homework at the end of each session. Couples should complete these assignments before returning the next week.

Robyn Huck aptly described the role of homework in counseling: "The purpose of homework is to help a counselee move forward, to make progress, and to grow. We are not just trying to improve basic habits; we are after something more specific and more personal. Good homework engages the person's struggles and situational difficulties directly."[43] Huck then explained homework greatly benefits the counseling process by: 1) carrying counseling out of counselors' offices and into their counselees' everyday lives; 2) allowing counseling goals to move forward; and 3) serving as a continuous thread that weaves individual counseling sessions together.[44] In a premarital counseling context, homework also helps counselors to know which principles couples readily absorb, and which concepts require additional attention.

Good homework assignments are not ambiguous or mechanical in nature. Rather, counselors should design them for use with specific couples that require assistance with particular issues. Counselors should regard

---

42. The above list draws heavily on certain aspects of Eyrich's helpful premarital counseling model. For a thorough discussion of the contents of his premarital counseling sessions, see Eyrich, *Three to Get Ready*, 71–159.

43. Huck, "Effective Homework," 77.

44. Ibid., 77–78.

exercises that others develop only as sample homework assignments rather than appropriating them as they stand into their own counseling sessions.[45]

Because the author is unaware of the existence of homework that focuses on the needs of multiethnic couples, a sample exercise is in order. The author has selected as an example one aspect of worldview that affects virtually every area of life: one's concept of time. While some people groups subscribe to the notion of time-orientation, others prefer event-orientation. Additionally, ideas regarding punctuality vary from culture to culture.

Multiethnic couples may not know that to a large extent, these deep-seated practices are a function of culture. If their understanding of promptness and tardiness differs from one another, frustration and conflict will be the inevitable results, especially if they misinterpret any worldview differences as disrespect. Counselors who observe through interaction with the couple that perceptions of time are a source of contention will want to explore the topic with them. They should then assign to them an exercise examining punctuality so they might become better attuned to each other's worldviews.

Possible questions to explore in homework exercises include the following inquiries: 1) "What are my personal beliefs concerning the issues of promptness and tardiness?" 2) "How important is promptness to me?" 3) "Do my potential spouse's habits regarding promptness and tardiness align with mine? Do they differ?" 4) "Do any of my potential spouse's habits regarding promptness and tardiness irritate me? If so, which ones?" 5) "Do any of my habits regarding promptness and tardiness irritate my potential spouse? If so, which ones?" 6) "What would I like to change about my potential spouse's concept of promptness?" 7) "What could I change about my concept of promptness?" 8) "What does 1 Cor 13:1–13 teach about biblical love?" 9) "What are some ways we can resolve our different views of promptness in a loving, patient way that strengthens our future marriage and honors Christ?"

During the following week, couples carefully will consider these questions and write or type their answers on a sheet of paper. At the next session, their counselor will examine the homework in order to surmise whether or not they tackled the problem in a biblical manner. A portion of the session

---

45. Mack, *Homework Manual*, 1:v; Adams, *Christian Counselor's Manual*, 298. Both of these resources provide a number of concrete assignments that serve as excellent models. Counselors would do well to review these examples as they develop homework activities for their counselees.

Premarital Counseling Propositions for Multiethnic Couples

will explore ways in which the couple can refine any deficient answers and defuse future disagreements in both a constructive and scriptural manner.

Jim Slack, a missiologist with extensive experience as an ethnographer and a field assessments consultant, developed a helpful worldview questionnaire.[46] The resource can assist counselors in developing relevant homework. Although Slack designed the survey with missionaries in mind, his keen understanding of diversity is applicable to the realm of multiethnic marriage.

The following exploratory inquiries are examples of Slack's cultural diagnostic questions that counselors may elect to give as homework assignments: 1) "Do members of your culture tend to be oral or literate communicators and learners?" 2) "How is the typical family organized in your culture?" 3) "What functional roles do family, friends, neighbors, community, and society play in a person's development of appropriate cultural behavior, beliefs, habits, and lifestyle as they age?" 4) "What are some of the most offensive cultural indiscretions or offences that a person could commit?" 5) "Who are the most respected persons within your culture?"[47] After directing counselees to discuss these issues with one another, in the next premarital session counselors will help them to explore their answers and learn to negotiate their differences.

CONCLUSION

Counselors who instruct multiethnic Christian couples must make certain they guide their counselees in both a biblically proficient and a contextualized manner. In order to accomplish these crucial tasks, counselors prepare for the momentous undertaking by 1) studying the issue of multiethnic marriage from a scriptural perspective; 2) becoming cognizant of the unique challenges intermarried couples encounter; and 3) structuring sessions in such a way that each meeting incorporates these topics into the corpus of premarital instruction. Practical homework lessons will focus on topics with which multiethnic couples struggle, helping them to solve their marital dilemmas in Christ-honoring ways.

---

46. Slack, "Worldview Research." In this document, Slack discussed the concept of worldview and provided "a basic twelve . . . question worldview instrument."

47. Ibid.

7

Conclusion

At present, North America is experiencing unprecedented numbers of multiethnic marriages. This trend is not merely operational in society at large, but within Christendom as well. Unfortunately, few volumes examine the topic of intermarriage from a Christian perspective. Virtually no resource offers guidance for biblical counselors who desire to prepare multiethnic Christian couples for marriage. The purpose of this study was to remedy this deficit by examining the topic from multiple perspectives.

In addition to providing the motivation for this study, chapter 1 charted the course of the investigation. The section established that Scripture addresses the theme of multiethnic marriage. It also emphasized the necessity of deriving one's views and counseling instruction from God's Word. Additionally, the chapter outlined each subsequent division of the study.

Chapter 2 examined the concept of multiethnic marriage within the Old Testament. Contrary to the opinions of some ancient, medieval, and modern commentators, the God of Israel did not condone xenophobic tendencies in this era. Granted, the Old Testament condemns a number of marriages that occurred between Israelites and other people groups, but not for ethnic reasons. In each instance, God disapproved of his people entering into marital unions with individuals who worshiped false gods. Toranic legislation warned Israelites not to associate with idolaters.

The Old Testament portrays other incidences of multiethnic marriage neutrally. In these instances, Scripture merely reports the fact that such unions occurred without offering any commentary about the cases. In each

Conclusion

situation, however, the Israelite partner made a positive contribution to the well-being of Israel.

Numerous Old Testament texts depict certain multiethnic marriages positively. Although Yahweh made a special covenant with Abraham and his descendants, people of foreign descent who forsook the gods of their countries could become God-fearers. These converts could participate in the religious life of Israel and intermarry with the Israelites without incurring God's wrath. In circumstances in which ethnically diverse husbands and wives were followers of Yahweh, multiethnic marriage was an acceptable practice.

Chapter 3 examined the concept of multiethnicity within the New Testament. Research revealed few explicit references to intermarriage. The contribution to the theme is the teaching that although cultural and ethnic differences are realities, all human beings descend from one common ancestor. In other words, multiple races of people do not exist. Rather, every individual is a member of a unified human race.

In a salvific sense, Jews had no advantage over other people groups because God is no respecter of persons. Multiple times throughout the New Testament, he expressed his desire that all should repent and confess his resurrected Son Jesus Christ as Lord. As a consequence of salvation, all believers become one in Christ.

According to the book of Revelation, in the future all Christians of every ethnicity and historical period will gather around God's throne to worship him and his Son. This unity underscores the harmony ethnically diverse believers enjoy by means of union with Christ. Multiethnic Christian spouses, therefore, do not violate the principle of the uneven yoke the Apostle Paul described in 2 Cor 6:14.

Chapter 4 surveyed the attitudes toward multiethnic relationships in North America over the past four hundred years. In the colonial era, Native Americans, Africans, and Europeans intermarried intermittently. Public opinion of the practice varied from colony to colony. As time passed, the colonies—and eventually the states—introduced progressively stricter legislation in order to prohibit intermarriage. Unfortunately, North American churches typically followed society's lead in this area rather than observing Old and New Testament teachings regarding multiethnicity.

This trend continued throughout United States history until 1967, when the Supreme Court ruled the Fourteenth Amendment forbade states from denying marriage licenses to multiethnic couples. Since then, citizens of the United States have grown more tolerant of intermarriage. The practice is more acceptable in the second decade of the twenty-first century than at any other time in American history.

Chapter 5 examined challenges multiethnic couples encounter. The purpose of this section was twofold. First, the investigation systematically categorized common interethnic difficulties in order to assist multiethnic couples to think deliberately and deeply about complications they likely will face. Second, the research helped biblical counselors to provide relevant premarital counseling material for multiethnic couples. Topics included familial and societal acceptance, worldview, communication, and day-to-day issues.

Chapter 6 synthesized the findings of the aforementioned portions of the study in order to offer pre-marital counseling propositions for multiethnic couples. This division of the study examined principles such as preparation for premarital counseling, giving hope, proper perspective, and the sufficiency of Scripture. The paradigm section of the study explored the structure of effective counseling sessions. It also suggested a list of discussion topics that concentrate on the specific needs of multiethnic couples. Finally, the chapter provided an example of a practical homework assignment designed to assist multiethnic couples to learn how to put the lessons they learn into practice.

Marriage is humankind's oldest and most intimate institution. In addition to establishing the marital covenant, God's Word gives principles by which husbands and wives should live. Couples do not grasp these teachings intuitively, but require the assistance of godly counselors who prepare counselees for married life. Intermarried couples require this same loving guidance. Their counselors must equip themselves to address the unique trials they endure. Multiethnic Christian spouses are equally yoked. With the proper biblical training, their marriages can glorify the Lord Jesus Christ as they serve him together within the bonds of matrimony.

Bibliography

"The 2000 Baptist Faith and Message." http://www.sbc.net/bfm2000/ bfm2000.asp.

Abraham, Jed D. "Esau's Wives." *Jewish Bible Quarterly* 24/5 (October–December 1997) 251–59.

Achtemeier, Paul J. *Harper's Bible Dictionary*. San Francisco: Harper & Row, 1985.

———. *Romans*. Edited by James Luther Mays et al. Interpretation. Atlanta: John Knox, 1985.

Acts and Resolves, Public and Private, of the Province of the Massachusetts Bay: To Which are Prefixed the Characters of the Province with Historical and Explanatory Notes, and an Appendix. Vol. 1, *1692–1714*. Boston: Wright & Potter, 1869.

Adams, Jay E. *The Christian Counselor's Manual: The Practice of Nouthetic Counseling*. Grand Rapids: Zondervan, 1973.

———. *Christian Living in the Home*. Phillipsburg, NJ: Presbyterian and Reformed, 1972.

———. *Competent to Counsel: Introduction to Nouthetic Counseling*. Grand Rapids: Zondervan, 1970.

———. *Critical Stages of Biblical Counseling*. Stanley, NC: Timeless Texts, 2002.

———. "Personal Data Inventory." http://www.nouthetic.org.nz/wpcontent/uploads/2011/02/PDI1.pdf.

———. *Solving Marriage Problems: Biblical Solutions for Christian Counselors*. Grand Rapids: Zondervan, 1983.

Adelakun, Adewale J. "Complementarians Versus Egalitarians: An Exegesis of Galatians 3:28 from Nigerian Cultural Perspective." *Ogbomoso Journal of Theology* 17/3 (2012) 77–95.

Akers, Matthew R. "What's in a Name? An Examination of the Usage of the Term 'Hebrew' in the Old Testament." *Journal of the Evangelical Theological Society* 55/4 (2012) 685–96.

Alupoaicei, Marla. *Your Intercultural Marriage: A Guide to a Healthy, Happy Relationship*. Chicago: Moody, 2009.

Amato, Paul R., and Frank F. Furstenberg. "Strengthening Marriage is an Appropriate Social Policy Goal (with Response)." *Journal of Policy Analysis and Management* 26/4 (Autumn 2007) 952–56, 963–64.

Anders, Max. *Galatians, Ephesians, Philippians, and Colossians*. Edited by Max Anders. Holman New Testament Commentary. Nashville: Holman Reference, 1999.

Anderson, Irving W., and William Clark. "Probing the Riddle of the Bird Woman." *Montana: The Magazine of Western History* 23/4 (Autumn 1973) 2–17.

Bibliography

Anderson, Rachel J. "African–American History in Nevada (1861–2011)." http: //scholars.law.unlv.edu/cgi/viewcontent.cgi?article=1706&context=facpub.

Andrews, George Reid. *Afro-Latin America, 1800-2000*. Oxford: Oxford University Press, 2004.

Arendt, Hannah. "Reflections on Little Rock." In *Interracialism: Black–White Intermarriage in American History, Literature, and Law*, edited by Werner Sollors, 492–502. Oxford: Oxford University Press, 2000.

Arnold, Bill T. *Genesis*. Edited by Ben Witherington III et al. New Cambridge Bible Commentary. Cambridge: Cambridge University Press, 2009.

Assmann, J. "Neith." In the *Dictionary of Deities and Demons in the Bible*, edited by Karel von der Toorn et al., 616–18. Grand Rapids: Eerdmans, 1999.

———. "Re." In the *Dictionary of Deities and Demons in the Bible*, edited by Karel von der Toorn et al., 689–92. Grand Rapids: Eerdmans, 1999.

Astle, Matthew J. "An Ounce of Prevention: Marital Counseling Laws as an Anti-Divorce Measure." *Family Law Quarterly* 38/3 (Fall 2004) 733–51.

Auld, Graeme A. *Jesus Son of Nauē in Codex Vaticanus*. Edited by Stanley E. Porter et al. Septuagint Commentary. Boston: Brill, 2005.

Avins Alfred. "Anti-Miscegenation Laws and the Fourteenth Amendment: The Original Intent." *Virginia Law Review* 52/7 (November 1996) 1224–55.

Bagby, Daniel G. *Before You Marry*. Nashville: Convention, 1983.

Bakon, Shimon. "Samson: A Tragedy in Three Acts." *Jewish Bible Quarterly* 35/1 (January–March 2007) 34–40.

Ball, William McK., and Samuel C. Roane, eds. *Revised Statutes of the State of Arkansas: Adopted at the October Session of the General Assembly of Said State, AD 1837, in the Year of Our Independence the Sixty-Second, and of the State the Second Year*. Boston: Weeks, Jordan, 1838.

Barkan, Elazar. *The Retreat of Scientific Racism: Changing Concepts of Race in Britain and the United States between the World Wars*. Cambridge: Cambridge University Press, 1992.

Barnett, Paul. *The Second Epistle to the Corinthians*. Edited by Ned. B. Stonehouse et al. New International Commentary on the New Testament. Grand Rapids: Eerdmans, 1997.

Barton, John. "Biblical Studies." In *The Blackwell Companion to Modern Theology*, edited by Gareth Jones, 18–33. Malden, MA: Blackwell, 2004.

Belleville, Linda L. *2 Corinthians*. Edited by Grant R. Osborne et al. IVP New Testament Commentary. Downers Grove, IL: InterVarsity, 1996.

Belli, Filippo. *Argumentation and Use of Scripture in Romans 9–11*. With a Preface by Jean Noël Aletti. Rome: Gregorian & Biblical, 2010.

Bellinger, W. H., Jr. *Leviticus, Numbers*. Edited by W. Ward Gasque et al. Understanding the Bible Commentary. Grand Rapids: Baker, 2012.

Benjamin, Gail R. "Tone of Voice in Japanese Conversation." *Language in Society* 6/1 (April 1977) 1–13.

Berger, Bethany Ruth. "After Pocahontas: Indian Women and the Law, 1830–1934." In *Mixed Race America and the Law: A Reader*, edited by Kevin R. Johnson, 71–80. New York: New York University Press, 2003.

Best, Ernest. *The Letter of Paul to the Romans*. Edited by P. R. Ackroyd et al. Cambridge Bible Commentary on the New English Bible. Cambridge: Cambridge University Press, 1967.

Bibliography

Black, Matthew. *Romans*. Edited by Ronald E. Clements and Matthew Black. New Century Bible. Greenwood, SC: Attic, 1973.

Block, Daniel I. *Judges, Ruth*. Edited by E. Ray Clendenen. New American Commentary 6. Nashville: Broadman & Holman, 1999.

"Bob Jones University Drops Interracial Dating Ban." http://www.christianitytoday.com/ct/2000/marchweb-only/53.0.html?paging=off.

Bond, Susan L. "Acts 10:34–43." *Interpretation* 56/1 (January 2002) 80–83.

Borchert, Gerald L. *John 1–11*. Edited by E. Ray Clendenen et al. The New American Commentary 25a. Nashville: Broadman & Holman, 1996.

Botham, Fay. *Almighty God Created the Races: Christianity, Interracial Marriage, and American Law*. Chapel Hill: University of North Carolina Press, 2009.

Brackenridge, Henry Marie. *Journal of a Voyage up the Missouri River in 1811*. Pittsburgh: Cramer, Spear, and Eichbaum, 1814. Kindle Electronic Edition.

Bradshaw, Bruce. *Changes across Cultures: A Narrative Approach to Social Transformation*. With a foreword by Paul G. Hiebert. Grand Rapids: Baker Academic, 2002.

Bramlett, M. D., and W. D. Mosher. "Cohabitation, Marriage, Divorce, and Remarriage in the United States." *Vital and Health Statistics* 23 (July 2002) 1–94.

Bratcher, Robert G., and Howard A Hatton. *A Handbook on Deuteronomy*. UBS Handbook. New York: United Bible Societies, 2000.

Brattain, Michelle. "Miscegenation and Competing Definitions of Race in Twentieth-Century Louisiana." *Journal of Southern History* 71/3 (August 2005) 621–58.

Bratter, Jenifer L, and Rosalind King. "'But Will it Last?' Marital Instability Among Interracial and Same-Race Couples." *Family Relations* 57 (April 2008) 160–71.

Breckenridge, James, and Lillian Breckenridge. *What Color is Your God? Multicultural Education in America: Examining Christ and Culture in Light of the Changing Face of Culture*. Wheaton, IL: BridgePoint, 1995.

Breger, Rosemary, and Rosanna Hill, eds. *Cross-Cultural Marriage: Identity and Choice*. New York: Bloomsbury Academic, 1998.

Breneman, Mervin. *Ezra, Nehemiah, Esther*. Edited by E. Ray Clendenen et al. New American Commentary 10. Nashville: Broadman & Holman, 1993.

Briggs, David. "The Ties that May Not Bind: Race, Religion, and Marriage." http://blogs.thearda.com/trend/featured/the-ties-that-may-not-bind-race-religion-and-marriage.

Brindle, Wayne A. "The Causes of the Division of Israel's Kingdom." *Bibliotheca Sacra* 141 (July–September 1984) 223–33.

Brown, Carolyn M., and Richard Segal. "Ethnic Differences in Temporal Orientation and its Implications for Hypertension Management." *Journal of Health and Social Behavior* 37/4 (December 1996) 350–61.

Brown, Francis, et al. *Enhanced Brown-Driver-Briggs Hebrew and English Lexicon*. Oak Harbor, WA: Logos Research Systems, 2000.

Brown, Phillip A., II. "The Problem of Mixed Marriages in Ezra 9–10." *Bibliotheca Sacra* 162/4 (October–December 2005) 437–58.

Browne, William Hand, ed. *Archives of Maryland: Proceedings and Acts of the General Assembly of Maryland: January 1637/8–September 1664*. Baltimore: Maryland Historical Society, 1883.

Browning, James R. "Anti-Miscegenation Laws in the United States." *Duke Bar Journal* 1/1 (March 1951) 26–41.

Bibliography

Bruce, F. F. *1 and 2 Corinthians*. Edited by Ronald E. Clements and Matthew Black. New Century Bible Commentary. Grand Rapids: Eerdmans, 1980.

———. *Commentary on the Book of the Acts: The English Text with Introduction, Exposition, and Notes*. New International Commentary on the New Testament 5. Grand Rapids: Eerdmans, 1980.

———. *The Epistles to the Colossians, to Philemon, and to the Ephesians*. Edited by F. F. Bruce. New International Commentary on the New Testament. Grand Rapids: Eerdmans, 1984.

Brueggemann, Walter. *1 and 2 Kings*. Smyth & Helwys Bible Commentary. Macon, GA: Smyth & Helwys, 2000.

———. *Genesis*. Edited by James Luther Mays et al. Interpretation. Atlanta: John Knox, 1980.

Brunsma, David L. "Interracial Families and the Racial Identification of Mixed-Race Children: Evidence from the Early Childhood Longitudinal Study." *Social Forces* 84/2 (December 2005) 1131–57.

Bryan, Christopher. "A Further Look at Acts 16:1–3." *Journal of Biblical Literature* 107/2 (June 1988) 292–94.

Burchard, C. "Joseph and Aseneth: A New Translation and Introduction." In *Expansions of the "Old Testament" and Legends, Wisdom and Philosophical Literature, Prayers, Psalms, and Odes, Fragments of Lost Judeo-Hellenistic Works*, edited by James H. Charlesworth, 2:177–247. Old Testament Pseudepigrapha. Peabody, MA: Hendrickson, 1983.

Bystydzienski, Jill M. *Intercultural Couples: Crossing Boundaries, Negotiating Difference*. New York: New York University Press, 2011.

Cadet, Danielle. "'The Jeffersons,' How Sherman Hemsley and the Sitcom Changed the Landscape of American Television." http://www.huffingtonpost.com/2012/07/25/the-jeffersons-show-legacy_n_1701026.html.

Carroll, Jason S., and William J. Doherty. "Evaluating the Effectiveness of Premarital Prevention Programs: A Meta-Analytic Review of Outcome Research." *Relations* 52/2 (April 2003) 105–18.

Carter, Clarence Edwin, ed. *The Territory of Louisiana-Missouri: 1806–1814*. The Territorial Papers of the United States 14. Washington, DC: United States Printing Office, 1949.

Chadwick, Jocelyn. "Forbidden Thoughts: New Challenges of Teaching Twain's 'The Tragedy of Pudd'nhead Wilson.'" *The Mark Twain Annual* 1 (2003) 85–95.

Choi, Andy S., Franco Papandrea, and Jeff Bennett. "Assessing Cultural Values: Developing an Attitudinal Scale." *Journal of Cultural Economics* 31/4 (2007) 311–35.

"Church Refuses to Marry Black Couple in Mississippi." http://www.cnn.com/2012/07/30/us/mississippi-black-couple-wedding/index.html.

Cillizza, Chris. "Is Barack Obama 'Black'? A Majority of Americans Say No." http://www.washingtonpost.com/blogs/the-fix/wp/2014/04/14/is-barack-obama-black.

Cleek, Margaret Guminski, and T. Allan Pearson. "Perceived Causes of Divorce: An Analysis of Interrelationships." *Journal of Marriage and Family* 47/1 (February 1985) 179–83.

Clift, Rebecca. "Irony in Conversation." *Language in Society* 28/4 (December 1999) 523–53.

The Code of Virginia with the Declaration of Independence and Constitution of the United States; and the Declaration of Rights and Constitution of Virginia: Published Pursuant

Bibliography

to an Act of the General Assembly of Virginia, Passed on the Fifteenth Day of August 1849. Richmond: William F. Ritchie, 1849.

Coggins, R. J. *The Books of Ezra and Nehemiah*. Cambridge: Cambridge University Press, 1976.

———. *The First and Second Books of the Chronicles*. Edited by P. R. Ackroyd et al. Cambridge Bible Commentary. Cambridge: Cambridge University Press, 1976.

Cohen, Shaye J. D. "Was Timothy Jewish (Acts 16:1–3)? Patristic Exegesis, Rabbinic Law, and Matrilineal Descent." *Journal of Biblical Literature* 105/2 (June 1986) 251–68.

Cole, R. Alan. *Exodus: An Introduction and Commentary*. Edited by D. J. Wiseman. Tyndale Old Testament Commentaries. Grand Rapids: InterVarsity, 1973.

Congressional Globe, Senate, 40th Congress, 3rd Session, Part 2, 1010. February 8, 1868.

Cope, R. Douglas. *The Limits of Racial Domination: Plebeian Society in Colonial Mexico City, 1660–1720*. Madison: University of Wisconsin Press, 1994.

Cotter, David W. *Genesis*. Edited by David W. Cotter et al. Berit Olam: Studies in Hebrew Narrative and Poetry. Collegeville, MN: Liturgical, 2003.

Cottrol, Robert J. "The Long, Lingering Shadow: Law, Liberalism, and Cultures of Racial Hierarchy and Identity in the Americas." In *Mixed Race America and the Law: A Reader*, edited by Kevin R. Johnson, 441–46. New York: New York University Press, 2003.

Court, John M. *Revelation*. Edited by A. T. Lincoln. New Testament Guides. Sheffield, UK: Sheffield Academic, 1994.

Cousar, Charles B. *Galatians*. Edited by James Luther Mays et al. Interpretation. Atlanta: John Knox, 1982.

Crohn, Joel. *Mixed Matches: How to Create Successful Interracial, Interethnic, and Interfaith Relationships*. New York: Ballantine, 1995.

Croly, David G. *Miscegenation: The Theory of the Blending of the Races, Applied to the American White Man and Negro*. New York: B. Dexter, Hamilton, 1864.

Crown, Alan D. "Redating the Schism between the Judeans and the Samaritans." *Jewish Quarterly Review* 82/1–2 (July–October 1991) 17–50.

Cuming, Fortescue. *Early Western Travels, 1748–1846*. Vol. 4, *Cuming's Tour to the Western Country (1807–1809)*. Edited by Reuben Gold Thwaites. Cleveland: Arthur H. Clark, 1904.

Cundall, Arthur E. *Judges: An Introduction and Commentary*. Edited by D. J. Wiseman. Tyndale Old Testament Commentaries. Downers Grove, IL: InterVarsity, 1968.

Cunnningham, Mark, and Arland Thornton. "The Influence of Parents' Marital Quality on Adult Children's Attitudes toward Marriage and Its Alternatives: Main and Moderating Effects." *Demography* 43/4 (November 2006) 659–72.

Curtiss, Samuel Ives. "Delitzsch on the Pentateuch." *The Hebrew Student* 1/1 (April 1882) 1–5.

Cypess, Sandra Messinger. *La Malinche in Mexican Literature: From History to Myth*. Austin: University of Texas Press, 1991.

Dahlen, Robert W. "The Savior and the Dog: An Exercise in Hearing," *Word and World* 17/3 (Summer 1997) 269–77.

Danker, Frederick William, ed. *A Greek–English Lexicon of the New Testament and Other Early Christian Literature*. 3rd ed. Chicago: University of Chicago Press, 2000.

Darwin, Charles. *Evolutionary Writings*. Edited by James A. Secord. Oxford: Oxford University Press, 2008.

Bibliography

Davis, John J. "Ahab." In the *Holman Illustrated Bible Dictionary*, edited by Chad Brand et al., 36–37. Nashville: Holman, 2003.
Dawkins, Richard. *The God Delusion*. New York: Mariner, 2008.
Del Agua Pérez, Augustín. "El 'Derás' Cristológico." *Scripta Theologica* 14/1 (January–April 1982) 203–17.
DeMarce, Virginia E. "Looking at Legends—Lumbee and Melungeon: Applied Genealogy and the Origins of Tri-Racial Isolate Settlements." *National Genealogical Society Quarterly* 81 (March 1993) 24–45.
Diamond, James A. "The Deuteronomic 'Pretty Woman' Law: Prefiguring Feminism and Freud in Nahmanides." *Jewish Social Studies* 14/2 (Winter 2008) 61–85.
Dixon, Thomas J., Jr. *The Leopard's Spots: A Romance of the White Man's Burden—1865-1900*. Rochester, NY: Starry Night, 1902. Kindle Electronic Edition, 2008.
Douaud, Patrick C. "Canadian Metis Identity: A Pattern of Evolution." *Anthropos* 78/1–2 (1983) 71–88.
Dozeman, Thomas B. "The Wilderness and Salvation History in the Hagar Story." *Journal of Biblical Literature* 117/1 (Spring 1998) 23–43.
Du Bois, W. E. B. "Intermarriage." *Crisis* 5/4 (February 1913) 180–81.
Dunn, James D. G. *The Epistles to the Colossians and to Philemon: A Commentary on the Greek Text*. Edited by I. Howard Marshall et al. New International Greek Testament Commentary. Grand Rapids: Eerdmans, 1996.
Eakin, Marshall C. *The History of Latin America: Collision of Cultures*. New York: Palgrave Macmillan, 2007.
Earl, Douglas S. "The Christian Significance of Deuteronomy 7." *Journal of Theological Interpretation* 3/1 (March 2009) 41–62.
―――. "Toward a Christian Hermeneutic of Old Testament Narrative: Why Genesis 34 Fails to Find Christian Significance." *Catholic Bible Quarterly* 73/1 (January 2011) 30–49.
Easley, Kendell H. *Revelation*. Edited by Max Anders. Holman New Testament Commentary. Nashville: Holman Reference, 1998.
Edwards, Leigh H. "The United Colors of 'Pocahontas,' Synthetic Miscegenation and Disney's Multiculturalism." *Narrative* 7/2 (May 1999) 147–68.
"El Chapulin Colorado 1978: El Retorno de Super Sam." http://youtu.be/2rTeiKzJE1Y.
Elias, Marilyn. "Tennessee Pastor Rails Against Interracial Marriage." www.splcenter.org/hatewatch/2014/02/19/tennessee-pastor-rails-against-interracial-marriage.
Elliot, Michael A. "Telling the Difference: Nineteenth-Century Legal Narratives of Racial Taxonomy." In *Mixed Race America and the Law: A Reader*, edited by Kevin R. Johnson, 116–17. New York: New York University Press, 2003.
Elmer, Duane. *Cross-Cultural Conflict: Building Relationships for Effective Ministry*. Downers Grove, IL: InterVarsity, 1993.
Epps, Garrett. "What's Loving Got to Do with It?" In *Mixed Race America and the Law: A Reader*, edited by Kevin R. Johnson, 481–83. New York: New York University Press, 2003.
Eyrich, Howard A. *Three to Get Ready: Premarital Counseling Manual*. 3rd ed. With a foreword by D. James Kennedy. Bemidji, MN: Focus, 2005.
Farber, Paul Lawrence. *Mixing Races: From Scientific Racism to Modern Evolutionary Idea*. Edited by Mott T. Greene and Sharon Kingsland. Johns Hopkins Introductory Studies in the History of Science. Baltimore: Johns Hopkins University Press, 2011.
"Fast Facts." Bob Jones University. http://www.bju.edu/about/fast-facts.php.

Bibliography

Fausz, J. Frederick. "An 'Abundance of Blood Shed on Both Sides,' England's First Indian War, 1609-1614." *Virginia Magazine of History and Biography* 98/1 (January 1990) 3-56.

Feldman, Louis H. "Josephus' Portrait of Jacob." *Jewish Quarterly Review* 79/2-3 (October 1998-January 1989) 101-51.

Firmin, Michael W., and Mark Tedford. "An Assessment of Pastoral Counseling Courses in Seminaries Serving Evangelical Baptist Students." *Review of Religious Research* 48/4 (June 2007) 420-27.

Foeman, Anita Kathy, and Teresa Nance. "From Miscegenation to Multiculturalism: Perceptions and Stages of Interracial Relationship Development." *Journal of Black Studies* 29/4 (March 1999) 540-57.

France, R. T. *The Gospel of Matthew*. Edited by Ned B. Stonehouse et al. New International Commentary on the New Testament. Grand Rapids: Eerdmans, 2007.

Freedman, Estelle B. *No Turning Back: The History of Feminism and the Future of Women*. New York: Ballantine, 2002.

Fung, Ronald Y. K. *The Epistle to the Galatians*. Edited by F. F. Bruce. New International Commentary on the New Testament. Grand Rapids: Eerdmans, 1953.

Gammel, H. P. N., ed. *The Laws of Texas: 1822-1897*. Vol. 1. Austin: Gammel, 1898.

Gangel, Kenneth O. *Acts*. Edited by Max Anders. Holman New Testament Commentary. Nashville: Broadman & Holman, 1998.

Garland, David E. *2 Corinthians*. Edited by E. Ray Clendenen et al. New American Commentary 29. Nashville: Broadman & Holman, 1999.

———. *Colossians and Philemon*. Edited by Terry Muck et al. NIV Application Commentary. Grand Rapids: Zondervan, 1998.

Garrison, David. *Church Planting Movements*. Richmond, VA: Office of Overseas Operations, Southern Baptist Convention, n.d.

Gaul, Theresa Strouth, ed. *To Marry an Indian: The Marriage of Harriett Gold and Elias Boudinot in Letters, 1823-1839*. Chapel Hill: University of North Carolina Press, 2005.

Glick, Thomas F., and Oriol Pi-Sunyer. "Acculturation as an Explanatory Concept in Spanish History." *Comparative Studies in Society and History* 11/2 (April 1969) 136-54.

Goodnick, Benjamin. "She Shall Mourn." *Jewish Bible Quarterly* 32/3 (July 2004) 198-201.

Grant, Tobin. "Opposition to Interracial Marriage Lingers among Evangelicals." http://blog.christianitytoday.com/ctpolitics/2011/06/opposition_to_i.html.

Gray, John. *Joshua, Judges, Ruth*. Edited by Ronald E. Clements and Matthew Black. New Century Bible Commentary. Grand Rapids: Eerdmans, 1986.

Grearson, Jessie Carroll. *Swaying: Essays on Intercultural Love*. Iowa City: University of Iowa Press, 1995.

Grenz, Stanley J., and Roger E. Olson. *20th-Century Theology: God and the World in a Transitional Age*. Downers Grove, IL: InterVarsity, 1992.

Grunlan, Stephen A., and Marvin K. Mayers. *Cultural Anthropology: A Christian Perspective*. With a foreword by Eugene A. Nida. Grand Rapids: Zondervan, 1979.

Guenther, Allen R. "Interpreting the Silences: Deuteronomy 24:1-4." *Direction* 24/1 (Spring 1995) 41-53.

Haddad, H. S. "The Biblical Basis of Zionist Colonialism." *Journal of Palestine Studies* 3/4 (Summer 1974) 97-113.

Bibliography

Hafemann, Scott J. *2 Corinthians*. Edited by Terry Muck et al. NIV Application Commentary. Grand Rapids: Zondervan, 2000.

Hamilton, Victor P. *The Book of Genesis: Chapters 18–50*. Edited by R. K. Harrison and Robert L. Hubbard Jr. New International Commentary on the Old Testament. Grand Rapids: Eerdmans, 1995.

Hamlin, E. John. *Joshua: Inheriting the Land*. Edited by George A. F. Knight and Fredrick Carlson Holmgren. International Theological Commentary. Grand Rapids: Eerdmans, 1983.

———. *Ruth: Surely There is a Future*. Edited by George A. F. Knight and Fredrick Carlson Holmgren. International Theological Commentary. Grand Rapids: Eerdmans, 1990.

Harris, Murray J. *Colossians and Philemon*. Edited by Murray J. Harris. Exegetical Guide to the Greek New Testament. Grand Rapids: Eerdmans, 1991.

———. *The Second Epistle to the Corinthians: A Commentary on the Greek Text*. Edited by I. Howard Marshall and Donald A. Hagner. New International Greek Testament Commentary. Grand Rapids: Eerdmans, 2005.

Harris, R. Laird, et al. *Theological Wordbook of the Old Testament*. Chicago: Moody, 1999.

Harrisville, Roy A. *Romans*. Augsburg Commentary on the New Testament. Minneapolis: Augsburg, 1980.

Hawk, L. Daniel. *Joshua*. Edited by David W. Cotter et al. Berit Olam: Studies in Hebrew Narrative and Poetry. Collegeville: MN, Liturgical, 2000.

Hawkins, Robert L. *A Pastor's Primer for Premarital Guidance*. San Diego: Robert L. Hawkins, 1978.

Heather, P. J. "The Anti-Scythian Tirade of Synesius' 'De Regno,'" *Phoenix* 42/2 (Summer 1988) 152–72.

Hendrickson, William. *Galatians, Ephesians*. New Testament Commentary. Grand Rapids: Baker, 1979.

Hening, William Waller. *Statutes at Large of Virginia*. Vol. 1. http://vagenweb.org/hening/vol01–06.htm.

———. *Statutes at Large of Virginia*. Vol. 2. http://vagenweb.org/hening/vol02–09.htm#bottom.

———. *Statutes at Large of Virginia*. Vol. 3, http://vagenweb.org/hening/vol03–06.htm.

———. *Statutes at Large of Virginia*. Vol. 3. http://vagenweb.org/hening/vol03–16.htm.

Henry, Sheila E. "Family Structure, Social Class, and Cultural Values." *Comparative Family Studies* 8/3 (Autumn 1977) 291–99.

Herodotus. *The Histories*. Translated by G. C. Macaulay. http://www.gutenberg.org/files/2707/2707-h/2707-h.htm.

Hertzberg, Hans Wilhelm. *1 and 2 Samuel: A Commentary*. Edited by G. Ernest Wright et al. Old Testament Library. Philadelphia: Westminster, 1972.

Hess, Richard S. *Joshua: An Introduction and Commentary*. Edited by D. J. Wiseman. Tyndale Old Testament Commentaries. Downers Grove, IL: InterVarsity, 1996.

Hiebert, Paul G. *Anthropological Insights for Missionaries*. Grand Rapids: Baker, 1985.

———. *Anthropological Reflections on Missiological Issues*. Grand Rapids: Baker, 1994.

Hiebert, Paul G., and Eloise Hiebert Meneses. *Incarnational Ministry: Planting Churches in Band, Tribal, Peasant, and Urban Societies*. Grand Rapids: Baker, 1995.

Higginbotham, A. Leon, Jr., and Barbara K. Kopytoff. "Racial Purity and Interracial Sex in the Law of Colonial and Antebellum Virginia." In *Interracialism: Black–White Intermarriage in America History, Literature, and Law*, edited by Werner Sollors, 81–139. Oxford: Oxford University Press, 2000.

Bibliography

Holder, Ann S. "What's Sex Got to Do with It? Race, Power, Citizenship, and 'Intermediate Identities' in the Post-Emancipation United States." *Journal of African American History* 93/2 (Spring 2008) 153–73.

Holzer, Harold, ed. *The Lincoln-Douglas Debates: The First Complete, Unexpurgated Text.* New York: Fordham University Press, 2004.

Honoratus, Maurus Servius. *Commentary on the Aeneid of Vergil.* http: //www.perseus.tufts.edu/hopper/text?doc=Perseus%3Atext%3A1999.02.0053%3Abook%3D2%3Acommline%3D504.

House, Paul R. *1, 2 Kings.* New American Commentary 8. Nashville: Broadman & Holman, 1995.

Howard, David M., Jr. *Joshua.* Edited by E. Ray Clendenen et al. New American Commentary 5. Nashville: Broadman & Holman, 1998.

———. "Philistines." In *Peoples of the Old Testament World*, edited by Alfred J. Hoerth et al., 231–50. Grand Rapids: Baker, 1994.

———. "Rahab's Faith: An Exposition of Joshua 2:1–14." *Review and Expositor* 95/2 (Spring: 1998) 271–77.

Hubbard, Robert L., Jr. *The Book of Ruth.* Edited by R. K. Harrison and Robert L. Hubbard Jr. New International Commentary on the Old Testament. Grand Rapids: Eerdmans, 1988.

Huck, Robyn. "Effective Homework in Counseling." *Journal of Biblical Counseling* 27/1 (2013) 77–83.

Inrig, Gary. *1 and 2 Kings.* Edited by Max Anders. Holman Old Testament Commentary. Nashville: Holman Reference, 2003.

Jackson, John C. *Children of the Fur Trade: Forgotten Métis of the Pacific Northwest.* Edited by Robert J. Frank. Corvallis: Oregon State University Press, 1996.

Jacobs, Margaret D. "The Eastmans and the Luhans: Interracial Marriage between White Women and Native American Men, 1875–1935." *Frontiers: A Journal of Women Studies* 23/3 (2002) 29–54.

Jandt, Fred E. *Intercultural Communication: An Introduction.* 2nd ed. Thousand Oaks, CA: Sage, 1998.

Jefferson, Thomas. *Writings: Autobiography, Notes on the State of Virginia, Public and Private Papers, Addresses, Letters.* Library of America 17. New York: Library of America, 1984.

———. *The Writings of Thomas Jefferson.* Vol. 16. Edited by Albert Ellery Bergh. Washington, DC: Thomas Jefferson Memorial Society, 1907.

Johnson, Kevin R. "A Mixed Race Society: The End of Racism?" In *Mixed Race American and the Law: A Reader*, edited by Kevin R. Johnson, 469–70. New York: New York University Press, 2003.

Johnson, Luke Timothy. "First Timothy 1,1–20: The Shape of the Struggle." In *1 Timothy Reconsidered*, edited by Karl Donfried, 19–40. Colloquium Oecumenicum Paulinum 18. Leuven: Peeters, 2008.

Johnson, Phyllis J., and Kathrin Stoll. "Remittance Patterns of Southern Sudanese Refugee Men: Enacting the Global Breadwinner Role." *Family Relations* 57/4 (October 2008) 431–43.

Johnson, Sherman E. "Paul in Athens." *Lexington Theological Quarterly* 17/3 (July 1982) 37–43.

Bibliography

Johnston, James Hugo. *Race Relations in Virginia and Miscegenation in the South: 1776–1860*. With a foreword by Winthrop Jordan. Amherst: University of Massachusetts Press, 1970.

Jones, Mark, and John Wertheimer. "Pinkney and Sarah Ross: The Legal Journey of an Ex-Slave and His White Wife in the Carolina Borderlands During Reconstruction." *The South Carolina Historical Magazine* 103/4 (October 2002) 325–50.

Josephus, Flavius. *The New Complete Works of Josephus*. Rev. ed. Translated by William Whiston. With commentary by Paul L. Maier. Grand Rapids: Kregel, 1999.

"Judge Leon M. Brazile, Indictment for Felony." http://lva.omeka.net/items/show/54.

Julia, Maria. "The Need for Cultural Considerations in Examining Puerto Rican Financial Retirement Planning." *International Review of Modern Sociology* 28/2 (Autumn 1998) 17–27.

Kaminsky, Joel S. "Did Election Imply the Mistreatment of Non-Israelites?" *The Harvard Theological Review* 96/4 (October 2003) 397–425.

Kane, J. Herbert. *Life and Work on the Mission Field*. Grand Rapids: Baker, 1980.

Kang-Yum, Elaine. "Cross-Cultural Miscommunication." *Hastings Center Report* 26/3 (May–June 1996) 46.

Kaplan, Sidney. "The Miscegenation Issue in the Election of 1864." *Journal of Negro History* 34/3 (1949) 274–343.

Kapur Devesh, and John McHale. "Migration's New Payoff." *Foreign Policy* 139 (November–December 2003) 48–57.

Keener, Craig S. *Acts: An Exegetical Commentary. Volume 2: 3:1—14:28*. Grand Rapids: Baker, 2013.

———. *Acts: An Exegetical Commentary. Volume 3: 15:1—23:35*. Grand Rapids: Baker, 2014.

———. *The Gospel of John: A Commentary, Volume 1*. Peabody, MA: Hendrickson, 2003.

———. *Matthew*. Edited by Grant R. Osborne et al. IVP New Testament Commentary. Downers Grove, IL: InterVarsity, 1997.

Kelly, Balmer H. "Revelation 7:9–17." *Interpretation* 40/3 (July 1986) 288–95.

Kennedy, N. Brent, and Robyn Vaughan Kennedy. *The Melungeons: The Resurrection of a Proud People*. Rev. ed. Macon, GA: Mercer University Press, 1997.

Kenney, Nick. "Commissioner Henri Brooks Surrenders at Jail East, Booked on Simple Assault." http://www.wmcactionnews5.com/story/25762184/police-investigate-shelby-co-commissioner-henri-brooks-for-simple-assault.

Kiddushin. http://halakhah.com/pdf/nashim/Kiddushin.pdf.

Kidner, Derek. *Genesis: An Introduction and Commentary*. Edited by D. J. Wiseman. Tyndale Old Testament Commentaries 1. Downers Grove, IL: InterVarsity, 1967.

———. *Ezra and Nehemiah: An Introduction and Commentary*. Edited by D. J. Wiseman. Tyndale Old Testament Commentaries. Leicester: InterVarsity, 1979.

King, Martin Luther, Jr. "Communism's Challenge to Christianity." http://mlkkpp01.stanford.edu/primarydocuments/Vol6/9Aug1953Communism%27sChallengetoChristianity.pdf.

———. *A Testament of Hope: The Essential Writings and Speeches of Martin Luther King Jr.* Edited by James Melvin Washington. New York: HarperOne, 1986.

Klein, William W., et al. *Introduction to Biblical Interpretation*. Nashville: Thomas Nelson, 1993.

Bibliography

Klingbeil, Gerald A. "Between 'I' and 'We,' The Anthropology of the Hebrew Bible and its Importance for a 21st-Century Ecclesiology." *Bulletin for Biblical Research* 19/3 (2009) 319–39.

Kraft, Charles H. *Worldview for Christian Witness*. Pasadena: William Carey Library, 2008.

Kurz, William S. *Acts of the Apostles*. Edited by Peter S. Williamson et al. Catholic Commentary on Sacred Scripture. Grand Rapids: Baker, 2013.

Kysar, Robert. *John*. Augsburg Commentary on the New Testament. Minneapolis: Augsburg, 1986.

Laërtius, Diogenis. *Lives and Opinions of Eminent Philosophers*. http: //www.mikrosapoplous.gr/dl/dlo1.html#thales.

Lane, Patty. *A Beginner's Guide to Crossing Cultures: Making Friends in a Multicultural World*. Downer's Grove: InterVarsity, 2002.

Lansing, Michael. "Plains Indians Women and Interracial Marriage in the Upper Missouri Trade, 1804–1868." *Western Historical Quarterly* 31/4 (2000) 413–33.

Larkin, William J., Jr. *Acts*. Edited by Grant R. Osborne et al. IVP New Testament Commentary. Downers Grove, IL: InterVarsity, 1995.

Larson, Jeffrey H., and Thomas B. Holman. "Premarital Predictors of Marital Quality and Stability." *Family Relations* 43/2 (April 1994) 228–37.

Larson, Knute. *1 and 2 Thessalonians, 1 and 2 Timothy, Titus, Philemon*. Edited by Max Anders. Holman New Testament Commentary. Nashville: Holman Reference, 2000.

Larson, Knute, and Kathy Dahlen. *Ezra, Nehemiah, Esther*. Edited by Max Anders. Holman Old Testament Commentary 9. Nashville: Holman Reference, 2005.

Launey, Michel. *An Introduction to Classical Nahuatl*. Translated by Christopher Mckay. Cambridge: Cambridge University Press, 2001. Kindle Electronic Edition.

Laws of the State of Delaware, from the Fourteenth Day of October, One Thousand Seven Hundred, to the Eighteenth Day of August, One Thousand Seven Hundred and Ninety Seven. Vol. 1. New Castle, DE: Samuel Adams and John Adams, 1797.

Leon, Sharon M. "Tensions Not Unlike That Produced by a Mixed Marriage: Daniel Marshall and Catholic Challenges to Anti-Miscegenation Statutes." *U.S. Catholic Historian* 26/4 (Fall 2008) 27–44.

Leslau, Wolf. "Harari Idioms." *Rassegna di Studi Etiopici* 19 (1963) 150–54.

Leslie, Okana. *How to Survive an International Marriage*. Bloomington, IN: AuthorHouse, 2004.

Leveen, Adrian B. "Inside Out: Jethro, the Midianites, and a Biblical Construction of the Outsider." *Journal for the Study of the Old Testament* 34/4 (October 2010) 395–417.

Lewis, Richard, Jr., and Joanne Ford-Robinson. "Understanding the Occurrence of Interracial Marriage in the United States Through Differential Assimilation." *Journal of Black Studies* 41/2 (November 2010) 405–20.

Liefeld, Walter J. *1 and 2 Timothy, Titus*. NIV Application Commentary. Grand Rapids: Zondervan, 1999.

Lincoln, Abraham. *Speeches and Writings, 1832–1858: Speeches, Letters, and Miscellaneous Writings, The Lincoln–Douglas Debates*. New York: Library of America, 1989.

———. *Speeches and Writings, 1859–1865: Speeches, Letters, and Miscellaneous Writings, Presidential Messages and Proclamations*. New York: Library of America, 1989.

Lingenfelter, Sherwood G., and Marvin K. Mayers. *Ministering Cross-Culturally: An Incarnation Model for Personal Relationships*. Grand Rapids: Baker, 1986.

Littlejohn, Janice Rhoshalle, and Christelyn D. Karazin. *Swirling: How to Date, Mate, and Relate—Mixing Race, Culture, and Creed*. New York: Atria, 2012.

Bibliography

Litwak, Kenneth D. "Israel's Prophets Meet Athens' Philosophers: Scriptural Echoes in Acts 17:22-31." *Biblica* 85/2 (2004) 199-216.

Loller, Travis. "Melungeon DNA Study Reveals Ancestry, Upsets 'A Whole Lot of People.'" http://www.huffingtonpost.com/2012/05/24/melungeon-dna-study-origin_n_1544489.html.

Loritts, Bryan. *Right Color, Wrong Culture: A Leadership Fable*. Chicago: Moody, 2014.

Loss, Myron. *Culture Shock: Dealing with Stress in Cross-Cultural Living*. Winona Lake, IN: Light and Life, 1983.

Lotz, Denton. "Peter's Wider Understanding of God's Will: Acts 10:34-38." *International Review of Mission* 77 (April 1988) 201-7.

Loum, John. "Diversity and Contextualization." *Missio Apostolica* 20/2 (November 2012) 172-80.

Luciani, D. "Samson: L'amour Rend Aveugle." *Vetus Testamentum* 59/2 (April 2009) 323-26.

Lueking, F. Dean. *Let's Talk Marriage: A Guide for Couples Preparing to Marry*. Grand Rapids: Eerdmans, 2001.

Luzbetak, Louis J. *The Church and Cultures: An Applied Anthropology for the Religious Worker*. Pasadena: William Carey Library, 1970.

Lyonnet, Stanislas. *Etudes sur L'Epître aux Romains*. Analecta Biblica 120. Rome: Editrice Pontificio Istituto Biblico, 1989.

MacArthur, John, Jr. *Colossians and Philemon*. MacArthur New Testament Commentary. Chicago: Moody, 1992.

Macchia, Frank D. "The Covenant of the Lamb's Bride: A Subsersive Paradigm." *Living Pulpit* 14/3 (July-September 2005) 14-15.

Mack, Wayne A. *Homework Manual for Biblical Living*. Vol. 1, *Personal and Interpersonal Problems*. Phillipsburg, NJ: P&R, 1980.

———. *Homework Manual for Biblical Living*. Vol. 2, *Family and Marital Problems*. Phillipsburg, NJ: P&R, 1980.

———. "Taking Counselee Inventory: Collecting Data." In *Introduction to Biblical Counseling: A Basic Guide to the Principles and Practice of Counseling*, edited by John F. MacArthur Jr. and Wayne A. Mack, 210-30. Nashville: Thomas Nelson, 1994.

Magonet, Jonathan. "Rabbinic Readings of Ruth." *European Judaism* 40/2 (Autumn 2007) 150-57.

Malina, Bruce J. *Christian Origins and Cultural Anthropology: Practical Models for Biblical Interpretation*. Atlanta: John Knox, 1986.

Mann, Charles C. *1493: Uncovering the New World Columbus Created*. New York: Knopf, 2011.

Marsh, John. *Saint John*. Edited by D. E. Nineham. Westminster Pelican Commentaries. Philadelphia: Westminster, 1977.

Martin, Troy W. "The Covenant of Circumcision (Genesis 17:9-14) and the Situational Antithesis in Galatians 3:28." *Journal of Biblical Literature* 122/1 (Spring 2003) 111-25.

———. "The Scythian Perspective in Colossians 3:11." *Novum Testamentum* 37/3 (July 1985) 249-61.

Mathews, Kenneth A. *Genesis 11:27—50:26*. Edited by E. Ray Clendenen et al. New American Commentary 1b. Nashville: Broadman & Holman, 2005.

Matthews, I. G. "Expository Studies in the Old Testament IX: Joshua, the Successor of Moses." *Biblical World* 30/3 (September 1907) 213-24.

Bibliography

McCann, J. Clinton. *Judges*. Edited by James Luther Mays. Interpretation. Louisville: John Knox, 2002.
McDougall, Donald G. "Unequally Yoked—A Re-Examination of 2 Corinthians 6:11– 7:4." *Master's Seminary Journal* 10/1 (Spring 1999) 113–37.
McGrath, Alister, and Joanna Collicutt McGrath. *The Dawkins Delusion? Atheist Fundamentalism and the Denial of the Divine*. Downers Grove, IL: IVP, 2007.
McLaren, Brian, and Duane Litfin. "Emergent Evangelism: The Place of Absolute Truth in a Postmodern World." *Christianity Today*, November 1, 2004, 42–43.
McNutt, Paul M. "The Kenites, the Midianites, and the Rechabites as Marginal Mediators in Ancient Israelite Tradition." *Semeia* 67 (1994) 109–32.
Meacham, Jon. *Thomas Jefferson: The Art of Power*. New York: Random House, 2012.
Melick, Richard R., Jr. *Philippians, Colossians, Philemon*. Edited by David S. Dockery et al. New American Commentary 32. Nashvile: Broadman, 1991.
Melville, Herman. *Redburn, White Jacket, Moby Dick*. London: Heritage Illustrated, 2014. Kindle Electronic Edition.
Menachoth 43b. http://halakhah.com/pdf/kodoshim/Menachoth.pdf.
Merrill, Eugene H. *Deuteronomy*. Edited by E. Ray Clendenen et al. New American Commentary 4. Nashville: Broadman & Holman, 1994.
Mesle, C. Robert. *Process Theology: A Basic Introduction*. Atlanta: Chalice, 1993.
Metzger, Bruce. *A Textual Commentary on the Greek New Testament: A Companion Volume to the United Bible Societies' Greek New Testament*. 4th rev. ed. Stuttgart, Germany: Deutsche Bibelgesellschaft United Bible Societies, 1994.
Miller, J. Maxwell, and Gene M. Tucker. *The Book of Joshua*. Edited by P. R. Ackroyd et al. Cambridge Bible Commentary on the New English Bible. Cambridge: Cambridge University Press, 1974.
Mills, Gary B. "Miscegenation and the Free Negro in Antebellum 'Anglo' Alabama: A Reexamination of Southern Race Relations." *Journal of American History* 68/1 (June 1981) 16–34.
Mitchell, James T., and Henry Flanders. *Statutes at Large of Pennsylvania from 1862–1801*. Vol. 4, *1725–1744*. Harrisburg, PA: C. E. Aughinbaugh, 1801.
Molldrem, Mark J. "A Hermeneutic of Pastoral Care and the Law/Gospel Paradigm Applied to the Divorce Texts of Scripture." *Interpretation* 45/1 (January 1991) 43–54.
Morris, Leon. *The Gospel according to John*. Rev. ed. Edited by Ned B. Stonehouse et al. New International Commentary on the New Testament. Grand Rapids: Eerdmans, 1995.
Mounce, Robert H. *The Book of Revelation*. Edited by F. F. Bruce. New International Commentary on the New Testament. Grand Rapids: Eerdmans, 1977.
Mudd, Emily Hartshorne. *The Practice of Marriage Counseling*. New York: Association, 1951.
Murphy, Lucy Eldersveld. *Gathering of Rivers: Indians, Métis, and the Mining in the Western Great Lakes, 1737–1832*. Lincoln: University of Nebraska Press, 2000.
Nash, Gary B. "The Hidden History of Mestizo America." *Journal of American History* 82/3 (December 1995) 941–64.
Nathan, Debbie. "Sending Love and Money: A Photo Essay on Mexican Migration." *New Labor Forum* 18/2 (Spring 2009) 52–59.
Netanyahu, B. "Américo Castro and His View of the Origins of the Pureza de Sangre." *Proceedings of the American Academy for Jewish Research* 46 (1978) 397–457.

Bibliography

Newport, Frank. "In U.S., 87% Approve of Black-White Marriage vs. 4% in 1958." http://www.gallup.com/poll/163697/approve-marriage-blacks-whites.aspx.

Ngewa, Samuel M. *Galatians*. Edited by Nupanga Weanzana and Samuel Ngewa. Africa Bible Commentary. Nairobi: Hippo, 2010.

Nguyen, Van Thanh. "Crossing Cultural Boundaries: Missiological Implications of Acts 10:1—11:18." *Missiology* 40/4 (October 2012) 455-66.

Nida, Eugene Albert. *Customs and Cultures: Anthropology and Christian Missions*. South Pasadena, CA: William Carey Library, 1975.

———. "The Other Message." *Occasional Bulletin of Missionary Research* 3/3 (July 1979) 110-12.

The NIV Archaeological Study Bible: An Illustrated Walk through Biblical History and Culture. Grand Rapids: Zondervan, 2005.

"North America: Mexico." https://www.cia.gov/library/publications/the-world-factbook/geos/mx.html.

Noth, Martin. *Leviticus: A Commentary*. Rev. ed. Translated by J. E. Anderson. Old Testament Library. Philadelphia: Westminster, 1997.

Novkov, Julie. "Racial Constructions: The Legal Regulation of Miscegenation in Alabama, 1890-1934." *Law and History Review* 20/2 (Summer 2002) 225-77.

Oates, Wayne E. *Premarital Pastoral Care and Counseling*. Nashville: Broadman, 1958.

O'Grady, William. "The Syntax of Idioms." *Natural Language and Linguistic Theory* 16/2 (May 1998) 279-312.

Oldmixon, John. *The British Empire in America, Containing the History of the Discovery, Settlement, Progress and Present State of all the British Colonies, on the Continent and Islands of America*. Vol. 2. London: King's Arms, 1708.

Olley, John W. *The Message of Kings: God is Present*. Edited by J. A. Motyer. The Bible Speaks Today. Grand Rapids: InterVarsity, 2011.

Ormond, John J., et al., eds. *The Code of Alabama*. With Notes by Henry C. Semple. Montgomery: Brittan and De Wolf, 1852.

Olsina, Eva Codó. "Managing Understanding in Intercultural Talk: An Empirical Approach to Miscommunication." *Atlantis* 24/1 (June 2002) 37-57.

Ostriker, Alicia. "The Redeeming of Ruth." *Studies in American Jewish Literature* 11/2 (Fall 1992) 217-19.

"Pace v. Alabama 106 U.S. 583 (1883)." https://supreme.justia.com/cases/federal/us/106/583/case.html.

Pandya, Sheel. "Racial and Ethnic Differences Among Older Adults in Long-Term Care Service Use." http://www.aarp.org/home-garden/livable-communities/info-2005/fs119_ltc.html.

Parsons, Mikeal C. *Acts*. Edited by Mikeal C. Parsons and Charles H. Talbert. Paideia Commentaries on the New Testament. Grand Rapids: Baker, 2008.

Pascoe, Peggy. "Miscegenation Law, Court Cases, and Ideologies of 'Race' in Twentieth-Century America." *Journal of American History* 83/1 (June 1996) 44-69.

Passel, Jeffrey S., et al. "Marrying Out: One-in-Seven New U.S. Marriages is Interracial or Interethnic." http://www.pewsocialtrends.org/2010/06/04/marrying-out.

Patterson, Dorothy. "The High Calling of Wife and Mother in a Biblical Perspective." In *Recovering Biblical Manhood and Womanhood: A Response to Evangelical Feminism*, edited by John Piper and Wayne Grudem, 364-77. Wheaton, IL: Crossway, 1991.

Patterson, Paige. *Revelation*. Edited by E. Ray Clendenen et al. New American Commentary 39. Nashville: B&H, 2012.

Bibliography

Paulin, Diana Rebekkah. *Imperfect Unions: Staging Miscegenation in U.S. Drama and Fiction.* Minneapolis: University of Minnesota Press, 2012.

Peace, Martha. "'Ashley' and Anorexia." In *Counseling the Hard Cases: True Stories Illustrating the Sufficiency of God's Resources in Scripture*, edited by Stuart Scott and Heath Lambert, 141–70. With a foreword by John MacArthur. Nashville: B&H Academic, 2012.

———. *The Excellent Wife: A Biblical Perspective.* Expanded ed. Bemidji, MN: Focus, 2005.

Pelikan, Jaroslav. *Acts.* Edited by R. R. Reno et al. Brazos Theological Commentary on the Bible. Grand Rapids: Brazos, 2005.

Pérez-Torres, Rafael. "Miscegenation Now!" *American Literary History* 17/2 (Summer 2005) 369–80.

Peterson, David G. *The Acts of the Apostles.* Edited by D. A. Carson. Pillar New Testament Commentary. Grand Rapids: Eerdmans, 2009.

Pexman, Penny M. "It's Fascinating Research: The Cognition of Verbal Irony." *Current Directions in Psychological Science* 17/4 (August 2008) 286–90.

Phillips, Anthony. *Deuteronomy.* Edited by P. R. Ackroyd et al. Cambridge Bible Commentary on the New English Bible. Cambridge: Cambridge University Press, 1973.

Phillips, Cyrus E., IV. "Miscegenation: The Courts and the Constitution." *William and Mary Law Review* 8/1 (1966) 133–42.

Pitta, Antonio. *Disposizione e Messaggio della Lettera al Galati.* Analecta Biblica 131. Rome: Editrice Pontificio Istituto Biblico, 1992.

"Plessy v. Ferguson 163 U.S. 537 (1896)." http://caselaw.lp.findlaw.com/scripts/ getcase.pl?court=US&vol=163&invol=537.

Polaski, Donald C., and Sandra Hack Polaski. "Listening to a Conversation: Divorce, the Torah, and Earliest Christianity." *Review and Expositor* 106/4 (Fall 2009) 591–602.

Pomeroy, James M., ed. *Debates and Proceedings of the Convention which Assembled at Little Rock, January 7th, 1868, under the Provisions of the Act of Congress of March 2nd, 1867, and the Acts of March 23rd and July 19th, 1867, Supplementary Thereto, to Form a Constitution for the State of Arkansas.* Little Rock: J. G. Price, 1868.

Powlison, David, and John Yenchko. *Pre-Engagement: Five Questions to Ask Yourselves.* New Jersey: P & R, 2000.

Prentice, Sartell. "Elijah and the Tyrian Alliance." *Journal of Biblical Literature* 42/1–2 (1923) 33–38.

Proudfoot, Shannon. "Number of Mixed-Race Couples on the Rise in Canada: StatsCan." http://www.canada.com/Number+mixed+race+couples+rise+Canada+StatsCan/2928592/story.html.

Pummer, Reinhard. "Genesis 34 in the Jewish Writings of the Hellenistic and Roman Periods." *Harvard Theological Review* 75/2 (April 1982) 177–88.

Qian, Zhenchao. "Breaking the Racial Barriers: Variations in Interracial Marriage between 1980 and 1990." *Demography* 34/2 (May 1997) 263–76.

Rad, Gerhard von. *Deuteronomy: A Commentary.* Edited by G. Ernest Wright et al. Old Testament Library. Philadelphia: Westminster, 1966.

Rah, Soong-Chan. *Many Colors: Cultural Intelligence for a Changing Church.* Chicago: Moody, 2010.

Rao, A. B. S. V. Ranga, and K. Sekhar. "Divorce: Process and Correlates, A Cross-Cultural Study." *Journal of Comparative Family Studies* 33/4 (Autumn 2002) 541–63.

Bibliography

Rastoin, Marc. *Tarse et Jérusalem: La Double Culture de L'Apôtre Paul en Galates 3:6—4:7*. Analecta Biblica 152. Rome: Editrice Pontificio Istituto Biblico, 2003.

Ribichini, S. "Melqart." In the *Dictionary of Deities and Demons in the Bible*, edited by Karel von der Toorn et al., 563–65. Grand Rapids: Eerdmans, 1999.

Rice, Gene. *1 Kings: Nations under God*. Edited by Frederick Carlson Holmgren and George A. F. Knight. International Theological Commentary. Grand Rapids: Eerdmans, 1990.

Robinson, Charles F. "Legislated Love in the Lone Star State: Texas and Miscegenation." *The Southwestern Historical Quarterly* 108/1 (July 2004) 65–87.

———. "'Most Shamefully Common,' Arkansas and Miscegenation." *The Arkansas Historical Quarterly* 60/3 (Autumn 2001) 265–83.

Rogers, Everett M., and Thomas M. Steinfatt. *Intercultural Communication*. Prospect Heights, IL: Waveland, 1999.

Romano, Dugan. *Intercultural Marriage: Promises and Pitfalls*. 3rd ed. Boston: Intercultural, 2008.

Romano, Renee C. *Race Mixing: Black-White Marriage in Postwar America*. Cambridge, MA: Harvard University Press, 2003.

Rowe, C. Kavin. "Romans 10:13: What is the Name of the Lord?" *Horizons in Biblical Theology* 22/2 (December 2000) 135–73.

Ruether, Rosemary Radford. "Feminism and the Future of Religious Studies." *Frontiers: A Journal of Women Studies* 6/1–2 (Spring–Summer 1981) 10–12.

———. "The Theological Vision of Letty Russell." In *Liberating Eschatology: Essays in Honor of Letty M. Russell*, edited by Margaret A. Farley and Serene Jones, 16–25. Louisville: Westminster John Knox, 1999.

Rutledge, Aaron L. *Pre-Marital Counseling*. Cambridge, MA: Schenkman, 1966.

Sanger, Margaret. "Letter from Margaret Sanger to Dr. C. J. Gamble." December 10, 1939. http://www.smithlibraries.org/digital/items/show/495.

———. "Unity!" *Birth Control Review* 5/11 (November 1921) 3–4.

Saunders, William L. ed. *Colonial Records of North Carolina*. Vol. 2, *1713–1728*. Raleigh: Josephus Daniels, 1886.

Sawchuk, Joe. "Negotiating an Identity: Métis Political Organizations, the Canadian Government, and Competing Concepts of Aboriginality." *American Indian Quarterly* 25/1 (Winter 2001) 73–92.

Scales-Trent, Judy. *Notes of a White Black Woman: Race, Color, Community*. University Park: Penn State University Press, 2001.

Schnabel, Eckhard J. *Acts*. Edited by Clinton E. Arnold, et al. Exegetical Commentary on the New Testament. Grand Rapids: Zondervan, 2012.

Schoff, Rebecca. "Deciding on Doctrine: Anti-Miscegenation Statutes and the Development of Equal Protection Analysis." *Virginia Law Review* 95/3 (2009) 627–65.

Schreiner, Thomas R. *Galatians*. Edited by Clinton E. Arnold et al. Exegetical Commentary on the New Testament. Grand Rapids: Zondervan, 2010.

Schüssler Fiorenza, Elisabeth. "Public Discourse, Religion, and Wo/men's Struggles for Justice." *DePaul Law Review* 51 (Summer 2002) 1077–1101.

Selman, Martin J. *2 Chronicles: A Commentary*. Edited by D. J. Wiseman. Tyndale Old Testament Commentaries. Downers Grove, IL: InterVarsity, 1994.

Bibliography

Semyonov, Moshe. "Labor Migration, Remittances, and Household Income: A Comparison between Filipino and Filipina Overseas Workers." *International Migration Review* 39/1 (Spring 2005) 45–68.

Shelling, G., and J. Frayser-Smith. *In Love But Worlds Apart: Insights, Questions, and Tips for the Intercultural Couple*. Bloomington, IN: AuthorHouse, 2008.

Sherwood, Stephen. *Leviticus, Numbers, Deuteronomy*. Edited by David W. Cotter et al. Berit Olam: Studies in Hebrew Narrative and Poetry. Collegeville, MN: Liturgical, 2001.

Simpson, E. K., and F. F. Bruce. *The Epistles to the Ephesians and Colossians*. Edited by F. F. Bruce. New International Commentary on the New Testament. Grand Rapids: Eerdmans, 1957.

Sire, James W. *The Universe Next Door: A Basic Worldview Catalog*. 4th ed. Downers Grove, IL: IVP Academic, 2004.

Sleeper-Smith, Susan. *Indian Women and French Men: Rethinking Cultural Encounter in the Western Great Lakes*. Edited by Colin G. Calloway and Barry O'Connell. Native Americans of the Northeast: Culture, History, and the Contemporary. Amherst: University of Massachusetts Press, 2001.

Sloan, Ja[me]s A. *The Question Answered; Or, Is Slavery a Sin in Itself (Per Se) Answered according to the Teaching of the Scriptures*. Memphis: Hutton, Gallaway. 1857.

Sloyan, Gerard S. *John*. Edited by James Luther Mays et al. Interpretation. Atlanta: John Knox, 1988.

Smedley, Audrey, and Brian D. Smedley. *Race in North America: Origin and Evolution of a Worldview*. 4th rev. ed. Boulder, CO: Westview, 2012.

Smith, Harold Ivan. *More Than "I Do," A Pastor's Resource Book for Premarital Counseling*. Kansas City, MO: Beacon Hill, 1983.

Smith, John. *The Generall Historie of Virginia, New-England, and the Summer Isles: With the Names of the Adventurers, Planters, and Governours from Their First Beginning, Ano: 1584. To This Present 1624*. Documenting the Southern South. http://docsouth.unc.edu/southlit/smith/smith.html.

———. *A True Discourse of the Present Estate of Virginia, and the Successe of the Affaires There Till the 18 of June, 1614*. American Memory from the Library of Congress. http://lcweb2.loc.gov/service/gdc/lhbcb/02778/02778.pdf.

———. *A True Relation of Such Occurrences and Accidents of Note as Hath Hapned in Virginia Since the First Planting of that Colony, Which is Now Resident in the South Part Thereof, Till the Last Returne from Thence*. London: John Tappe, 1608. Kindle Electronic Edition.

Smithers, Gregory D. "The 'Pursuits of Civilized Man': Race and the Meaning of Civilization in the United States and Australia, 1790s–1850s." *Journal of World History* 20/2 (June 2009) 245–72.

Sohoni, Deenesh. "Unsuitable Suitors: Anti-Miscegenation Laws, Naturalization Laws, and the Construction of Asian Identities." *Law and Society Review* 41/3 (September 2007) 587–618.

Sollors, Werner. *Interracialism: Black–White Intermarriage in American History, Literature, and Law*. Oxford: Oxford University Press, 2000.

———. "'Never was Born,' The Mulatto, an American Tragedy?" *Massachusetts Review* 27/2 (Summer 1986) 293–316.

Sowell, Thomas. *Intellectuals and Race*. New York: Basic, 2013.

Bibliography

Sperling, Melanie, Deborah Appleman, Keith Gilyard, and Sarah Freedman. "Voice in the Context of Literacy Studies." *Reading Research Quarterly* 46/1 (January–March 2011) 70–84.

Spickard, Paul R. *Mixed Blood: Intermarriage and Ethnic Identity in Twentieth-Century America*. Madison: University of Wisconsin Press, 1989.

Stulman, Louis. "Encroachment in Deuteronomy: An Analysis of the Social World of the D Code." *Journal of Biblical Literature* 109/4 (Winter 1990) 613–32.

Sumney, Jerry L. *Colossians: A Commentary*. Edited by C. Clifton Black et al. New Testament Library. Louisville: Westminster John Knox, 2008.

Talbert, Charles H. *Ephesians and Colossians*. Edited by Mikeal C. Parsons and Charles H. Talbert. Paideia: Commentaries on the New Testament. Grand Rapids: Baker, 2007.

Thai, Hung Cam. "Money and Masculinity Among Low Wage Vietnamese Immigrants in Transnational Families." *International Journal of Sociology of the Family* 32/2 (Autumn 2006) 247–71.

Thiselton, Anthony C. *The First Epistle to the Corinthians: A Commentary on the Greek Text*. Grand Rapids: Eerdmans, 2000.

Thomas, Hugh. *Conquest: Montezuma, Cortés, and the Fall of Old Mexico*. New York: Simon & Schuster, 1993.

Thompson, J. A. *1–2 Chronicles*. Edited by E. Ray Clendenen et al. New American Commentary 9. Nashville: Broadman & Holman, 1994.

———. *Deuteronomy: An Introduction and Commentary*. Edited by D. J. Wiseman. Tyndale Old Testament Commentaries. Grand Rapids: InterVarsity, 1974.

Throntveit, Mark A. *Ezra–Nehemiah*. Edited by James Luther Mays. Interpretation. Louisville: John Knox, 1991.

Tocqueville, Alexis de. *Democracy in America and Two Essays on America*. Translated by Gerald E. Bevan. With an introduction and notes by Isaac Kramnick. London: Penguin, 2003.

"Transcript of Civil Rights Act." http://www.ourdocuments.gov/doc.php?flash=true&doc=97&page=transcript.

Trible, Phyllis. *Texts of Terror: Literary-Feminist Readings of Biblical Narratives*. Philadelphia: Fortress, 1984.

"U.S. Supreme Court: Loving v. Virginia, 388 U.S. 1." 1967. http://supreme.justia.com/cases/federal/us/388/1/case.html.

Viars, Steve. "'Brian' and Obsessive-Compulsive Disorder." In *Counseling the Hard Cases: True Stories Illustrating the Sufficiency of God's Resources in Scripture*, edited by Stuart Scott and Heath Lambert, 57–84. With a foreword by John MacArthur. Nashville: B&H Academic, 2012.

Volpp, Leti. "American Mestizo: Filipinos and Anti-Miscegenation Laws in California." In *Mixed Race America and the Law: A Reader*, edited by Kevin R. Johnson, 86–93. New York: New York University Press, 2003.

Vroom, Jonathan. "Recasting Mišpāṭîm: Legal Innovation in Leviticus 24:10–23." *Journal of Biblical Literature* 131/1 (2012) 27–44.

Wadlington, Walter. "The Loving Case: Virginia's Anti-Miscegenation Statute in Historical Perspective." *Virginia Law Review* 52/7 (November 1966) 1189–1223.

Walden, Wayne. "Galatians 3:28 Grammar Observation." *Restoration Quarterly* 51/1 (2009) 45–50.

Walfish, Barry Dov. *Esther in Medieval Garb: Jewish Interpretation of the Book of Esther in the Middle Ages*. Albany: State University of New York Press, 1993.

Bibliography

Wallace, Daniel B. *Greek Grammar Beyond the Basics: An Exegetical Syntax of the New Testament*. Grand Rapids: Zondervan 1996.

Wallenstein, Peter. *Tell the Court I Love My Wife: Race, Marriage, and Law—An American History*. New York: Palgrave MacMillan, 2002.

Walsh, Jerome T. *1 Kings*. Edited by David W. Cotter et al. Berit Olam: Studies in Hebrew Narrative and Poetry. Collegeville, MN: Liturgical, 1996.

Wang, Wendy. "The Rise of Intermarriage: Rates, Characteristics Vary by Race and Gender." http://www.pewsocialtrends.org/2012/02/16/the-rise-of-intermarriage.

Webb, William J. "Unequally Yoked Together with Unbelievers." *Bibliotheca Sacra* 149 (January–March 1992) 27–44.

———. "What is the Unequal Yoke (ἑτεροζυοῦντες) in 2 Corinthians 6:14?" *Bibliotheca Sacra* 149 (April–June 1992) 162–79.

Wenham, Gordon J. *Numbers: An Introduction and Commentary*. Edited by D. J. Wiseman. Tyndale Old Testament Commentaries. Downers Grove, IL: InterVarsity, 1981.

Whitacre, Rodney A. *John*. Edited by Grant R. Osborne et al. IVP New Testament Commentary. Downers Grove, IL: InterVarsity, 1999.

Williams, Sam K. *Galatians*. Edited by Victor Paul Furnish et al. Abingdon New Testament Commentaries. Nashville: Abingdon, 1997.

Williamson, Joel. *New People: Miscegenation and Mulattoes in the United States*. Baton Rouge: Louisiana State University Press, 1995.

Wilson, Judith. "Optical Illusions: Images of Miscegenation in Nineteenth- and Twentieth-Century American Art." *American Art* 5/3 (Summer 1991) 88–107.

Wood, Charles A., Jr. "Premarital Counseling: A Working Model." *Journal of Pastoral Care* 33/1 (March 1979) 44–50.

Woodson, Carter G. "The Beginnings of Miscegenation of the Whites and Blacks." In *Interracialism: Black-White Intermarriage in America History, Literature, and Law*, edited by Werner Sollors, 42–54. Oxford: Oxford University Press, 2000.

Worthington, Everett L. *Counseling Before Marriage*. Edited by Gary R. Collins. Resources for Christian Counseling 23. Dallas: Word, 1990.

Woudstra, Marten H. *The Book of Joshua*. Edited by R. K. Harrison. New International Commentary on the Old Testament. Grand Rapids: Eerdmans, 1981.

Wright, Christopher J. H. *Deuteronomy*. Edited by W. Ward Gasque et al. Understanding the Bible Commentary. Grand Rapids: Baker, 1996.

Yamauchi, Edwin. "The Scythians: Invading Hordes from the Russian Steppes." *Biblical Archaeologist* 46/2 (Spring 1983) 90–99.

Yancey, George A. "Unequally Yoked by Race or by Faith?" *Criswell Theological Review* 6/2 (Spring 2009) 65–75.

Yodanis, Carrie, and Sean Lauer. "Managing Money in Marriage: Multilevel and Cross-National Effects of the Breadwinner Role." *Journal of Marriage and Family* 69/5 (December 2007) 1307–25.

Zeitlin, Solomon. "Judaism as a Religion: An Historical Study. Part 6: Galuth–Diaspora." *Jewish Quarterly Review* 34/2 (October 1943) 207–41.

Zimmermann, Jens. *Incarnational Humanism: A Philosophy of Culture for the Church in the World*. Downers Grove, IL: InterVarsity, 2012.

Author Index

Adams, Jay, 125, 128–29, 131
Alupoaicei, Marla, 119
Anderson, Rachel, 91
Andrews, George Reid, 75
Avins, Alfred, 99

Bakon, Shimon, 37
Bellinger, William H., Jr., 32
Benjamin, Gail, 114
Brackenridge, Henry, 77
Bramlett, M. D., 122
Bratter, Jenifer L. 122
Brindle, Wayne, 23
Brueggemann, Walter, 18

Coggins, Richard James, 14, 26
Cole, R. Alan, 30
Cotter, David, 16
Cousar, Charles, 60
Croly, David Goodman, 43–45
Cuming, Fortescue, 89
Curtiss, Samuel, 13

Darwin, Charles, 51, 96
Dawkins, Richard, 8, 40
Dixon, Thomas, Jr., 98
Du Bois, W. E. B., 98

Edwards, Leigh H., 78
Epps, Garrett, 78
Eyrich, Howard A., 112, 131

Firmin, Michael W., 123
Frayser-Smith, J., 121

Grunlan, Stephen, 116

Hamilton, Victor, 20
Hamlin, E. John, 35, 36, 39
Hendrickson, William, 60
Herodotus, 63–64
Hess, Richard, 33
Hiebert, Paul, 111
Honoratus, Maurus Servius, 63
Howard, David, 33
Hubbard, Robert L., Jr., 38
Huck, Robyn, 133

Jacobs, Margaret D., 82
Josephus, 46

Keener, Craig, 50, 52
King, Martin Luther, Jr., 55–56, 60–61
King, Rosalind, 122

Laërtius, Diogenis, 58
Lane, Patty, 120
Leveen, Adriane, 29
Lingenfelter, Sherwood, 112
Lueking, F. Dean, 122
Luzbetak, Louis, 120

Macarthur, John, 62
Macchia, Frank, 68
Mack, Wayne, 124
Marsh, John, 47
Mayers, Marvin, 112
Melville, Herman, 89
Mesle, Robert, 60
Meyers, Marvin, 116

Author Index

Mosher, W. D., 122

Nash, Gary B., 80, 106
Ngewa, Samuel M., 61
Nida, Eugene, 115–16
Noth, Martin, 30
Novkov, Julie, 93

Oldmixon, John, 79

Parsons, Mikeal, 48
Rad, Gerhard von, 10
Rice, Gene, 24
Rogers, Everett, 110
Romano, Renee, 105

Sanger, Margaret, 97
Scales–Trent, Judy, 106

Shelling, G., 121
Sire, James, 107
Slack, Jim, 135
Sloan, James A. 44–45, 52
Smith, John, 78
Sohoni, Deenesh, 81
Steinfatt, Thomas, 110
Synesius, 64

Tedford, Mark, 123
Tocqueville, Alexis de, 88–89

Walfish, Barry Dov, 15
Walsh, Jerome, 23
Wood, Charles, 5

Yamauchi, Edwin, 63
Yancey, George, 55, 58

Subject Index

Aaron, 31–32
Abolitioniss, 43, 92
Abraham, 12, 13, 15, 16–17, 19, 25, 27, 28, 29, 35, 36, 40, 49, 54, 62, 69
Abram. See Abraham.
Adam, 17, 52, 58
Adams, John, 127
Aeneid, 63
African Americans, 8, 43, 44, 45, 61, 88–89, 90, 91, 92, 93, 94, 95, 96, 97, 98, 100, 101, 106, 118
Africans, 75, 81, 82, 87
Aha ben Jacob, Rabbi, 58
Ahab, 24–25, 27
Ahasuerus, 14–15
Alabama, 90
All in the Family, 101
amalgamation, 89, 93
America, 18
American Association of Retired Persons (AARP), 118
Americans. See North Americans.
Ammonites, 23
Amnon, 19
Amorites, 50
angels, 48
anthropologists, 52
Antioch, 59
apostasy, 26
Aqiba, 127
Arabia, 12, 28
Areopagus, 51
Arikaras, 77
Arizona, 123
Arkansas, 90, 93

Asenath, 12–13
Asherah, 25
Ashtoreth, 23
Asians, 91, 97, 98, 118
Assyrian Conquest, 26
Assyrians, 45
Athenians, 51, 52
Athens, 51
Attica, 51
Atum, 13
autochthonism, 51
Aztecs, 74

Baal, 25, 27, 39
Baal Melqart, 24
Baal of Peor, 29
Babylonian Captivity, 25
Balaam, 39
Baptist Faith and Message, 127
Barbarians, 58, 62–65
Barnabas, 59
Bathsheba, 21–22, 27
Bath-Shua, 21.
Bazile, Leon Maurice, 7
Beor, 39
Berbers, 64
Bethlehem, 38, 39
Boaz, 38–40
Bob Jones University, 7
Britton, James, 3
Brooks, Henri, 120
Bunker, Archie, 101

Cain, 16
Caleb, 34–36, 40

Subject Index

calpa mulattos, 76
cambujos, 76
Canada, 2, 74
Canaan, 8, 9, 10, 18, 19, 20, 21, 27, 33, 34, 35
Canaanites, 18, 19, 20, 21, 27, 33
castizos, 75
Catholics, 8, 77
Caucasians, 1, 3, 8, 43, 45, 52, 61, 77, 83, 84, 85, 86, 87, 88, 89, 90, 91, 92, 93, 94, 95, 96, 97, 98, 99, 100, 101, 105, 106, 111, 123
Central America, 3
Chapulin Colorado, 109–10
Charbonneau, Jean Baptiste, 77
Charbonneau, Toussaint, 77
Chemosh, 23
childrearing, 119
Chilion, 38
chinos, 75
Chippewa, 88
Christ. See Jesus.
Church of England, 85
circumcision, 20, 59, 67
Civil Rights Act, 99
Civil War, 43, 91, 93
Clark, William, 77
Colossians, 62
Columbus, Christopher, 73
communication, 113–15
community, 108
compatability, 125
concubine, 12, 13
Congo, 53
Connecticut, 88
Conquest, 32
Constitution, 2
contextualization, 132
Corinthians, 56
Cornelius, 48, 54
Cortés, Hernán, 74
Cortés, Martín, 74
covenant, 12, 16, 17, 19, 20, 21, 26, 27, 40, 49, 50, 59
Cox, Mary, 95
Critical Stages of Biblical Counseling, 131
cultural diagnostic questions, 135

cultural implementation, 120
culture, 108, 129
culture shock, 120
Cush, 31, 32, 40

Dan, 13, 30, 31, 36
Darwin, Charles, 51, 96
data gathering, 131
David, 21–22, 24, 27, 30, 38, 39
Davis, Hugh, 80
Delaware, 85, 86
Delaware (Native Americans), 88
Delilah, 36
Derbe, 66
Descent of Man, 51, 96
desegregation, 55
Dibri, 31
Dinah 19–21, 27
discrimination, 61
divorce, 123
Doolittle, James R., 93
Douglas, Stephen A., 91–93

East Louisiana Railroad, 95
Ebenezer Baptist Church, 60
Ecuador, 117
Edomites, 23, 34, 35
Egypt, 30, 31, 35
Elimelech, 38
Emancipation Proclamation, 43, 93
Ephraim, 13
Ephraimites, 14
Epicureans, 51
epistemology, 124
Esau, 12, 18–19, 27
Esther, 14–15
Eth-baal, 24, 25
Ethiopia, 31
Ethiopian eunuch, 48
ethnos, 49, 51, 69
eugenics, 97
Evangelicals, 8, 113
Eve, 17
Ezra, 25–26

family, 105
female roles, 112–13
Fertile Crescent, 63

Subject Index

finances, 117–19
First Baptist Church of Crystal Springs, 61
food, 116–17
Fourteenth Amendment, 2, 100, 102, 137
France, 76

Galatia, 59
Gamble, C. J., 97
geneticists, 52, 87
Gerizim, 46
Germans, 112
Gershom, 30
gibaros, 75
Gibeonites, 34
Gómez Bolaños, Roberto, 110
gospel, 53
Gray, William, 94
Great Commission, 49
Greeks, 51–53, 58, 62–65
Guatemala, 117

Hadassah. See Esther.
Hagar, 16–17, 27, 28
halo data, 124–25
Ham, 44
Hamor, 20
Heaven, 68, 70
Hebron, 34, 35
Henry, Patrick, 88
Hermippus, 58
Hillel, 127
Hiram, 14
Hispanics, 97, 116, 118
Histories, 63
Hittites, 18–19, 21, 22, 23, 35, 50
Hivites, 20, 21, 27
homework, 133–35
Homogenocene Era, 3, 73
hope, 124–25
Hosea, 53
Houston, 111
Huram-Abi, 13–14
Hurrians, 35
Hyrcanus, John, 46

I don't understand thee (racial designation), 76
Iconium, 66
identity, 107–9, 119
idioms, 115
idolatry, 19, 25, 27, 29, 33, 37, 51
i-Mazigh-en, 64
individualism, 108
Isaac, 12, 18
Isaiah, 53
Ishmael, 12, 17, 18
Ishmaelites, 35
Israelites, 8, 9

Jacob, 12, 18, 19, 20, 21, 39
James, King of England, 78
Jamestown, 78
Japanese, 114
Jefferson, George, 101
Jefferson, Thomas, 88, 127
Jeffersons, 101
Jehiel, 26
Jephunneh, 34
Jericho, 32, 33
Jeroboam, 13, 24
Jerusalem, 34, 46, 54
Jerusalem Council, 53, 66–67
Jerusalem Temple, 14, 15, 45, 46
Jeshua, 45
Jesus, 4, 22, 33, 38, 41, 42, 45–48, 50, 51, 53, 54, 55, 57, 58, 59, 61, 62, 65, 68, 69, 71, 107, 121, 126, 127, 132, 137, 138
Jeter, Mildred. See Mildred Loving.
Jethro. See Reuel.
Jezebel, 24–25, 27
Johanan, Rabbi, 66
John, 69, 70
Johnson, Lyndon B., 99
Joppa, 48
Jordan River, 33
Joseph, 12–13, 15, 35
Josephus, 46
Joshua, 34, 36
Josiah, 23
Judah, 21, 34, 35, 36, 39
Judah, Rabbi, 58
Judaizers, 59

163

Subject Index

Judea, 47

Kansas, 101, 123
Kenaz, 34
Kenites, 35
Kenizzites, 34, 35
Kenya, 101
Keturah, 12, 13, 16, 19, 28
Kiddushin, 66
King, Martin Luther, Jr., 55–56, 60–61
Korah, 35
kosher food, 48

language, 114–15
language acquisition, 119
Latin Americans, 112, 116
Leah, 39
Leopard's Spots, 98
lepers, 47
lepers (racial designation), 75
Levi, 20
Levite, 14
Lewis and Clark Expedition, 77
Lewis, Meriwether, 77
Lincoln, Abraham, 43, 44, 91–93
Lives and Opinions of Eminent Philosophers, 58
London, 79
Louisiana, 95, 98
Loving, Mildred, 1–2, 7, 99
Loving, Richard, 1–2, 7, 99
Loving v. Virginia, 1–2, 99
Luke, 67
Luter, Fred, Jr., 61
Lystra, 66

Maccabeans, 46
Mahalath, 18
Mahlon, 38
male roles, 112–13
Malinalli, 74
Manasseh, 13
Marina. See Malinalli
Mars Hill, 51
Maryland, 81, 82, 84
Massachusetts, 85, 90
materialism, 109
Matoaka. See Pocahontas.

Maynard v. Hill, 100
Mediterranean, 63
Melungeons, 87
Memphis, 120
merismus, 65
Messiah. See Jesus.
mestizos, 2, 75, 77
métis, 77
Mexicans, 2, 106
Mexico, 74, 75, 109
Miami (Native Americans), 88
Micronesia, 112
Midian, 12, 28
Midianites, 28, 29, 35
Milcom, 23
Miriam, 31–32, 40
miscegenation, 43–45
Mishnah, 58
Mississippi, 44
Moab, 29
Moabites, 23, 30, 39
Molech, 23
Montezuma. See Moteuczoma.
Mordecai, 14
moriscos, 75
Moses, 8, 9, 28–29, 30, 31–32, 40, 46, 54
Moteuczoma, 74
mulattos, 75, 83, 84, 85, 91, 96
mustees, 83

Nahuatl, 74
Naomi, 38
Natchez, 89
Nathan, 22
Native Americans, 75, 79, 83, 84, 88, 97
Nazirite vow, 36
Nehemiah, 45
Neith, 13
Nevada, 91
New Covenant, 65
New World, 76, 80
New York World, 43
Nigeria, 35, 105
Noah, 44
non-materialism, 109
nonverbal communication, 114, 115–16
North Americans, 19, 45, 52, 61, 101, 102, 105, 112, 114, 136

Subject Index

North Carolina, 85, 86, 90, 98–99

Obama, Barack, 101
Obed, 39
octoroons, 83, 95, 96
Oklahoma, 99, 123
Omri, 24
On, 13
Opechancanough, 79
Othniel, 35

Pace, Tony, 95
Pace v. Alabama, 95
Pacific coast, 91
Pacific Islanders, 97
Paul, 4, 51–53, 54, 55, 56, 57, 58, 59, 60, 62, 63, 64, 65, 67, 69, 70, 71, 102, 126, 132
Pennsylvania, 86, 90
Perez, 39
Persia, 14
Personal Data Inventory (PDI), 130–31
Peru, 117
Peter, 48–53, 54, 59, 67, 102
Pharaoh, 12, 23
Pharisees, 127, 128
Philip, 47, 48
Philippines, 117
Philistines, 36, 37, 40
Pithecia satanas, 96
Planned Parenthood, 97, 125
Plessy, Homer, 95
Plessy v. Ferguson, 95
Pocahontas, 78, 79, 99
polygamy, 77
polytheism, 24, 25, 27
Potawatomi, 88
Potiphar, 17
Potiphera, 12
Powhatan Confederacy, 78, 79
propitiation, 50
Protestants, 8
punctuality, 112, 135
Punjabis, 106

quadroons, 83, 85, 96

Rabina, 66

race, 52, 53, 70, 105, 106
Rachel, 39
Rahab, 32–34, 36, 40
rape, 19, 20, 73
Re, 13
Redburn, 89
Rekem, 35
remittances, 118
remnant, 26
Republicans, 43
Reul, 28, 29
Rolfe, John, 78, 79, 99
Rolfe, Rebecca. See Pocahontas.
Rolfe, Thomas, 78
Romans, 60, 64
Ross, Pinkney, 94
Ross, Sarah, 94
Russia, 63
Ruth, 30, 38–40

Sacagawea, 77
Saigon, 110
Salmon, 32–34
Salvadorans, 106, 111–12
Samaria, 45, 47
Samaritans, 27, 45–48, 67, 70
Samson, 36–38, 40
Sanger, Margaret, 97
Sarah, 12, 16–17
Sarai. See Sarah.
scientific racism, 97
Scythians, 62–65
segregation, 61
Shamgar, 35
Shammai, 127
Shecaniah, 26
Shechem, 19–21, 27
Shelomith, 30–31, 40
Shema, 35
Shittim, 29
Sidon, 24
Sidonians, 23
Simeon, 20
Simeon ben Yohai, Rabbi, 66
Simon Peter. See Peter.
Sinai, 29
Skinner v. Oklahoma, 100
slavery, 44, 73, 80, 81, 92

Subject Index

Smith, John, 78
Socrates, 58
Solomon, 14, 22–24, 27
soteriology, 55, 137
South Africa, 52
Southern Baptist Convention, 61
Spaniards, 75
stay in the airs (racial designation), 76
step backwards racial designation), 75, 76
Stoics, 51
Strive Toward Freedom, 55
Super Sam, 109
Superman, 109
Supreme Count, 1–2, 95, 96, 99, 100, 102, 137
Sychar, 46, 47
syncretism, 19, 24, 45

Tabasco, 74
Talmud, 66
Tamar, 19
Temple. See Jerusalem Temple.
Tennessee, 87
Tenochtitlan, 74
Texas, 89–90, 123
Thales, 58
Theophilus, 66
Third World, 111
time, 111–12
Timnah, 36
Timnites, 37
Timothy, 65–68, 70, 71, 120
Titus, 66
tone, 114, 115
Torah, 4, 9, 11, 19, 26, 29, 38, 53, 54, 59, 66, 102, 128
Transjordan, 28
Tyre, 13, 14, 24

Uncle Sam, 109
Uncle Tom's Cabin, 98
United States, 35, 110, 122
Uriah, 21, 22

Valdés, Ramón, 110
values, 109–10
Vashti, 14
verbal communication, 114–15
verbal irony, 114
Vietnam, 110
Virgil, 63
Virginia, 1, 7, 78, 79, 80, 81, 82, 83, 84, 87, 90
Virginia Company of London, 78

Wahunsonacock, 78
Warren, Chief Justice Earl, 2
Western culture, 1, 18, 52, 69, 108, 112, 117, 126, 128
Willis, Helen, 101
Willis, Tom, 101
wolves, 75
World War I, 97, 106
worldview, 107–13, 115, 125

xenophobia, 79, 91, 136

Yahweh, 19, 21, 23, 24, 28, 29, 30, 31, 32, 33, 34, 35, 36, 37, 38, 39, 40, 41, 46, 54, 69, 137
Yapese, 112

zambaigos, 76
Zaphenath-paneah, 12
Zerubbabel, 45
Zion, 54
Zipporah, 28–29, 40
zoology, 52

Scripture Index

Genesis

1:27	128
2:24	119, 128
3	16
3:17	17
4	16
9:20–27	44
11:1–9	65
14:13	17
15	16
15:5–6	16
15:12–16	19, 20
15:12	27
15:19	34
16:1–3	16, 17
16:2	17
16:10	17
16:11	17
17	17
17:1	21
17:8	21
17:18–19	17
22:15–18	59
22:17	12
22:18	50, 69
25	16
25:1	12
25:1–4	28
25:1–6	12
25:12–18	12
25:19–34	12
26:34	18
26:34–35	19
28:1–9	18
28:1–5	18
28:6–9	18, 19
33:17–23	29
34	19, 20, 21
34:1–4	20
34:1	20
34:2	19
34:5–24	20
34:13–17	20
34:21	21
34:25–31	20
34:26	20
34:30	20
36:9–43	12
36:11	34
36:16	35
37:28	28, 35
38:2	21
38:8	38
38:12	21
41:14–44	12
49:5–7	20
50:20	37

Exodus

2:11–12	29
2:15	28
2:16–21	28
12:38	30, 31, 35
18:17–27	29
20:4–5	27
20:6	50
20:7	30
20:14	27

167

Exodus (continued)

25:8	57
32:1–6	10

Leviticus

24:10–16	30
24:10–11	30
24:11	31
24:12	30
24:16	30, 31
24:22	31
26:12	57
27:7	66

Numbers

3:18	35
6:1–21	36
12:1–15	31
12:1	31, 32
12:2	31
12:4	31
12:8	32
12:13–15	32
14:6–9	34, 35
20:8–13	29
22:1–24:22	39
25:1–16	39
25:1–9	29
25:1–3	10
25:16–18	29

Deuteronomy

1:1–4:49	9
5–11	9
6:7–8	11
7:1–6	8–10, 23, 27, 37
7:1	20
7:2–4	25
7:3	26
7:4	24
8:3	102
17:17	23
19:1–22:8	10
20:10–15	10
20:16–18	10
21:10–14	10–11
22:10	57
23:3–4	39
24:1–4	11
24:1	127
25:5–6	38
30:14	54
34:10	29

Joshua

2	32
2:3–7	33
2:9–11	33
2:12–14	33
2:17–20	33
6:23	33
6:25	33
9:1–27	34
13:21	35
14:1–14	34
14:13–14	35
14:6	34
15:13–19	34
15:17	35

Judges

1:13	35
3:9	35
3:31	35
13:1	36
13:3–5	36
13:5	37
14–16	36
14:1–4	37
14:1	36
14:2	36
14:3	36
14:4	36, 37
14:9	36
14:10–11	36
15:1–5	37
15:6–8	37
15:15	36
16:7	36
16:19	36
17:6	36

Scripture Index

21:25	36	**1 Chronicles**	
		1:32	12
Ruth		2:3	21
		2:11	33
1:1–14	38	2:42	35
1:16	38	2:43	35
2:1–2	38	2:55	35
4:1–10	38	3:5	21
4:11	39	4:13	34
4:12	39	6:33–38	14
4:18–22	38, 39		
		2 Chronicles	
1 Samuel		2:13–14	13
1:1	14		
15:22	50	**Ezra**	
16:17	36	4:1–3	45
		4:4–6	45
2 Samuel		9:1	25
7:8	57	9:2	25
7:14	57	9:3	26
11	21	9:6–15	26
11:1–4	22	9:8	26
11:5–25	22	9:13	26
12:9–10	22	9:14	26
12:13	22	9:15	26
12:15	22	10:1–4	25, 26
13:14	19	10:3	26
21:17	22	10:18–44	26
23:39	21	10:26	26
1 Kings		**Nehemiah**	
7:13–14	13	4:2	45
8:27	49		
11:1–13	24	**Esther**	
11:9–13	24	2:10	14
11:1–2	23	2:17	14
11:3	23	7:1–6	15
16:29–33	24	8:9–14	15
16:31	25		
16:32	25	**Psalms**	
16:33	25	51	22
2 Kings			
17:24–41	45		

Scripture Index

Proverbs
15:1   115, 130

Ecclesiastes
1:9   126

Isaiah
8:14   53
11:10   69
28:16–17   54
28:16   53
42:6–7   69
43:6   57
49:6   47, 69
52:10   47
52:11   57
52:15   69
56:6–8   43, 50

Jeremiah
3:17   69
31:9   57
32:38   57
44:7   26
44:12   26
44:14   26
44:28   26

Ezekiel
16:3   50
20:34   57
20:41   57
37:27   57

Hosea
2:23   53

Joel
2:29   113
2:32   54

Amos
3:13   57
4:13   57

Matthew
1:1–17   38
1:4   33
1:6   22
4:4   102, 127
5:32   128
5:37   132
7:21   42
10:5–6   47
10:14   53
19:3–9   4, 127
19:4–6   16, 119
19:4–5   128
19:6   128
19:9   128
19:26   65
28:19   49, 69

Mark
7:9–13   119
10:8   110

Luke
1:1–4   66
10:30–37   47
14:28   119
17:11–19   47

John
3:1–21   47
4:1–42   45–48, 70
4:9   46
4:20   46
4:22–23   46
4:22   46
4:27   46
4:35   47
4:42   47
4:44   47
14:15   50

Scripture Index

Acts

1:1–2	66
1:8	47, 49
2:1–11	65
8	48
8:4–24	47, 48
8:25–40	48
10:1–48	48–50, 52, 54, 71
10:1–35	117
10:2	48
10:3–8	48
10:9–16	48
10:34–35	48
10:35	49
13:51	53
15:1–31	53
15:1–29	67
15:1	59
15:19–20	117
16:1–3	65, 68, 70
16:1–2	66
16:3	67
17	52
17:16–31	51–53, 70
17:16–21	51
17:22–31	51
17:26	44, 51
17:30–31	52
18:6	53

Romans

2:11	49
2:25–3:8	59
2:25–29	67
3:1	67
2:24	107
3:29–30	55
4:9–12	67
5:12	52
5:15–17	52
6:3	107
6:6	107
6:11	107
6:23	107
8:1	107
8:2	107
8:17	126
8:28	37
8:39	107
9–10	53, 55
9:1–5	53
9:30–33	54
10:1–13	53–55, 71
10:1–4	54
10:8	54
10:9–10	54
10:11–13	54, 55
14:11	54
11:1–36	34
12:3–5	126
12:5	50, 107
15:17	107
16:7	107

1 Corinthians

1:30	107
4:15	107
4:17	66
7:15	4
7:19	59, 67
10:31–32	117
10:31	132
10:32–33	67
12:13	59, 65
13:1–13	126, 134
13:4	110
15:45	52

2 Corinthians

5:17–19	57
5:17	42, 59, 65, 69, 126
6:11–7:4	56
6:11–18	55–58, 70
6:14–7:1	57
6:14	56, 57, 137

Galatians

2:6	49
2:11–14	67, 69
2:11–13	59
2:20	107
3:16	50
3:26–28	59

Scripture Index

Galatians (continued)

3:26	59
3:28	58–61, 62, 65, 71, 113
3:29	59
4:21–31	17
5:1–15	59
5:1–6	67, 69
5:13	126
6:15	59, 67, 69

Ephesians

2:11–22	67
2:13	59
3:6	55
4:15	132
4:24	107
4:26	130
6:9	49

Philippians

2:11	54
3:1–6	67

Colossians

2:8–15	67
2:19–24	66
3:1–7	62
3:5–9	62
3:8–9	62
3:9–11	62–64, 71
3:12–17	62
3:25	49
4:10–12	67

1 Timothy

1:2	66
5:8	119

2 Timothy

3:16–17	70
3:16	5, 102, 126

Titus

1:4	66
1:10–16	67

Hebrews

11:6	27
11:31	34

James

1:19	130
2:25	34

1 Peter

1:25	103
3:7	121

2 Peter

1:19–21	5, 102
3:9	71

1 John

2:2	50

Revelation

7:4–8	68
7:4	69
7:9	68–70, 71
7:10	68
7:11–12	68
14:8	68
18:1–2	68
19:7–8	65
20:11–15	69
21:1–4	68
21:8	69

www.ingramcontent.com/pod-product-compliance
Lightning Source LLC
Chambersburg PA
CBHW050811160426
43192CB00010B/1721